Mothering Inner-City Children

MOTHERING INNER-CITY CHILDREN

The Early School Years

KATHERINE BROWN
ROSIER

RUTGERS UNIVERSITY PRESS
New Brunswick, New Jersey, and London

Library of Congress Cataloging-in-Publication Data

Rosier, Katherine Brown.
  Mothering inner-city children : the early school years /
Katherine Brown Rosier.
     p.   cm.
  Includes bibliographical references and index.
  ISBN 0-8135-2796-1 (cloth : alk. paper) — ISBN 0-913527-97-X (pbk. : alk.
paper)
     1. Socially handicapped women—Indiana—Indianapolis—Interviews.
  2. Women heads of households—Indiana—Indianapolis—Interviews.
  3. Afro-American single mothers—Indiana—Indianapolis—Interviews.
  4. Socially handicapped children—Indiana—Indianapolis—Case studies.
  5. Socially handicapped children—Education—Indiana—Indianapolis—Case
  studies.   6. Education—Parent participation—Indiana—Indianapolis—Case
  studies.   7. Child rearing—Indiana—Indianapolis—Case studies.   I. Title.

HV1447.I53 R67 2000
362.83—dc21   99-055855

British Cataloging-in-Publication data for this book is available from the
British Library

Manufactured in the United States of America

For my Grandma,
who also always said . . .

Contents

Acknowledgments

Portions of this research were supported by grants from two foundations. William A. Corsaro's ethnographic research in the Head Start center was supported by The Spencer Foundation, and small grants from Spencer and from the W. T. Grant Foundation funded portions of the longitudinal extension of the study. I am also grateful for the dissertation fellowship and the encouragement I received from The Spencer Foundation, and especially thank Catherine Lacey.

I thank Indianapolis Public Schools for granting us permission to conduct research in the schools during the children's first-grade year. More pointedly, I thank all the kindergarten and first-grade teachers who graciously participated in this study. I am also grateful for the cooperation of the Head Start center's administrators, especially the classroom teachers. These exemplary preschool teachers, like so many others in their field, are far too seldom recognized for their skills, compassion, and patience, and for the "head start" they so capably provide.

I acknowledge and thank Sheldon Stryker, Donna Eder, David Heise, and William J. Reese, of Indiana University, for their confidence, encouragement, and insightful criticism. My most profound thanks go to Bill Corsaro, who so expertly and unselfishly nurtured my professional development, and so generously shared with me the unique, insightful perspective he brings to the study of children's lives. These fine mentors' support has enabled me to sustain the belief that caring about people has a place in academe, and I am fortunate indeed to have had such models for my own relationships with students. My colleagues at Louisiana State University also deserve thanks for their patience and support, as do my many enthusiastic students.

Two Rutgers editors have shown great enthusiasm and sensitivity; I wish to thank Martha Heller for giving me a chance and David Myers for his compassionate and skillful handling of my peculiarities, insecurities, and stubbornness. Working with these individuals and others at Rutgers University Press has been a genuine pleasure.

I also thank my family, who have shown patience and understanding beyond the call. My husband, parents, brother, and sister have all encouraged me, and sweet little "Wolfy" has helped me keep my child eyes. I have special gratitude for my dear daughter, Mary, who for so long has motivated and inspired me. Mary's active involvement helped create the warm and mutual climate that was so important to the research, and here I thank her and am very proud of her.

It is, of course, the mothers, children, and their families to whom I owe the greatest debt. Without the mothers' gracious hospitality, their candid participation, and their often keen insights, this work would not have been possible. My gratitude for their contributions is immense, and they deserve most of the credit for anything and all that is of value in this work. They, like all others mentioned, deserve no blame for its flaws. I have the greatest respect and admiration for each of these mothers, and am grateful for the many ways they enriched my life and my daughter's. I am forever changed for having known them, and my personal thanks are boundless.

Mothering Inner-City Children

MOTHERING IN THE INNER CITY

This book is about mothers, their young children, and the various contexts—families, schools, neighborhoods, and the larger society—in which their lives are embedded. It is a book about child-rearing strategies and practices, and children's transition from home to school. It is a book about living daily lives, about interpreting and negotiating the complexities of the social environment. As such, it is a book about the familiar, and the somewhat mundane.

This book is also about a segment of Americans who have been increasingly demonized and set apart from the mainstream. It is a book about low-income inner-city black mothers and their children, whose mention often evokes powerful negative images and stereotypes (for example, see Gresham 1989; Sidel 1996). As such, it is a book about "others," and despite pervasive stereotypes, it is a book about people largely unknown to mainstream, and particularly mainstream white, Americans.

Rhonda Craft is one of those mothers. Pregnant at seventeen, Rhonda dropped out of high school in 1984, during her junior year.[1] By the time she was twenty, she had three children by three different fathers and she had never married. Reliance on AFDC, or welfare, had been a constant in Rhonda's life, both as a child and as a mother.[2] When I met her in the summer of 1990, she lived in the same public housing project where she'd spent most of her own childhood. This was a bleak, dangerous place, and I always saw much evidence of drug and gang activity when I visited there. Rhonda often spoke of the devastation wrought by drugs and violence on the lives of her family, friends, and neighbors.

Among the nine women portrayed in this book, Rhonda best fits the stereotype of the poor black inner-city mother. But Rhonda is also thoughtful and poignantly articulate, industrious, and intelligent. She is extremely proud of her three delightful children, who have become bright and successful students. She is actively involved in their schooling and a strong advocate on their behalf. She is also proud of and dedicated to her large, extended family, which has taught her to deal with adversity through honesty, loyalty, and perseverance.

Rhonda once described her family like this: "We're not Ozzie and Harriet, but we're not the Addams Family either!" Her remark purposefully evoked a sanitized image of the mainstream, nuclear-family ideal on the one hand, and an image of the deviant inner-city black family stereotype on the other. As mainstream American families have increasingly abandoned the Ozzie and Harriet ideal, the Addams Family–like stereotype of black families seems to have gained currency. The latter image, however, depicts inner-city "others" no more accurately than the former depicts most middle-class white families. Debunking the Addams Family myth through the telling of nine families' stories is also what this book is about.

This book is lengthy and I have much to say, but it is difficult to begin. Part of the difficulty arises from questions about my right to say it, and questions about the perspective from which I speak. I constantly urge my students to ask "Who says so?" when they are told this or that about contemporary family life. I urge them to learn and understand what they can about where speakers and authors are "coming from" before they buy into the arguments they present. I tell them, too, that this is critical, because what we find in our research is so often shaped by where we look, what we ask, and what our own self-interests are.[3] So they must be very cautious, and mindful of the power of perspective. And now comes me, a fortyish middle-class white academic, from small-town middle-class origins, asking readers to accept my examination and portrayal of the poor black inner-city mothers and children who people this book.

There is currently much written and much debate about "Who Can Speak?" for and about disempowered groups who are constrained from speaking for themselves.[4] A good deal of discussion is focused on race and ethnicity: Can white academics such as myself legitimately conduct research, report findings, write articles and books about racial and ethnic groups whose worlds we can never truly experience and know? Do we do more harm than good as we necessarily portray and interpret their lives through the lenses of our own cultural backgrounds and understandings? Do our analyses and interpretations dilute or negate what little power they have to speak for themselves? Do we exploit them for our own career gains?

I cannot pretend certainty in response to such questions. But I can say that I am clearly more than my Anglo heritage and my current middle-class-academic status; like everyone else, I draw upon a unique collection of experiences and statuses as I observe, inquire, analyze (and hazard) my way through the situations and encounters that make up my life. Part of that "more" that I am is quite relevant to my perspective and understanding of these mothers' experiences parenting in poverty, and a recent incident that helped me to understand my own perspective may do the same for readers.

I routinely teach a senior-level "Sociology of the Family" course, with a heavy focus on social policy. I also routinely share with students my own history as an Aid to Families with Dependent Children (AFDC) recipient, sometimes tossing down on a startled front-row student's desk a stack of monthly "Determination of Benefits" forms that illustrate the paucity of AFDC allowances for housing, food stamps, child care, and "personal needs" allocations. This, I explain to them, was the nature of AFDC in the "Welfare Wonderland" that was Michigan in the mid-1980s. I benefited from Michigan's generosity, which consistently placed it near the top in state rankings of AFDC grant amounts, while my students' own state, Louisiana, generally has only Mississippi keeping it from the absolute cellar of this list.[5] Michigan also was unusual in that it allowed the pursuit of a four-year degree as a legitimate activity for welfare recipients. "I would not be here," I tell my students very sincerely, "if the current punitive welfare regime had existed in my state a decade ago."[6]

These classes quite effectively encourage students to make the so often elusive link between the "private troubles" and "public issues" (Mills 1959) of contemporary family life. But during a recent semester, as I began this discussion, I was choked in midsentence by sudden tears that shocked me as much as the silent room of fifty students. I laughed these off—"Where did *that* come from?"—and continued after only a moment's pause. Perhaps my emotional display contributed to an even more effective classroom experience, but it is surely not one I hope to repeat.

Readers should not suppose I am embarrassed, or ashamed, or guilty about my experiences as a young, single mother on AFDC. I am not. What I occasionally am—and clearly was in this instance—is quite pained at the memory of poverty. I have not forgotten what it's like to have to decide whether to take the last five bucks out of the bank and have dinner, or leave it in there, still have a place to cash checks, and eat crackers. I also have not forgotten what it's like to be the mother of a poor kid, a kid with little compared to most American children, who understands too early that it's best not to ask.

I was a single parent and a welfare recipient nearly continuously from the time my daughter, Mary, was born in 1982 until I started graduate school at Indiana University in 1988. As noted above, I benefited from the "generosity" of my state, and I also benefited from quite privileged access to knowledge, information, and a middle-class social network. The story of how I made it out of my own dire straits is a long one, and I may tell it—someday. But this is not a book about me, and here it is enough to say that like many welfare recipients (see Edin and Lein 1997), I had help. Now, what feels like a lifetime later, in my middle-class job in my middle-class world, I always feel something of a stranger here; like someone watching a movie, I step back, shake my head and smile—"What are *you* doing here?"

In qualitative studies like the one reported here, encouraging the development of initial trust and liking is always a challenge, for the investigator must rely on participants' candid cooperation for the success of the research. The challenge is certainly magnified when the group of interest is marginalized and has reason to be distrustful of mainstream representatives. Expecting suspicion, therefore, goes with the territory, and any reasonable researcher thinks long and hard on strategies she will employ to encourage rapport. When I met first the children, and later the mothers, who are the focus of this study, during my second year of graduate school, I knew that my experiences gave me an advantage relative to most researchers who hope to understand the world from their subjects' perspective. And I purposely communicated those experiences to each of the mothers before turning on my tape recorder for our first interviews.

I told the mothers I was a single parent of an eight-year-old daughter, and I had a rather extensive history of AFDC receipt. I knew firsthand some of the difficulties of parenting in poverty, and I also knew that without assistance I'd received in the past from others, I would never have finished college and gone on to graduate school. I told them, too, that like their children, my daughter had also participated in a Head Start program in another community.[7] And in our later meetings, my self-disclosures continued, as I deemed appropriate given the various contexts and contents of our conversations. As the mothers and I became increasingly comfortable with each other, their questions about my life were asked and answered in what seemed a sort of quid pro quo exchange typical of other reciprocal relationships.[8]

These disclosures seemed to matter. While I cannot know how the mothers would have responded in the absence of this information, their knowledge of our shared experiences surely helped to shape the way they viewed and interpreted me and my research.[9] They came to see me as someone who could indeed hear their voices, understand their lives, and treat them fairly and well. Rhonda, whose voice is among the clearest throughout this book, once described her own qualms about participation and the resolution that she reached. More than a year after our first meeting, she told me that "people are askin' me all the time, what do you mean somebody doin' research on [her daughter] Cymira?" She reportedly "tried to tell them," but they just said, "No". Rhonda dismissed others' disapproval, she said, because "this is how I see you: You're not gonna go for no stereotype. You're gonna show the other side. We are not all the same; we are all different. . . . You want to know what it's like, and you're gonna show something good about us."

I do not take such confidence lightly, and its implications contributed to much personal anguish as well as satisfaction as I completed the research, and later, this book. For now, I hope readers will suspend their own judgments of "who can speak" at least temporarily as they read this examination of the complex demands, challenges, and rewards of mothering inner-city children through the transition into school.

A BRIEF DISCUSSION OF METHOD

In addition to the bases for initial rapport and connections I've described above, my prior relationships with the mothers' children may also have added to the relative ease with which our acquaintances began. This study began when, throughout the 1989–90 school year, I assisted William A. Corsaro of Indiana University in an ethnographic study of children's peer cultures, which included his weekly, daylong observations in two classrooms at a Head Start center in Indianapolis.[10] I accompanied Bill on his classroom visits during the last several months of the school year, in the course of which I learned a great deal about the individual children and developed quite friendly relationships with them. Our observations at the center had convinced us that to better understand the children's peer culture, we needed to develop understanding of their lives outside the center, in their homes and communities. This was the impetus for my initial contact with the mothers. When this contact was made, they knew I had already spent considerable time getting to know their children during my visits to the center. This also likely contributed to their trust in me and their willingness to grant initial interviews to discuss their perceptions concerning the Head Start program, and other child-rearing issues and concerns.

The ten mothers I contacted had either shown an interest in the Head Start research, or had children who participated in particularly interesting episodes of peer interaction that we videotaped at the Head Start center.[11] Nine of those mothers agreed to be interviewed, and all of those continued to participate for the duration of the study. Table 1.1 describes the mothers and their families when we met for the first round of interviews. All the mothers were black, and in each family there was a five-year-old child expecting to begin kindergarten in the fall of 1990. All but one of these families had been AFDC recipients at some time, but the considerable variation in family structure and household composition begins to demonstrate Rhonda's comment that "we are not all the same; we are all different." Family members also varied a good deal in age, educational background, and employment status and occupational history. And as will become apparent in subsequent chapters, over the course of the study there were many changes in these families' circumstances.

The mothers' warmth, enthusiasm, and apparent candor encouraged me to extend both the scope and the duration of the study. Beginning with these first interviews in June 1990, I eventually completed four rounds of intensive, open-ended interviews in the homes of each of the nine mothers, during (or at the close of) their children's Head Start, kindergarten, and first- and second-grade years. Data collection formally ended in the summer of 1993.[12] The interviews with mothers were wide-ranging, and their focus evolved over time. I also observed the families in their homes

Table 1.1 Family Characteristics, June 1990*

MOTHER AND AGE	NO. OF CHILDREN	HOUSEHOLD COMPOSITION	EMPLOYMENT STATUS	MOTHER'S EDUCATION	WELFARE STATUS
Amy 29	1, age 5	self mother 2 brothers son	full-time full-time full-time	1 year college, no degree	Past AFDC, currently no assistance
Denise 40	5, ages 1–13	self 4 children at time of interview	no	High school graduate	First time on AFDC, since January 1990
Tasha 34	6, ages 2–17	self husband 5 children	part-time part-time	GED. Some college classes	Food stamps only, past AFDC receipt
Rhonda 23	3, ages 3–5	self mother brother 3 children	no no no	Did not graduate high school	AFDC
Harriet 25	4, ages 4mo.–9 yrs.	self landlady 2 children	full-time social security	Did not graduate high school, certificate from 9-mo. nursing assistant program	Medicaid only (grace period) just off AFDC, food stamps

Table 1.1 (Continued)

MOTHER AND AGE	NO. OF CHILDREN	HOUSEHOLD COMPOSITION	EMPLOYMENT STATUS	MOTHER'S EDUCATION	WELFARE STATUS
Annette 29	6, ages 1–7	self husband 6 children	no full-time	High school graduate	Past AFDC, currently no assistance
Samantha 39	4, ages 5–19	self 3 children	full-time teen empl. part-time	Some college classes. Certified hematologist. Bachelor's degree	Past AFDC, currently no assistance
Evelyn 38	2, ages 5 and 9	self 2 children	full-time		Never
Marissa 23	3, ages 3–5	No stable residence moves between relatives' and partner's homes	Lost job week prior to initial interview	Did not graduate high school	Off & on AFDC last 5–6 yrs, currently receiving food stamps only

*This table appears in Rosier and Corsaro (1993), "Competent Parents, Complex Lives: Managing Parenthood in Poverty." *Journal of Contemporary Ethnography* 22(2):171–204.

and in other settings in their communities. For example, I observed and participated in both regular services and special programs at five different Indianapolis churches with four of the families. I attended school programs, including a "Parent Appreciation" program, a kindergarten graduation ceremony, a program celebrating Black History Month, and a midyear student award ceremony. More informal visits with families included spending evenings in conversation over dinner, observing the activities of children in their neighborhoods, and in several instances, attending morning church services and then returning to the home for the rest of the day and dinner. I occasionally drove mothers around town on various errands, and at these and other times, met extended family members of all but two of the families (sometimes providing them with transportation as well). My daughter, Mary (three years older than the study children), often accompanied me to church and school activities, and she became an important participant in the research as well. Many mothers began to ask that Mary come along when I visited—for formal interviews as well as informal visits and activities—and she frequently did so.

To some extent the relationships that developed among myself, my daughter, the mothers, and their children resembled cooperative friendships. It certainly is true that the families became very dear to me, and in many cases I am sure the feeling was mutual. But it is important to note that these friendships were an added bonus, and not in any way a cover for the ongoing research. I repeatedly reminded the mothers that I was "always collecting data," and I have no doubt they understood this.[13]

Following interviews with the Head Start teachers in the spring of 1990, we also interviewed the nine children's kindergarten and first-grade teachers. These interviews focused on the teachers' views and experiences regarding teaching and parental involvement, major organizational features of their classrooms, and their evaluations of the particular children and their mothers. In addition, we were interested in how Head Start practices prepare children for public school and the expectations of teachers there, and the extent to which Head Start teachers' philosophies and emphases differed from those of teachers the children encountered later. We also looked for similarities and differences in parents' versus teachers' goals, practices, and assessments of the children, and further considered teacher remarks as checks on the mothers' reports of their own activities to promote their children's academic achievement. We also completed brief observations in several first-grade classrooms, which supplemented the extensive observational data collected in the Head Start center.[14]

The initial interviews with the mothers were quite structured explorations of their views of the Head Start program, their expectations for their children's futures, and their current family circumstances and routines. Over time, however, later interviews evolved to reflect various themes that emerged as I got to know the families more intimately. Although the overarching theme of the study is young children's experiences as they negotiate the transition from home to formal schooling, this focus very often took a backseat to other child-rearing and socialization issues that were clearly important to various mothers (for example, overseeing their children's interaction with dangerous environments; managing family needs in the face of often severe economic and other constraints; and enlisting the involvement of others in their children's lives). Their concerns reflected family and local cultures, neighborhood features, and larger social environments, all of which provided the contexts of these families' lives and helped to shape both the children's experiences in various settings and the mothers' attempts to make sense of and manage those experiences. As the study progressed, it became clear that my own understanding of these contexts was inadequate, and I pursued additional information both in interviews and through study of local history, neighborhood census data, and social policy.

In addition, because the mothers revealed so much about their own histories as they answered my questions about their children, I followed their lead and focused considerable attention on their past as well as present lives. Features of the mothers' biographies had a profound influence on the children's experiences, the mothers' interpretations of them, and the translation of those interpretations into daily practice and child-rearing strategies. While this is, then, a study of children's movement into formal schooling, it is primarily in the context of their mothers' lives and through their mothers' eyes that this transition is examined.

PROMINENT THEMES

The mothers' biographies were clearly important for shaping their responses to the demands of parenting in difficult, complex circumstances, and that fact to some extent dictated the organization of this book. Rather than organizing chapters around prominent themes or issues, and bringing in data from various families to illustrate and develop these themes, I use a family narrative analy-sis strategy, presenting the families' stories one by one. In these nine chapters, I am able to detail the mothers' particular past expe-riences that seemed most influential for their later parenting, and I link the mothers' interpretations of their pasts with both their child-rearing views and practice, and their prospective thinking about the children's futures. The family narrative chapters thus develop particularistic themes, detailing patterns apparent over time that were more or less unique to the individual families in question.

But these are not merely individual stories; the chapters iden-tify and develop many more general themes, patterns apparent in the lives of all or nearly all the families. A brief preview of these general themes will help to orient the reader.

The negative stereotypes that abound concerning low-income black families include beliefs that black children are inadequately socialized by families who lack motivation, resources, and child-rearing knowledge and skills. This "inadequate socialization" theory is often evoked to explain black children's frequent failure to achieve, and the intergenerational transmission of poverty among the so-called underclass. Black inner-city community members are no strangers to these negative stereotypes, and the mothers I came to know incorporated such beliefs into their own definitions of the situations they confronted. Their discussions of child-rearing tac-tics were often accompanied by claims of family difference, which they used to set themselves apart from the well-known images of supposedly typical inner-city others. These claims also helped mothers to ward off feelings of fatalism, and maintain hopefulness about their own children's futures despite the dismal outcomes they saw for so many adolescents in their communities.

Despite the mothers' defenses against them, feelings of fatal-ism and hopelessness did nonetheless arise. One mother expressed such attitudes quite clearly when she said that "you can go on and on and on and on, and make 'em do this or that, and they still may not, so what difference does it make?" But fatalistic attitudes were resisted through active strategies to encourage children's academic achievement, moral development, and sense of self-reliance and independence. This latter emphasis, a strong and important find-ing in its own right, begins to suggest another central theme of the book, that is, the complexities and many contradictions that seemed inherent in the child-rearing demands these mothers con-fronted. The creeping sense of fatalism we detected in the mothers' views seemed to grow as the children matured and made increasing demands for freedom. It was clear to mothers that granting increased freedom to explore and negotiate their neighborhoods meant that their children would encounter many negative and potentially dangerous situations, and surely all the mothers at least considered attempting to isolate their children and forbid as much as possible their interaction with others in the community. But there was a palpable tension between the desire to restrict and control in order to keep their children safe on one hand, and the desire to encourage independence they felt was necessary for their children's eventual success on the other. And as this tension played itself out in various families' strikingly different daily practice, the critical nature of the mothers' own histories was very clear indeed.

My own attention to the mothers' biographies was not so much a conscious and well-considered decision followed by probing inquiries as it was merely the result of acknowledging and respecting the explanations the mothers themselves repeatedly offered for their views and practices. A general theme that will be developed is related to the mothers' routine practice of explaining their child-rearing by locating it in biographic context—that is, the mothers' often acute awareness of social reproductive processes that were manifested in successive generations of their families. "It had to plant something," one mother insightfully said of her own mother's attitudes, and she and other mothers described their efforts to foil the cycles that were repeatedly apparent when they surveyed their family histories. Recognition of the ways their own lives often mirrored those of their mothers and other family members also contributed to the mothers' sense of fatalism. But these mothers were anything but passive. They actively resisted feelings that their efforts on their children's behalf might be for naught, and their strategies were perhaps all the more impressive given their suspicions of the futility of these efforts.

As Tasha did when she spoke of the planting and growth of important attitudes, the mothers often employed highly stylized, metaphoric language, especially when they discussed their children's education. This colorful and often powerful imagery was an important socialization resource for mothers, called upon to help communicate values and to warn their children of the dangers of adolescence. Such stylized talk, most often apparent when the mothers' words took on an air of folk wisdom being handed down, aided in the transmission of particular, traditional cultural values.

Among those traditional emphases are the importance of

often complex networks of support that include both kin and nonkin members, and the high valuation of religion and religious participation. Both patterns are noted and developed throughout the family narratives, and both take on increased importance as strategic emphases that helped combat the negative community features and processes that were never far from the mothers' minds. Perceived threat and constant reminders of violence and gang activity, early school leaving and pregnancies, and crippling poverty increased the urgency of the mothers' desires to provide alternative sources of both support and interaction for their children, away from the distrusted and always uncertain influence of other neighborhood occupants. Nearly always, a lack of material resources dictated possible strategies, and the constraints that poverty placed on these families' child-rearing efforts is another theme that is woven throughout the narratives.

The mothers' search for alternatives also extended to the schools, and several chapters illustrate the strategy of seeking workable alternatives to traditional public elementary classrooms. Primarily restricted to alternative programs within public schools, several families attempted to increase their children's chances of success in this manner. These efforts were far from cure-alls, but they illustrate the mothers' strong desire to take action on their children's behalf and in support of the high value they place on educational achievement.

This is perhaps the clearest of all general themes—the mothers' unanimous strong valuation of education and their high expectations for their children's achievement. Despite an often severe lack of resources, they actively promoted this value through their involvement in their children's schooling. This involvement took many forms, which are detailed in the narratives. However, many of the mothers' more private activities (that is, away from school) often went unrecognized by teachers. In fact, another prominent theme involves the teachers' strong desire for parent involvement, but as several chapters clarify, teachers unfortunately tended to employ rigid definitions of what counts as participation. Rather ritualized occasions like Open House and Parent-Teacher Conferences were granted remarkable significance, and teachers were highly critical of mothers who failed to show for such events.

Throughout the discussions of children's experiences at school, tensions are apparent between community influences, family practices, school policy, and teachers' expectations for children and parents. The fit—or lack of fit—between family and classroom practice is repeatedly examined, as are the manifestations of mothers' emphases in children's classroom behavior. I also explore the apparent effect of systemic features of the schools; of particular importance here are the school system's busing policies, and the related policy of nonmandatory kindergarten attendance. Both features of the system had implications for the continuity of children's schooling experiences, which is a critical contributor to children's educational success. Other features of the schools, and characteristics of the individual teachers, are also considered throughout. (At this and at later points, readers may wish to refer to the "School Features" table in the appendix, which describes the children's teachers, the schools they attended, and the schools' surrounding neighborhoods.)

The narrative chapters integrate these general themes with discussion of particular family themes and circumstances. It is, of course, the more general rather than particular patterns that most interest sociologists and others who wish to better understand the collective experience of groups. This, too, is my objective, but I know that neglect of individual peculiarities leads to overdeterministic conceptualizations of social processes, conceptualizations that too often downplay human agency and fail to highlight the interpretive procedures that underlie behavioral choices. The narrative chapters allow us to see how general patterns are constituted through daily practice in homes and schools, thereby promoting greater understanding not only of socialization practices in low-income black families, but also of interaction processes and interpretive procedures more generally.

ORGANIZATION

I have organized the narratives with two considerations in mind. First and most important, the ordering reflects concerns of thematic development. Certain families represent the best illustration of certain general themes, and themes introduced in earlier narratives are elaborated by narratives presented later. The second consideration is the mothers' age. As table 1.1 illustrates, this is a diverse group of families in terms of family composition, mothers' education and labor-force participation, and mothers' age. When the mothers are grouped in terms of age, it is possible to recognize specific influences on their own lives and on the way they view their children's lives.

All the mothers began their lives in a city that purposely and effectively segregated them residentially and educationally from white children, and did little to hide the fact that blacks were considered second-class citizens. The city historically maintained strict residential segregation, with nearly all blacks living on the north, near northeast, and near northwest sides of the central business district. The influence of the city's unofficial red line at 27th Street (referred to by some in the 1920s as the "White Supremacy Dead Line"; see Hooper and Neal 1993) is still clear in the distribution of Indianapolis blacks today.

Perhaps even more important historical influences are the mothers' own experiences as schoolchildren. The women I group together as "older mothers" all attended one of two traditionally black high schools in Indianapolis, either Crispus Attucks or Shortridge High.[15] They completed high school before desegregation efforts were under way in the city, and all but one—whose family lived in a middle-class white neighborhood—attended segregated black schools throughout their years in Indianapolis Public Schools (IPS).[16] These mothers' educational experiences helped shape their perceptions of their own children's schooling.

Two mothers fall between the "older" and "younger" mothers. These "middle" (or "on-time") mothers both graduated from high school in 1979, six years after the onset of busing to desegregate Indianapolis Public Schools. They began their public schooling in all-black elementary schools, attended IPS throughout the system's within-district desegregation process, and graduated from high school before the implementation of the controversial busing of inner-city blacks to suburban townships of Indianapolis. Although they experienced school changes and uncertainty due to reorganization of the school system, they were spared the upheavals and anger that accompanied this latter stage of IPS's desegregation.[17]

The final group, the "young" mothers, spent their entire educational careers within a system continuously in flux while desegregating its schools to accommodate court orders. Beginning school just after the courts originally ordered the system's desegregation, and leaving without credentials shortly after busing to suburban schools began, these women experienced a chaotic system that inspired little confidence and could offer students and parents little security or continuity. While none of the women involved in this study were bused to suburban schools, this most controversial reorganization influenced the climate at all IPS schools, and Rhonda, Marissa, and Harriet were surely affected.

I begin the narrative chapters with the two mothers—Amy

Stevens and Annette Richy—who were twenty-nine years of age when we completed our first interviews. Their children, Jeremiah and Alysha, were both born when their mothers were in their mid-twenties, an age seen by many as the ideal for having children. Amy has only one child while Annette has many, but none of Annette's children were born while she was in her teens. These mothers, then, avoid the many pressures, as well as the stereotypes, especially associated with early childbearing.

Amy and Annette were quite similar in some respects, yet they differed radically in others. One important characteristic they shared was their devotion to their children. As the result of very different processes, both women gave up their own aspirations for education and career success, and both appeared to have placed their dreams in their children (see Collins 1991a). Like other mothers involved in this research, Amy and Annette also shared a strong belief in what they perceived as their families' "difference" from other families in their communities, and I introduce and begin to develop the "claims of family difference" theme in these first two narrative chapters. These first two narratives also introduce the importance of support networks in the mothers' lives.

Rhonda Craft, Marissa Dunbar, and Harriet Heath-Mathews—who head the three families depicted in chapters 4 through 6—make up the second group of mothers. These women, aged twenty-three to twenty-five at the time of our first interviews, are the young mothers. They all had children while in their teens, and none graduated from high school. They were also more persistently poor, and decidedly less likely to marry their children's fathers than were the older mothers. But they were not all cut from the same cloth; their differences were as striking as their similarities. While they did indeed come closest to the all-too-well-known stereotypes of poor urban black mothers, only one had no formal employment history, while the others had extensive employment histories in low-income, "pink collar ghetto" (Sidel 1992) occupations. Each of these families faced monumental struggles, and the chapters devoted to them depict their various difficulties as well as their strengths. These chapters also most clearly speak to social policy issues concerning welfare and work for low-income mothers. Finally, within these chapters the mothers' awareness of social reproductive processes, and the creeping sense of fatalism are perhaps most poignantly demonstrated.

In chapters 7 through 10, the families of women who might be considered older mothers are depicted. Ranging in age from thirty-four to forty in the summer of 1990, Tasha, Samantha, Evelyn, and Denise made up the most diverse group. Two came from middle-class backgrounds, while the others' families were always quite poor. All had high school credentials, but their educational backgrounds were not uniform—one was a college graduate, two had some college experience (one with a GED), and the fourth did not continue her education beyond high school. One mother's oldest child was nine when the study began, another was already a grandmother, and a third had grandchildren before data collection was concluded. These mothers' marital status also varied and changed in the course of the study, as did their employment situation.

These older mothers' stories also illustrate claims of family difference, awareness of reproductive processes, and emerging fatalism, and these themes are further elaborated. The presence of teenage children added complexity to several of these families' lives, and inspired both additional insight into processes affecting children's outcomes, and reasons for anxiety. As is true in earlier chapters, three of the older mothers' narratives highlight the critical importance of social networks and religious participation for these families. And these final narratives, like all the others, underscore the tremendous complexity of child-rearing, and of daily life in general, in these challenging inner-city environments.

The Head Start center where this study began was located in one of Indianapolis's poorest neighborhoods (see appendix, "Neighborhoods" table, tract B.3). Like all but one of the children, the teachers in the two classrooms we studied were black, and they lived in nearby communities. This probably contributed to teachers' genuine valuation of and comfort with the children's experiential backgrounds, and the atmosphere of mutual respect that we perceived among the adults and children. This was reflected in the unflappable teachers' calm reactions even to some of the children's most outrageous or disconcerting remarks. Children's talk about horror movies, police and arrests, drugs and pushers, fights and spousal abuse, and their occasional sharing of some of the more distasteful rap lyrics—to give a few examples—were met with matter-of-fact responses that never suggested aversion or dismay. Although teachers at times suggested, "Let's not talk about that," I never saw children's contributions treated disrespectfully.

Children's role play and peer interaction at the center often incorporated many issues and themes relevant to their families' economic status (see Corsaro and Rosier 1992; Rosier and Corsaro

1993). In addition to the persistent theme of police making arrests, the children at times enacted roles of employees in fast food restaurants, parents taking sick babies to the clinic, and mothers frustrated by their children's many demands. Head Start teachers took this in stride, and seemed to quite routinely legitimate the children's experiences in a way that other teachers in this study found difficult to do. For example, on a bus ride through downtown Indianapolis during a field trip, children pointed out buildings they recognized, including a bank ("My mom comes here to cash her check"), a food stamp office ("My mom goes here and then we get to go shopping"), and the city jail. Several children noted they knew people who'd been in the jail, and one boy exclaimed, "My dad's been in there for drinkin' too much!" Ms. Murdock responded that "I know people who've been in there, too," and the children then turned their attention to other matters. This stood in marked contrast to a white first-grade public school teacher who described her upset when a student answered her question about where her mother had been: "In jail for fighting." After that, Ms. Majors was careful not to ask such questions, and she also reported that she did not mention children's fathers unless she was certain they were in the home.

Unlike in middle-class American preschools (see Corsaro 1994), a great deal of teasing, good-humored opposition, and insults were the norm among the Head Start children. The teachers' interaction styles were quite similar, as teachers too participated in mild teasing and oppositional tactics to control the children's behavior. Teachers were also at times physically affectionate with their students, and although the children seemed to respond quite favorably, many rolled their eyes or in other ways feigned impatience with these displays.

In these and other ways, routine interaction at the center seemed to build upon what children brought with them to the classrooms, contributing to feelings of competence and self-confidence. Although they all had their bad days, in general these were children who—by the end of the school year—were excited about learning, confident about themselves and their place in the school culture, and prepared to move on to new challenges in new environments.

When William Corsaro and I traveled to and from the Head Start center throughout the spring of 1990, the hour-long drive between Bloomington and Indianapolis provided us considerable opportunity to discuss our observations at the center and the children we had come to know there. While we did not record these discussions, some of them were particularly important in our decisions to extend the research—first, to include interviews with some of the children's parents, and second, to follow these children through their transition into elementary schooling. I recall the distinct sadness I could not shake after one of my earliest visits. What delightful, interesting, confident, and competent children most seemed to be! "This is hard," I told Bill as we drove back to Bloomington, "to come to know these kids and also know what will likely happen to so many of them once they get to public schools." It was this simple and sad recognition of the risks these children faced—in and out of school—that inspired the longitudinal focus of this study. What does happen to the enthusiasm and the clear promise of such children? Perhaps by documenting the experiences of these children and families in the early years of schooling, this study can uncover some of the processes that intervene between early promise and later heartache.

2

PARENTAL INVOLVEMENT AND CLAIMS OF FAMILY DIFFERENCE

Many of the major themes developed throughout the book are introduced in this first narrative chapter devoted to Amy Stevens and her son, Jeremiah. As the chapter title suggests, two themes are of particular importance. The first is parental involvement in children's schooling: In both her daily in-home practice and her knowledge of activities at school, Amy stands out among the mothers as the extreme example of high parental involvement. While all the mothers attempted to support their children's education, and all developed strategies to enhance their children's achievement, the intense control and involvement Amy demonstrated were unmatched. Amy's own earlier experiences as a successful student helped to shape her tactics in support of this high valuation of and expectations for her son's education.

As I emphasize throughout the book, mothers' practices were strongly influenced by their own experiences as children in family, community, and school settings. Amy recalled her own mother's strict parenting style with much admiration, and she clearly tried to reproduce tactics she viewed as highly effective and successful. Amy's response to neighborhood and school environments was mediated by these recollections of her childhood, which provided her with a strong model to emulate. It is clear that the mothers' pasts played a critical role in shaping their parental practice, and my analysis emphasizes how Amy's strategies reflected her interpretations of both the objective conditions of her family's current circumstances and unique features of her own biography.

Amy also provides the clearest examples of the mothers' routine claims of family difference. Repeatedly, and with great clarity and conviction, she set herself apart from others in her neighborhood, whom she viewed as grossly neglectful of their own children's best interests. Her view of other neighborhood parents and children was translated into restrictive strategies intended to isolate Jeremiah from feared negative influences of the community, and she attempted attempts to exercise complete control over all his activities.

When I began this study, I thought Amy's distrust of and disdain for others in her neighborhood would be unusual among the mothers, but this was not the case. In fact, virtually every mother expressed similar sentiments about other families, parents, and children. At some time or other, all the mothers made claims about their own families' distinctiveness, respectability, or decency, and contrasted this with the lax or "street" values of other nearby families. Regardless of the grounds for these claims, perceptions of family difference seemed to both prompt and justify many of the mothers' child-rearing practices, and I became convinced that this was a critical pattern.

Two other themes introduced in this chapter deserve mention. First, this narrative briefly introduces the theme of mothers' encouragement of autonomy and independence. Amy's words in support of this value rang rather empty in light of her controlling behavior, and only in later chapters do we see families who succeed in more consistently expressing this emphasis in both their words and their behaviors. And finally, this chapter begins to illustrate the importance of networks of support that not only added to the quality of these families' lives but also at times made it possible for them to maintain their homes and families. Amy and Jeremiah's extended family network provided emotional and material support, stability, and connectedness to others that enriched their lives immeasurably. At the same time, Amy's contributions and her sense of obligation to her family were clear as well, and this and other narratives support well-known findings concerning the prevalence and importance of reciprocal support networks for African-American families.

AMY'S NARRATIVE: FAMILY TRADITIONS AND FAMILY BOUNDARIES

When we met in the summer of 1990, Amy Stevens lived with her son, her mother, and two of her adult brothers in a two-story duplex apartment where the family had lived since Amy's elementary school years. Their street, which runs only four blocks off a busy throughway, is like many in this city; almost exclusively single-family homes, many well kept by long-term residents, but others, presumably rentals, fallen into disrepair. Still, this is a street where residents look up, and sometimes wave, as cars enter and leave. I never went here feeling anonymous or unobserved, nor did I ever feel threatened. On several occasions when Amy was a passenger in my car, neighbors waved and shouted greetings as we passed.

At twenty-nine, Amy had seemingly boundless energy, and at times seemed uncomfortable sitting still during our lengthy interviews. She was quite articulate and talked very fast, smoked a lot, and was extremely intense. But she was also quick to smile and laugh, and I was struck by the way Jeremiah's expressions and mannerisms mirrored his mother's.

After her high school graduation in 1979, Amy completed one semester of college at a large state university, but did not continue. She never married, and was the only mother in this study with just one child. Jeremiah's father had been active in his life until he died in a car accident before Jeremiah's second birthday. Jeremiah had the support of a large extended family network composed primarily of Amy's siblings and their children, but his father's family never took an interest or an active role in his life.

All adults in this household worked full-time. Amy's brothers were employed as a factory worker and a junior accountant, and Amy and her mother provided unlicensed family day care for as many as twenty children a day. Their clients, primarily relatives and family friends, paid what they could, and although Amy rarely complained about finances, Jeremiah was eligible for free school lunch throughout his early elementary years. Amy also routinely utilized a summer lunch program offered through a neighboring church, and she, Jeremiah, and all of the "baby-sittin' kids" would walk several blocks to the church each day in the summer. However, although Amy received AFDC for several years after Jeremiah was born, she was not on welfare at any time during our acquaintance, and her income remained relatively stable and dependable, though modest.

Reciprocal support and obligation characterized the members of this family. Amy's two brothers both moved in 1993, but they remained in close contact. All the other surviving children in the Stevens family also live in Indianapolis, and they were in regular, often daily, contact with one another. Various siblings routinely took Amy and her mother shopping and running errands, a critical service since neither woman drove. They, in turn, regularly provided child care for several of Jeremiah's cousins, and one cousin lived with them on weekends.

Although Amy was a single parent, Jeremiah never lacked the involvement of other caring adults in his life, and here Amy's brothers were particularly important. One brother taught Jeremiah a great deal about computers and often took him and several cousins to special events around the city. The other provided Jeremiah with a series of swimming lessons. Amy both made considerable investments in, and received many benefits from, this extended family network, which provided critical support for her in raising Jeremiah.

My first interview with Amy was the first I conducted with any of the mothers. She welcomed me into the house, helped me set up my tape recorder at the kitchen table, and then called Jeremiah downstairs to say hello. We visited briefly until Amy told him to return to his play upstairs. Throughout the interview, a girl slightly younger than Jeremiah sat at the table with us, and Amy's mother also joined us for a portion of the interview. Several other children came in and out of the kitchen for various reasons that day, which was described as "a light day," with "eleven or twelve" children in the Stevenses' small home.

I began these first interviews with a short series of demographic questions, and Amy answered these quickly and then produced a detailed description of Jeremiah's typical day. I then asked Amy to describe the "kinds of things you think are important for Jeremiah to learn and know in order to get along well in his community," and I was startled by her reply:[1]

> OK, the first thing, especially in this community where I live, you have to be very particular about who you play with. You need to protect your child like this, because there's gang problems over here bad. Now, like up these stairs right here, I do not allow him to go up here, 'cause there's lots of trouble, and I do not allow him to play with anybody who lives up there [a long flight of concrete steps rose up the steep hill directly behind the Stevenses' apartment; at the top was Philadelphia Gardens, a small and rundown public housing project]. You know, and really, other than kids we're baby-sittin' and his cousins, he don't interact with any in the community, because I just don't trust 'em. The community, this community, that is. 'Cause there's so many problems here.

She then noted exceptions—two children from known families were acceptable playmates, but "I'd rather for them to come over here, because he does not go outside without me, even if he's goin' to sit in front of the house." She then continued: "And that's about it in the community, 'cause there's not too many little kids his age, except for up there, . . . they let their kids run wild, do anything. I do not allow that. And 'course I'm very strict about study. Even though he's five years old, I am just too strict. Like I said, he has to write his ABC's every day. . . ."

Amy's strong distrust of and isolation from most other community members was striking. She clearly differentiated herself and her family from these others—"They let their kids run wild. . . . I do not allow that." She also noted exceptions to her tight restriction of Jeremiah's neighborhood interaction, especially one child's family, who "don't allow the [same] things I don't allow." Amy then reintroduced the topic of Jeremiah's in-home educational activities, which had been the focus of her earlier description of his typical day.

This excerpt neatly depicts the two most prominent themes of my series of interviews with Amy, both of which were evident in each of our four interviews. One is Amy's intense concern with and active involvement in Jeremiah's education. The other is her claims of family difference.

Routine Claims of Family Difference

This was the first interview I conducted with any of the mothers, and Amy's indictment of her neighborhood occurred just ten minutes after we began. For me, this was a powerful and unsettling introduction into the field. I was not expecting to hear such sentiments, but rather had admittedly idealistic, romantic notions of cooperative communities providing all kinds of instrumental and emotional support for one another (see Stack 1974; also see Heath 1983). What I found was quite different.

Like other mothers, Amy often evoked a notion of family difference when she talked about Jeremiah, her activities with him, and decisions she made regarding his upbringing. Most other examples are not nearly as striking as the first, however, primarily because they appear as asides over the course of other discussions. The offhand manner in which these examples arise is important in itself, because it demonstrates the routine way in which Amy called upon this notion of difference to make sense of her experiences, and decide upon and explain her actions. Another example, from our fourth interview, illustrates this pattern. I asked Amy a simple question about whether there was a special man in her life, and she produced this complex response:

K: What about you now? Is there any relationship, or man in your life? [laugh]

A: Uh, no. Not really. There's not that one special person. I'm not into runnin' a lot of men in and out of his life. You know, it might be this man today, this man tomorrow. Naw. It's not like that.

K: Yeah. The reason I asked that question is, if so, what is the relationship of this person with Jeremiah?

A: I can't see—See, my mother, once our father died, she never remarried. So, I never believed in stuff like that. . . . Until you meet that one special person. Then, you know, then it's you, your son, and him. But until then, he might "Hi, how you all doin'?" But other than that, not no personal contact like, "Can I come over, and—" No. No. I don't like that. That just teaches them wrong family values. 'Cause if they see you doin' this, what they gonna do when they get older? They might think it's OK, you know, "Oh, I'll have this girl this week, this girl next week." So, usually when I go out, he's always in bed, asleep. . . . But see, most young ladies are not like that. Whoever's in their life, they's just in their life. And that's not good. It's not good to have different men runnin' in and out of a kid's life. That's not a stable environment, I think.

Amy first answered no, she was not seeing anyone special, and—anticipating the reason behind my question—she indicated this was a decision made on Jeremiah's behalf. She said, "I'm not into runnin' a lot of men in and out of his life. . . . It's not like that." She then went on to give three different reasons for her decision not to openly date men at that time. First, she evoked memories of her own childhood and indicated that she wanted to reproduce the behavior of her own mother. Next, she noted the importance of her behavior as a model for Jeremiah, and explained that by not openly dating, she felt she was setting a good example for him and discouraging him from taking dating relationships lightly. Finally, she explained her behavior by contrasting it to the behavior of other single mothers—of whom she clearly disapproved—saying that "most young ladies are not like that. And that's not good."

Amy's conversations were full of contrasts between her own values and behavior and those of other parents, and often her statements concerned others' lack of involvement in their children's schooling. During a telephone conversation in the fall of 1993, Amy told me about the new school Jeremiah had begun attending as a result of the Select Schools public school-choice program that had begun in the city that year.[2] She asked if I'd heard of problems with busing routes and schedules at the beginning of the year, and I said I'd been following it in the news. She then offered this analysis of the problem: "A lot of people are blamin' it on the school system. But it's not the school system, it's the parents." When I asked what she meant, she recalled the forms sent home in the spring: "A lot of people just didn't do it, didn't even send it back. Or they did it wrong. I'm sorry, I'm not blamin' the school system. Parents just didn't do it." Finally, I asked, "Why not, do you suppose?" and she quickly replied: "Lazy. Triflin', I'll tell you the truth. 'Cause it only took like three seconds. Everybody's complainin' now, but it's all your own fault."

That parents would fail to attend to or correctly fill out the forms sent home in preparation for the new school choice program was indicative, in Amy's mind, of serious failings on their part. Her conclusion that "a lot of parents" were lazy or unconcerned contrasted sharply with her own conscientious attention to all matters concerning Jeremiah's education. Amy's claims of family difference were based most firmly on her devotion to her son's schooling.

Intense Involvement in Jeremiah's Schooling

Perhaps the most striking thing about Amy was her in-depth knowledge and discussion of her son's educational activities and routines. I began each interview by asking the mother to describe her child's typical day. While all mothers told me, for example, about what time the child went to school and came home, and all related something about their understanding of the general daily routine in the classroom, no one else gave the kind of detailed reports that Amy produced. For example, she always knew which extra classes (gym, music, art) were on which days. She knew when Jeremiah had reading and math, what days he received instruction in science, what time he ate lunch, and she told me all these things and more each time we talked. On each visit, she also produced a large folder that appeared to contain every paper Jeremiah had brought home during the school year, which she displayed and discussed at length.

In addition, Amy described the tight schedule she enforced for Jeremiah's homework. Every day, at the same time each day, there was a set amount of time he must devote to school-related work. If he finished required work before that time was up, then he could choose other school-related activities, such as reading, making up math problems, or writing sentences. During our third interview, Amy described their nightly reading routine. This excerpt contains only a small portion of her description: " . . . if you miss too many words on one page, you automatically have to do it over. . . . The first book was *Best Friends*, then *Mortimer Frog*, now *Mr. Big*. So we're reading "Hello Momma," which he has to read all by hisself without missin' any words, 'cause we done read that story twice. And then we'll go over "Tap, Tap, Tap," together, then he has to read it by hisself. And if there's any time left over, he has flash cards that the teacher sends home that he's havin' a little problem with, so we'll go through the flash cards." Here Amy was actually remembering and telling me the names of all the reading books Jeremiah had gotten through, and the names of the stories in these books! In addition, she also went into great detail about how they read together. For his homework, they didn't just read; there were precise rules this reading activity must follow, and she explained those rules to me.

Every interview with Amy included such extended (and often quite tedious!) talk with much detail about every aspect of Jeremiah's schooling—his performance, his behavior, his teacher, his homework schedule, and importantly, how Amy carefully linked his schooling to his everyday life at home. This was a mother who clearly and consistently defined her child's student role as most important, regardless of the setting or what activities he was involved in. This excerpt (from our second interview) demonstrates how Amy linked Jeremiah's home life and leisure activities with his educational pursuits:

> Like I say, "Jeremiah, what you wanna be when you grow up?" He said, "Well, I wanna be like Air Jordan." I said, "Well, Air Jordan has an education. I bet you Air Jordan didn't play in school. . . . Now if you wants to be like him, you have to work on your studies. Like knowin' your ABCs, knowin' them when you see 'em. Not like 'Momma, how you make a W? How you make a F?' " I said, "You're not bein' like Air Jordan. You have to practice every day, every day." . . . I might take him down to the little court every other day, and I said, "Now if I take you to the basketball court, what are you gonna do for Momma?" He said, "Well, I'll practice writin' names, or I'll do my rhyming words, when we get back.' " I always say, "If I give you somethin', you gonna have to give me somethin' in return. And I don't want your money, I don't want no kisses, I don't want no hugs. . . . No. You're gonna have to do somethin' educational-wise for me."

Two things are especially important in this excerpt. First, Amy's talk about Michael Jordan; to paraphrase: If you want to be like Air Jordan, you have to concentrate on study. Sure, Jordan can play basketball, but not only that, he's a glowing example of the value of practice and repetition. Amy artfully used her son's admiration of Michael Jordan to help justify her own high expectations and strictness about study, and she routinely drew on interests in sports and sports personalities that she shared with Jeremiah as a resource in support of her child-rearing practices.

But the second point this excerpt brings to light is the way Amy connected Jeremiah's privileges, and her activities with him, to his willingness to expend extra effort on his student role. She would take Jeremiah to play basketball only if he would do something "educational-wise" for her in return. And both Amy and her mother told me of other instances when Jeremiah's participation in leisure activities was contingent upon his satisfactory performance in school, and his willingness to study at home.

Amy's Past in Family and School

Amy not only had high standards and expectations for Jeremiah; she also had very strong ideas about her own role in his education, and she translated these ideas into routine strategies aimed at encouraging his educational success. In addition to her participation in and close monitoring of Jeremiah's homework, she also routinely communicated with his teachers and at times attempted to influence their practices. She clearly had great confidence in her own tactics, and she described her activities with obvious pride. Amy's past clearly formed the basis of her specific child-rearing practice. Unique features and events in Amy's life influenced her interpretations of her situation and resulting child-rearing practices. By considering the unique biographical contexts in which more general patterns of family life arise, we can better understand variations in the ways that general patterns are manifested in daily practice.

Although Amy seemed a generally optimistic and happy person, there was no disputing she'd had a difficult life. Amy was one of the middle children of seven. When she was four years old, her father became mysteriously ill at work, was hospitalized for an extended period, and eventually died. Amy's mother, "Miz" Stevens, told me they were never sure what caused his illness, but "I guess there was a lot of things they didn't know anything about back then."

Soon after her husband's death, Miz Stevens began working days in a restaurant, and evenings cleaning an office building. She put her oldest daughter in charge of the other children. Because Miz Stevens was rarely home, she laid down strict rules that the children were to follow while they were home alone. As Amy said of her own routine as a schoolchild, "You come straight home, you come straight in the house, you do not let nobody in the house, you do not open the door."

Several times, Amy noted that she and her siblings had little contact with other neighborhood children. Instead, they were expected to find companionship with one another. During our third interview, Amy recalled this aspect of her own childhood in support of her own strict limits on Jeremiah's neighborhood interaction. I wanted to follow up on Amy's statements in earlier interviews about the neighborhood where they live, so I asked:

K: I wonder if conditions in the neighborhood have changed at all, or if there's been anything going on that is different, or that worries you, or any improvements in//

A: //If anything, it done got worse. He's six years old [actually, nearly seven] and I still don't like him to go outside by hisself. If I don't have time to go outside, I'm sorry, you just can't go outside, because little kids around here? Parents don't care what they do, where they at and stuff. . . .

At this point, as she did during our first interview, she again stressed that "if I don't know you, he really ain't gonna play with you," and "I don't let little kids come over here, and he do not go to no little kids' house and play. Nobody's. Nobody's." "Really?" I asked, somewhat incredulously. And Amy then explained her restrictions by linking them to her own upbringing: "See, I was always brought up, it's OK to play, but you don't go in people's house and play. You know, that's the way I was brought up. And when I was little, it was seven of us, why should I go somewhere else and play? . . . And, you know, there's always somebody here for him to play with, until the evenin', and when everybody go home, it's homework and bedtime anyway, so you don't have no time to play."

In addition to again illustrating the general theme of family difference, these excerpts demonstrate that Amy's isolationist practices arose not only in response to objective neighborhood conditions. They were also grounded in memory of her own mother's actions, her belief in the appropriateness and success of these practices, and the parallels she drew between her own childhood and her son's. Although Jeremiah was an only child, their home was typically filled with other children. Amy defined his situation as quite similar to her own when she was young, and she clearly believed similar rules and restrictions were appropriate.

In formulating and justifying her own practices, Amy not only drew on recollections of her life within the family as a youngster; she also often reflected upon her past experiences as a student. During two interviews, Amy revealed especially important information about how her own experiences informed her thinking about Jeremiah's schooling. In the first excerpt (from our second interview in February 1991), Amy had been talking about Jeremiah's school ("The school is beautiful, beautiful, [with] the best library of any public school I've ever seen"), and about his kindergarten teacher. She noted her pleasure to discover that "it's not just me, you know, pushin' him. The school is also doin' it." This then led to recollections of her own experiences as a student in the same elementary school:

> It wasn't like that when I grew up. Because—huh!—[PS#X] used to be a hole in the wall that they sent us to school in. Even when I was in the fifth grade, we did not have a desk in our classroom, nothin' but carpet. . . . We barely did schoolwork. Our teacher, he didn't care if we learned somethin'. And I think we got our first desk when we was in fifth grade, a glass cabinet fell on him, he was sittin' in his rocking chair and it fell over on his head. After that, we got desks, and things changed a little bit. . . . But it was too late then, you know, I was in the fifth grade then! . . . And when I got to the seventh grade, we got bused out to a white school. And I was truly far behind. . . . And I had to work so hard just to catch back up. . . . And when I got my first report card, I was shocked. I had one C and all the rest were As. And I didn't show her [Miz Stevens], because of that one C. . . . I tell Jeremiah's teacher everyday when I pick him up, "You tell me whenever, even if he's just talkin' too much, you let me know, and I will straighten it out." Back then they didn't care, they did not care. But my son will never get like that. Never. 'Cause when it comes time to work, you have to work. And I told 'im, "As you get older, you will understand that school is nothin' you play around with. . . ." And he has a history up here. When it comes to first grade, then he have to start all over? What if he gets sick at school? How am I gonna get way out here to get you? . . . [Next year] he'll catch the bus right down here on the corner. I don't want my child standin' out on no corner eight o'clock in the mornin'.

Amy's story of deplorable conditions she endured prior to the desegregation of IPS was told to contrast with the "beautiful" facilities and expanded opportunities she believed her son enjoyed in the same building where she'd spent her own elementary years. Not only did Jeremiah have the benefit of greatly improved material conditions in school; in addition, Amy also believed school personnel now truly cared about and pushed students to achieve, and she did whatever she could to make sure that Jeremiah took full advantage of opportunities that for her were unavailable.

Amy was bused to a distant "white school" midway through her seventh-grade year (at that time, elementary schools included K–8 students).[3] Although Amy found herself "truly far behind," through hard work (inspired in part by her mother's high standards) she recovered from her dismal early academic preparation. Amy ended this discussion as she so often did when talking about her past, by relating it to concerns about Jeremiah's schooling, and actions she took on his behalf. Through close monitoring of his schoolwork and behavior, she would make sure Jeremiah never got far behind, or let behavioral problems get out of hand. However, Amy was clearly concerned about the coming year, when Jeremiah would, like his mother, also participate in the system's mandatory busing.

Nearly two years later, I asked Amy to talk more about her experiences with busing. I wondered about her social life after she was bused in seventh grade, and although I expected she would report feelings of alienation, her response (again) defied my expectation. She described her experiences, then linked them to her feelings about Jeremiah's placement in a distant school:

K: . . . So how did you feel about bein' bused to the one school? And were you satisfied, like with your social life out there? Just describe to me what it was like.
A: [laugh] It was fun!
K: It was?
A: I didn't have to worry about my momma walkin' up to school and checkin' on me; she couldn't get way out there! I could just about get away with anything. I did my work, now don't get me wrong! I kept good grades; my momma don't believe in bad grades. . . . But I just had so much fun! I got away with as much as I could. You know, you know what buttons to push, what you could do or couldn't do. You do somethin' too bad, they gonna call your parents. I would never cross that line. I'd never want Momma to know what I be doin' in school. It was—an experiment that I think every child should have at least one year. Jeremiah done had two years down

here at [PS#XX]; he need to go to a neighborhood school so I can go check on him every day.

K: [both laugh] Well, I wondered, how did you feel your experiences with busing when you were growing up had influenced how you felt about him goin' out there?

A: Now, when he was in kindergarten, I took 'im to school, I picked him up, I usually know if he was havin' a bad day, good day. . . . But now, it's like it was when I got bused. He knows how far to go, before crossin' that line where they gonna get in contact with parents. . . . That's why I stressed to [his teacher], if it's anything, let me know, 'cause I want to keep on top of it. And like I told him, all the little things can add up to one great big ol' thing. So you don't wanna get too many little bitty things. . . .

Laughingly and with obvious enjoyment, Amy recalled the freedom from parental monitoring that busing provided her, as well as her response to that freedom. She clearly relished these memories, when she "didn't have to worry about my momma checkin' on me," and was able to "just about get away with anything!" Her tone changed, however, to one of great seriousness as she related these experiences to her desire that Jeremiah return to a nearby school so she could resume her practice of "check[ing] on him every day." Amy's own behavior as a bused student ("I got away with as much as I could") contributed to her conviction that she must continue her close monitoring of Jeremiah. She felt that, as was true for herself, he too had likely come to understand the line he shouldn't cross, and she was convinced her own persistent monitoring was required to prevent things getting out of hand.

Family Obligations and Family Ties

For high school, Amy returned to a nearby school where she continued to accept her mother's tight restrictions on her social life and demands that Amy work hard and earn good grades. After graduation in 1979, she began college at Indiana University, planning to major in business administration. At that point, it looked as though Amy's and her mother's efforts would soon pay off in her successful completion of college and eventual upward social mobility. However, before she had finished an academic year, her schooling was abruptly terminated when her mother suffered a severe stroke during the winter and was unable to care for herself. Two of Amy's younger siblings were still at home and in high school, but it was clear that Miz Stevens needed around-the-clock care. Amy and her siblings agreed that the two youngest children must finish high school, so the responsibility for Miz Stevens's care could not fall upon them. All the other children were either in college or working. Amy reported that "we all sat down—we had a family meeting, and we all sat down and I just volunteered to do it." She left college, and soon afterward began providing day care for a few children. As Miz Stevens's health gradually improved somewhat, she joined her daughter in this growing enterprise.

Amy's commitment to her family was clear in this instance, and she viewed her decision to leave college to care for her mother as unremarkable (she never volunteered this information, and I had to ask her explicitly about these events in order to learn what had transpired). Just as Miz Stevens' devotion to her children after their father died led her to take extraordinary steps to ensure their well-being—working two jobs while remaining highly involved in their education—when circumstances required, Amy made similar sacrifices on her mother's behalf, apparently without question. Amy's sense of family loyalty and devotion was very keen, and this, too, was a quality she hoped to develop in Jeremiah. She reportedly attempted to teach him that "your family come first . . . and everything else is secondary."

One final event in Amy's life may have contributed to her very protective and controlling parenting style. Several months before this study began, Amy's twin brother had died of a progressive illness left untreated for too long. When Amy told me this, she quickly added, "But he hadn't been livin' here. I think if he had been livin' here, it would be different." The only one of Amy's six siblings to ever leave Indianapolis for reasons other than college, Lyle had moved to another state. There he became quite ill but refused to see a doctor. By the time friends called his family, it was too late, and he died a few weeks later. Amy and her brothers were convinced Lyle would have lived had he not left the city, and this event underscored the importance and the protective function of family in Amy's mind. Families don't just protect their members from influences encouraging dropping out of school, criminal activities, or early parenthood. Family monitoring keeps members alive.

JEREMIAH'S NARRATIVE:
SCHOOLING UNDER AMY'S WATCHFUL EYE

Amy's experiences, her parenting concerns, and the child-rearing strategies she employed in the face of these concerns are fascinating in their own right. But the question of greater concern is: How do Jeremiah's experiences in school reflect his mother's practices?

According to his kindergarten teacher, Jeremiah began public school with skills and knowledge that placed him well above the average of his classmates. As he moved into later grades, however, he was more aptly described as a solid but not exceptional student who typically received Bs and Cs, and occasional As, on report cards. Jeremiah was a great deal like his mother—small and wiry, with a quick and expressive smile and energy that at times seemed nearly uncontrollable. Despite this, his manners were generally impeccable and quite formal unless he was excited. For example, although I introduced myself as "Katy" to the children, and all of them called me this (or "Miss Katy," as their mothers instructed), only Jeremiah routinely called me "Ma'am" in Amy's presence. At the Head Start center and on other occasions when I saw him apart from Amy, however, he too addressed me by my informal first name. This was a pattern evident in Jeremiah's behavior more generally. At home, and at school when Amy was present, Jeremiah was polite, reserved, and occasionally nervous and obviously concerned with pleasing his mother. I do not want to overstate this, however—despite occasional apparent anxiety, Jeremiah did not appear unhappy, and he clearly returned the devotion he received from Amy.

Yet his demeanor and behavior were quite different in other settings. His kindergarten teacher noted that "he's very active, very active," and "he easily becomes overexcited." This characterization fit well with our observations from the Head Start classroom. Here it was clear that Jeremiah sought rambunctious play and had little interest in crafts, puzzles, or other such activities. Rather, his free-time choices reflected a desire for physical play with other boys, with materials like blocks, toy cars, or barbershop paraphernalia. At times, while he obviously was excited, he seemed to lose control and became too physical with playmates, resulting in minor altercations and a few tears. In one instance, Jeremiah and Anthony played with tubular blocks, transforming them into telescopes and cameras that they held to their eyes in order to survey the room. As Anthony held a block to his eye, Jeremiah's block became a hammer (a typical transformation of these toys) and he hit it smartly against Anthony's, causing surprise and considerable pain. Anthony began crying and bid for a teacher's attention, and Jeremiah worriedly asked, "Are you gonna tell on me?" Anthony did tell, but after the teacher suggested it was accidental ("Did he mean to?") and extracted an apology from Jeremiah, the incident was forgotten.

This resolution was typical of how disputes were handled at the center, and only on rare occasions did teachers enforce punishments or inform parents. In contrast, Jeremiah's misbehavior at home led to more serious consequences. For example, Amy enforced time-outs when Jeremiah fought with his cousin or other children, or withdrew television or snack privileges when things got too rough. It is quite possible that as early as his Head Start year, Jeremiah was learning that he could get away with things at school that were dealt with much more harshly at home.

Jeremiah's teachers reported similar behavior (in kindergarten, first grade, and—according to Amy—second grade as well), often involving physical play that appeared to get out of hand. This and other roughhousing (for example, sliding under bathroom stalls in second grade, and doing cartwheels and flips in the first-grade classroom) contrasted sharply with Amy's expectations for Jeremiah's behavior. Although his teachers seemed to view such incidents as relatively minor, Amy took these reports very seriously and often suspended Jeremiah's privileges at home in response. Despite consequences, Jeremiah's misbehavior persisted.

Jeremiah's misconduct at school could be seen as assertions of his independence from his mother, and certain statements Amy made suggested that she might view this as somewhat desirable. For example, Amy repeatedly noted her desire that Jeremiah "find [his] own road and follow it," and she told him that "you have a mind—use your own mind." As my understanding of Amy's strategies deepened over time, however, I realized that her urgings that Jeremiah "use his own mind" applied only to his relations with peers, not to his dealings with adult authorities.

In addition, even Amy's frequent assertions that she wanted Jeremiah to take greater responsibility for his own care, possessions, and schoolwork seemed rather empty, as she continued to direct and control even his most mundane activities (bathing, for example) as he got older. Remarkably, Amy's mother observed this inconsistency between her daughter's words and actions, and shared her observations with me. Early in our fourth interview, Amy happily noted that Jeremiah's second-grade teacher was stressing that the children take responsibility for getting their own work done, and she then went upstairs to fetch a folder containing Jeremiah's school papers. During Amy's brief absence, Miz Stevens commented that "his teacher is teachin' him responsibility, and his mother don't." I asked her, "Why do you say that?" and she bluntly replied: "Because she doesn't." Amy returned at that point and Miz Stevens did not elaborate, but she made similar remarks when she and I spoke by phone nearly a year later. She noted that Jeremiah had been getting in trouble at home and at Drill Team, and she offered this explanation for his difficulties: "Jeremiah has a problem with responsibility. His mother doesn't make him be responsible." She complained about Jeremiah's "attitude," but said she could not discuss these things with Amy, who became defensive and upset (but could with me!).

Jeremiah's small bids for independence were complemented by complaints to his mother about the control she exerted over both his schoolwork, and his activities in the neighborhood. Amy assured Jeremiah he would understand the importance of school when he got older, and she linked conscientious attention to educational matters with the success of admired personalities. Essentially, she met his resistance with sympathetic explanations coupled with unrelenting insistence. When it came to his bids for more interaction with children outside school, however, Amy demonstrated some willingness to adjust her practices. Although in the early spring of 1994 Amy still would not allow Jeremiah, then nearly nine, to play outside unless she was with him or could see him from the window, she had begun to involve him in activities that allowed more interaction with peers while maintaining adult control over that contact. For example, during his first- and second-grade years, Jeremiah participated in swimming lessons, a summer garden club at the neighborhood school, organized baseball, and a church drill team.

Teachers Reactions to Amy's Tactics

Amy's intense involvement and control over Jeremiah was not lost on his kindergarten and first-grade teachers, who both acknowledged her conscientious attention to all matters concerning Jeremiah's education. They did, however, differ somewhat in their feelings about Amy's tactics. While Jeremiah's first-grade teacher offered unconditional praise of Amy's activities, his kindergarten teacher's assessment was quite mixed.

Jeremiah's kindergarten teacher was a white woman of about fifty who had taught for twenty years in several school systems, and in a variety of elementary grades. This was Ms. Sampsel's second year in her current position. Her students were from the surrounding low-income, primarily black neighborhood, and of the twenty-seven children in Jeremiah's afternoon class, only two or three were white.

Ms. Sampsel confirmed much of what Amy had reported about her activities in support of Jeremiah's education, including her pattern of checking daily about his schoolwork and behavior. The teacher offered both praise for Amy's involvement and concern that she might be overdoing it somewhat. Before I had asked Ms. Sampsel any questions about Amy, she introduced the topic while she discussed Jeremiah's performance in her class: "...His attendance is excellent. His mom is very much into his [laugh] performance, probably to a fault. . . . I think while he's doing a task, on the top of his mind is 'If I don't get this done right, I'm gonna be in deep trouble.' . . . He knows if he—like if he misses something, maybe Amy won't let him play for a couple days. . . . She kind of does overkill on things. So I think he does become very uptight, he doesn't want to fail."

Ms. Sampsel also noted that despite these problems Jeremiah "works hard," is "persistent" and "finishes tasks," and "is just right up there with the kids that know what they need to know." Later, Ms. Sampsel again brought up Amy's tactics, this time articulating the "fine line" she felt Amy walked between pressure and control that would encourage Jeremiah's success in schooling, and pressure and control that might instead lead to destructive rebellion. She said:

> "[Amy] obviously takes very good care of this little guy. And she's just putting a lot of herself into his upbringing. . . . I don't think Jeremiah's one of these kids who can grow up Topsy-like, and they still know everything, and toe the line, and do fine. I think if he wouldn't have gotten into Head Start, if Amy would not work so hard with him, I think that he would be having some struggles. And I don't know how that's gonna work itself out. . . . And I think a lot of these black mothers also see what happens to little black boys when they get about fifth grade. And I think that she's determined that this is not gonna happen. She's not gonna let it happen . . . there's a fine line. And I think even at this point he is rebelling against that, and you can see it in his reaction to her. And sometimes I'll try to balance that a little bit in the classroom; I'll cut him a little slack sometimes. Or say to her, "Be sure and compliment Jeremiah; he did a good job doing this." Because I think often she does bear down on things, [and] I wouldn't want to see him become so paranoid about that that he really is afraid to take a guess, take a gamble on an answer.

Finally, however, she concluded: "If she's consistent in it, hey—that's better than somebody who doesn't give a rip."

Clearly, Ms. Sampsel had a great deal of knowledge about Amy and her practices with Jeremiah, and she shared my own growing concern that perhaps Amy pushed too hard and was too concerned about every facet of his education. It was fascinating to hear how Ms. Sampsel had attempted to offset what she perceived as excessive pressure by cutting Jeremiah "some slack" in the classroom, and making a special effort to communicate to Amy his positive accomplishments. It was also clear at other points that Ms. Sampsel downplayed Jeremiah's minor misbehaviors—especially his tendency to become overexcited—in light of her concern that Amy might overreact.

The following year, Jeremiah rode the bus for twenty minutes to a school located in a working-class white neighborhood. He entered a class of only fourteen students, of whom he and two other bused children were the only blacks in the class. Jeremiah's teacher was a black woman in her mid-thirties, completing her first year in her current position. Ms. North had taught second and first grade in another IPS school for seven years, and before that was briefly employed in an all-black inner-city school in a major northeastern city.

This year, Amy could no longer regularly converse with his teacher, or drop in for unexpected visits. In fact, although she found a ride to the parent-teacher conference in the fall of the year, this was one of only three times she visited the school throughout Jeremiah's first-grade year. Although the school's distance clearly limited her participation, Amy kept herself informed through frequent phone calls and correspondence with Ms. North and, especially, through supervision of Jeremiah's work. In addition, Amy also attempted to influence the teacher's standards for acceptable work. Early in the school year, Amy used the parent-teacher conference to stress the high standards she held for her son, and to complain that Ms. North at times appeared to give high marks for what she considered shoddy work. She recalled telling Jeremiah, "Your teacher accept this sloppy stuff? And you got a smiling face on this? Well, I don't like it. You don't ride your bike today."

According to Amy, Ms. North responded by advising her to "be hard, but don't be that hard, 'cause he's doing very well compared to some of the kids." When I spoke with the teacher later in the school year, she too recalled this conversation and said that while Jeremiah's work might appear "not good to her, judging him by the class he's doing good." However, Ms. North also noted that "sometimes I think I'm a little more critical with him, in light of

the fact that I know he can do so much better." This example
demonstrates that Amy did more than just support and reinforce
school learning. She also tried to shape teachers' expectations
and evaluations of her son to more closely match her own higher
standards.[4]

As was true the year before, there was again evidence Jeremiah
was rebelling against his mother's tactics. Both Amy and Ms. North
reported he occasionally "lost" or "forgot" to deliver notes between
the two women. In fact, when Amy tried to communicate with Ms.
North about my research and our hope that the teacher would
grant an interview, Jeremiah repeatedly "forgot" to deliver this
note. When Amy finally told him, "That note is about Katy," he
reportedly replied, "Oh! Mom, I can't find it. I lost it." Amy wrote a
new note, which he then happily delivered.

Despite such small acts of resistance on Jeremiah's part, and
although Amy was rarely able to visit the school, Ms. North was
impressed with her consistent involvement. Like Jeremiah's
kindergarten teacher, Ms. North recognized that Amy exercised
tight control over Jeremiah's schooling, saying that "she gets on
'im, pretty much, she's hard on him when it comes to school."
This teacher, however, gave no indication that Amy's strategies
might be excessive. In fact, she argued that "she needs to be [hard
on him], especially with the boys, today." I asked her to elaborate,
and she continued:

> She doesn't let 'im get away with things, when he know he's sup-
> posed to do somethin', she makes him do it. No ands, ifs, or buts
> about it . . . she just makes sure he's doin' what he's supposed to
> do when it's supposed to be done. You know, she doesn't give 'im a
> whole lot of room for error. And the reason I said that boys today
> need it, especially black boys, they just don't have the role models,
> they don't have the self-esteem that they should have, the morals
> either, you know. [small laugh] And it's not *all*, but it's a lot, it's more
> than it should be. And when I was teachin' in a school where it was
> all black kids, I was a lot harder on my class. Because I didn't want
> them goin' out here and endin' up bein' a statistic. Either dead, or in
> jail, or on drugs. I feel that she's gonna make sure he's gettin' a
> education. He's not gonna be a dropout, 'cause she's not gonna let
> 'im. You need to have someone that's gonna be right on them when
> they're not doin' what they should be doin'.[5]

Although Jeremiah's kindergarten and first-grade teachers differed somewhat in their feelings about the appropriateness of
Amy's monitoring and control, they both believed that her tactics

could indeed help Jeremiah avoid negative outcomes all too common for "black boys" from low-income families and neighborhoods. Both also believed that without his mother's constant pushing, Jeremiah would have had more difficulties.

Academically, Ms. North described Jeremiah's grades as "just basically Cs and Bs," and Amy often lamented his many near-misses of honor roll status.[6] Ms. North was also disappointed with his performance, and she emphasized her belief that Jeremiah could achieve at a higher level. She reportedly "told him often that you can do better than this, and I've written to his mother that I don't think I'm gettin' his best effort."

While I did not interview second-grade teachers, I did meet Jeremiah's second-grade teacher and observed briefly in her classroom one morning when Amy and I attended a midyear awards ceremony. Before the start of the program, we watched as the children went through their morning routine in the classroom. Ms. Roth then distributed report cards. Jeremiah had seen his report card the day before, and he'd already told Amy that once again he'd "just missed" honor roll. But as the teacher distributed the cards, she announced that "there's somebody who doesn't think they made the honor roll, who actually did," and she beamed at Amy and stood beside Jeremiah's desk to examine his card with him. Unfortunately, Jeremiah had Cs in language and in reading, and was therefore ineligible. Everyone was disappointed as this confusion was resolved, but I was fascinated by the teacher's obvious desire for Jeremiah to do better than he actually had, both for his own sake and for his mother's.

Jeremiah's kindergarten, first-grade, and second-grade teachers, then, all demonstrated their desires and their expectations that he achieve at a higher level than he typically did. They appeared convinced he was capable of doing "so much better" and, in line with these convictions, they pushed him to improve upon his grades (which were, of course, really quite decent though not exceptional). In addition, they attributed his failure to excel to factors other than ability. In kindergarten, Ms. Sampsel interpreted Jeremiah's reluctance to offer answers and delays in completing his work as nervousness about his mother's potential disapproval. She did not seem to consider the possibility that he simply might not have the skills, knowledge, or motivation to do better. Similarly, Ms. North also did not appear to consider that Jeremiah's grades might truly reflect his abilities. Rather, this teacher was concerned that rushing to finish so he could socialize and have fun affected Jeremiah's performance.

These teachers perceived in Jeremiah capabilities beyond those he displayed, and it seemed that Amy's activities played a role in these perceptions. The teachers' awareness of Amy's clear devotion to her son, her concern for his success, and her extremely high valuation of educational achievement seemed to influence their assessments of his abilities. Part of the explanation for the teachers' beliefs that Jeremiah was a brighter student than he typically demonstrated could lie in their strong beliefs that parents' educational values have powerful effects on both children's motivation and ability to achieve. In my interviews with teachers, this was one of the most consistent themes—parents' valuation of education, as expressed through their apparent involvement, was viewed as perhaps the most important predictor and motivator of children's academic success. Certainly Jeremiah's teachers' knowledge of Amy's activities and values can help explain their convictions that this was a child who could be an excellent student, despite his failure to demonstrate such academic aptitude. Other children who performed comparably were seen by teachers in a much different light (see especially chapter 5, concerning Zena).

On the whole, Jeremiah's transition into schooling was generally positive and laid a foundation for future achievement as well as productive collaboration between home and school. Amy's painstaking work with Jeremiah prior to his entry into public school, coupled with his Head Start experiences, prepared him well for the initial transition into kindergarten. Once there, his kindergarten teacher's insight concerning Amy's perhaps overzealous participation contributed to action on her part that to some extent shielded Jeremiah from parental control that might otherwise have overwhelmed or immobilized him.

When Jeremiah was bused to a distant school the following year, his mother and teacher both expressed quite negative views about mandatory busing, as did virtually every teacher who addressed this issue. Amy argued during our second interview: "It's such a shame that you can't go to the school in your neighborhood. . . . I can see if busing was helping. Back then, it helped, now I don't think it's helpin' . . . So, why bus?" And Ms. North noted how pleased she was with the high level of parental involvement in the daily activities at the school, but she added that, unfortunately, "I haven't had any [parental help] from my bused children, which is understandable. All the parents that come out and help are the neighborhood parents." Despite these negative perceptions about mandatory busing, for Jeremiah, this systemic requirement may actually have positively contributed to his transition, providing him with a degree of independence from his mother's scrutiny, which otherwise might have become unbearable.

At the same time, the routine activities that structured his time at home likely helped offset the potentially unsettling and alienating effects that too often do accompany mandatory busing of students away from neighborhood schools (see Calabrese 1990). Indeed, the importance of Amy's insistence on rigid in-home routines cannot be overemphasized: the sense of security and predictability provided by routine in one sphere greatly enhances children's ability to cope with change and uncertainty in other areas (Corsaro 1985, 1988). And Jeremiah did indeed seem to cope well with the changes that accompanied his movement into first grade. Although he was not a model student, he dealt with his transition into a full-day program in an unfamiliar environment with ease and with obvious enjoyment. After busing, Jeremiah's grades remained slightly above average, he made friends and easily integrated himself into the peer culture, and, importantly, his first-grade teacher reported none of the nervousness that had so worried Ms. Sampsel.

While I have struggled with my own perceptions that Amy's tactics were excessive, I must point out that Jeremiah's smooth adjustment to busing differed sharply from the experiences of the three other children who were also bused in their first-grade year (Zena, Tamera, and Sheila—all girls). Undoubtedly, Amy's adherence to demanding routines at home contributed to Jeremiah's easy adjustment, while the other children's more difficult experiences may have been exacerbated by their less predictable home lives (see chapters 5, 6, and 7). Of course, the remarkable stability and continuity of Amy's residence, her income and employment situation, and her relationships with members of her extended family likely contributed to her ability to maintain these routines.

CONCLUSION

When the study children began third grade in the fall of 1993, they did so in the context of a new school-choice program. Not surprisingly, Amy chose to move Jeremiah to a school closer to home. Although her first choice was the neighborhood school he'd attended for kindergarten, he was assigned instead to her second-choice school, somewhat more accessible via public transportation, but still too distant for Amy to visit Jeremiah's classroom regularly. And Jeremiah continued to begin and end each school day with a bus ride, albeit a shorter one.

Amy was disappointed with this placement, but she had already demonstrated her ability to make such a situation work for her and her son. I had little doubt that patterns established in Jeremiah's earlier years of schooling—for example, Amy's strict control over Jeremiah's activities, the high level of support she demonstrated for teachers' demands, and her active advocacy on her son's behalf—would continue as he moved into the new school and into the upper elementary grades. Amy's involvement would likely help to shape teachers' perceptions and expectations of Jeremiah and his experiences there.

In addition to portraying the somewhat unique circumstances of Jeremiah's transition into schooling, this narrative has introduced themes that will reemerge repeatedly in coming chapters. Amy provides the exemplar for two of these themes to which other mothers' and children's experiences should be compared; for both claims of family difference, and involvement in children's schooling, Amy and Jeremiah represent the extreme case.

In this research, mothers' interpretations of their circumstances, and their translations of those interpretations into practice, reflected many similarities among them, and many similar assessments of the environments in which they were raising their children. All the mothers viewed themselves as different from the families who shared their neighborhoods, and they all saw their neighborhoods as somewhat dangerous places to live. They all also had strategies for protecting their children from the threats they perceived. In addition, all the mothers demonstrated their valuation of education and their beliefs that through education, their children could avoid negative outcomes that were common among residents in their communities. But the strategies of various mothers were different, and even when they were basically the same, they differed in degree. Understanding these differences in practice requires examination of the mothers' biographies, and consideration of their own earlier experiences in family, school, and community settings. Amy's history in both family and school provided her with critical resources she could draw upon in formulating her own strategies. Several other mothers appeared to have few similar resources available as they negotiated their children's transition into formal schooling. And while other mothers attempted to isolate their children from negative neighborhood influences, all allowed more freedom than did Amy. Likewise, Amy's involvement in Jeremiah's schooling was unmatched.

The final theme introduced in this narrative concerns the critical support often provided by the mothers' networks. For Amy, the exchange of practical and emotional support among extended-family members added stability and opportunities to her son's life. While all the mothers relied on support networks to some extent to enhance their children's lives, not all of these networks were peopled so heavily with extended family members. The next chapter, devoted to Annette and Alysha Richy, describes a primarily church-based network, and the role of religion in the Richys' daily life.

3

LOOKING FOR A PLACE TO SING

Several mothers in this study were deeply involved in their churches, and religious themes were clear and common as they talked about their lives and their parenting. This was nowhere more true than with Annette Richy, and in this narrative I describe how church and religion permeated the Richys' family life. Just as Amy's extended family influenced and supported her child-rearing efforts, Annette's church provided her with moral and practical support that helped her both interpret and negotiate her social environment. Annette's young daughter, Alysha, drew on her own religious understandings and faith as she negotiated a place among her peers in educational settings.

While Amy's version of "family values," and her devotion to Jeremiah's schooling, provided the foundation for her "claims of family difference," Annette felt it was her family's religiosity that set them apart from others in their community. Annette was less judgmental than Amy, and her interaction with both me and her children's teachers displayed a tentativeness that suggested considerably less self-confidence. This lack of confidence was limited to her own efficacy, however, and Annette's utter faith in her religious beliefs was clear.

My fears about what the practice of her faith would entail contributed to expectations that Alysha's freedom and autonomy would be severely limited. These concerns, however, were misplaced, and in this chapter I begin to examine the encouragement of autonomy and independence (through both words and deeds) that characterized many mothers' child-rearing practices. For her part, Alysha seemed to be developing a strong, independent personality—encouraged by both her mother's tactics and her experiences in Head Start. But this chapter is also the first to examine the clash that was often apparent between the emerging personalities and styles of the children, and the styles and expectations of teachers and peers. This was particularly problematic for children who attended distant, majority-white schools. Jeremiah was exceptional in his easy adaptation to this situation, while Alysha had much more difficulty. As the experiences of Alysha and several other children demonstrated, the skills, knowledge, and behavioral styles that served children well in Head Start classrooms were often ill suited and ill received in new classroom settings with culturally different peers and adult authorities.

Finally, this narrative underscores the unfortunate repercussions of stereotypical thinking about families and children. Stereotype-driven definitions of both Annette and Alysha seemed to take on a life of their own, and I participated in the perpetuation of some of those stereotypes right along with Alysha's teachers. While I have many regrets about my own prejudices concerning this family, I believe I eventually arrived at an appropriate interpretation of Annette and Alysha's family culture and their experiences in educational settings.

ANNETTE'S NARRATIVE: MY BIASES
AND AN UNFORTUNATE BEGINNING

Before ever meeting Annette, I unfortunately had quite negative preconceived notions about her and her family. These were based on comments by the teachers at the Head Start center, and on observations of Alysha's interaction with teachers and peers. From the teachers, I knew Annette had many young children and—after the birth of another child in early 1990—they felt that "enough was enough!" In fact, I learned during our first interview in July 1990 that Annette and her husband, Manny, had six children under the age of seven (another child born in 1991 brought the family total to three girls and four boys). I admittedly shared the teachers' feelings that the family had "enough" children, and that some effort to limit future childbearing was called for.

In addition, early on in this research I struggled with quite negative feelings about "fundamentalist" religion, and my biases were undeniable in my perceptions of Annette and her family. While many children at the Head Start center occasionally mentioned God, Jesus, or attending church, Alysha most routinely brought religious issues and comments into her interaction with peers and teachers. My own agnostic beliefs contributed to expectations that Alysha's family would be closed-minded, authoritarian and patriarchal.[1] Although I came to respect and in many ways admire Annette over time, I never totally overcame my initial discomfort in the face of the extreme religiosity I observed in this family.

For her part, Annette may have sensed my uneasiness, and she perhaps reciprocated by never quite opening up the way other mothers did. In addition, Annette considered herself a naturally reserved and private person, as she said at the end of our first interview: "I'm somewhat of a shy person, and I feel like I'm not very articulate, and so a lot of times I just keep my thoughts to myself." Interviews with Annette were by far the shortest I conducted, and they contained occasional uncomfortable silences. Despite this awkwardness, Annette was unfailingly pleasant, cooperative, and even affectionate at times, and she made it clear she appreciated and valued my interest in her daughter and their lives.

Valuing Religion, Education, and Autonomy

Like Amy, Annette was twenty-nine years of age when we first met. Also like Amy, she had graduated from the Indianapolis Public Schools in the late 1970s. During our first interview, Annette described herself as a "full-time mother," and with her many closely spaced children, this was a very demanding occupation indeed. Annette noted several times that she had persistent misgivings about not continuing her education—she thought, perhaps, she would have made a good teacher. However, after graduation from high school she met and married her husband, Manny, and never pursued any higher education.

At the time of our first interview, Manny Richy was employed at a religious radio station. He was trained in broadcasting, and had worked in both television and radio. Because his work often fell short of full-time, he sometimes held several jobs to support his family (including work as support staff in the public schools). Although the Richys had received AFDC for a brief period during the 1980s, they never received AFDC or food stamps during our acquaintance. However, like Jeremiah, the Richy children met eligibility criteria and received free school lunch throughout the years of this study.

The Richys lived in a large single-family rental home on a relatively quiet street that runs just one block between a busy major street and a small city park. In addition to other equally large, single-family homes, there are two churches on their block. Rundown homes—some deserted and many graffiti-covered—fill the surrounding neighborhood, which is generally considered quite "bad," but the Richys' block stands out as something of an anomalous enclave in an otherwise threatening and depressing area. Despite the seeming safety and quiet, Alysha and her siblings were forbidden to leave their home and large front porch to play in the neighborhood unless they were accompanied by an adult. However, Annette told me, this precaution was not necessarily in response to the particular neighborhood. "At their age," she said, "I would be concerned about any neighborhood I lived in. . . . Someone could snatch a child from any area, from anyplace. . . . If they were a little older, I might be more concerned about them being involved in activities that I don't condone. Like maybe a gang, maybe running with other children whose parents don't have the same values as myself."

Relatives were much less visible in the daily lives of this family than was true for Amy and for most other families represented here. In particular, the Richy children did not enjoy the involvement of grandparents in their lives on a regular basis. Manny's mother had passed on, and although Annette's parents lived in the city, the Richys typically saw them only once every couple of weeks. Annette described her mother as a young working woman whose busy life constrained involvement with her daughter's family.

Instead of extended family, this family depended primarily on their church congregation (which did include some of Manny's siblings) for both practical and emotional support, and church activities were central to their daily lives. On Sundays, they attended both Sunday school and regular services at their Apostolic church. As I discovered when Mary and I spent a Sunday with the Richys in December 1992, these activities lasted from morning to evening, with an afternoon break for socializing and eating the packed lunches many people brought with them. In addition, the Richys also attended "at least" two other evening services during the week at their Apostolic church. Manny was a member of the church's board, and on the day we attended, he read the week's announcements and sat at the front of the church throughout the service. During my interviews with Annette, the few times the telephone rang or someone knocked on the door, she explained the interruptions by saying, "That was so-and-so, from the church. . . ."

The Richys' friends were members of their congregation, and Annette rarely mentioned activities that did not revolve around the church or church members. They regularly socialized with Manny's siblings—two brothers and two sisters, all with older children—and, more often, with Annette's best friend, who had five children in the same age range as the Richys'. Annette felt fortunate, she said, to have these families in their lives. Not only did they share her interests and values—she also noted that since they are "better off financially," they served as "good role models for me and the children" (Annette was one of several mothers who felt it important their children socialize with children from more affluent families). In addition, these other families were occasionally willing to share their resources, "so we're able to participate in activities we might otherwise not have the chance to do" (for example, attending the fair, circus, or Ice Capades).

During our third interview, while discussing the family's regular activities, I mentioned the Women's Auxiliary group at Annette's church, and wondered "if you're still involved in that and if that's still a source of support for you." She replied that it was, then added that "the church itself is a big support for me." She described their church as "an anchor," "our family's foundation," and concluded that "the church, it's like a springboard, for our whole lifestyle."

Annette's comments confirmed my impression of the primacy of the church for this family. In her characteristically self-effacing manner, she then continued this discussion and speculated on what made her family "different" from other large black families who struggle financially:

> . . . As a matter of fact, that's what helps us to cope with all of the problems that come up on a daily basis. You know, I guess our family is—well, if you have any other families [involved in this research] that attend church, or feel like the church is their backbone, too, that's great. But I guess I could say that is one difference in us and maybe some other large families, that don't have some type of religion or place of worship, so to speak. We're always looking for a brighter day, tryin' to cope within our situation the best way we can, righteously. . . . Not to say that we're perfect and that we don't make mistakes, but we are generally pretty good people. And we

try to put good values in our children. . . . We try to maintain a goodness in our house.

Here Annette introduced the theme of family difference that was so prevalent in interviews with Amy Stevens. As was true for Amy, Annette's notions that her family was somehow different from (and superior to) others in similar situations were based on her apparent sense that other families lacked "good values." But while Annette was occasionally mildly and subtly critical of other families, she seemed to take great care not to appear judgmental of others. Amy clearly had no such reservations. This difference in the forcefulness of the two women's "claims" may be attributable to Annette's identification of her religion as the source of her family's values, goodness, and ability to cope. She was willing to take very little personal credit for positive aspects of her family. Instead, the credit lay elsewhere, and it was clear in other instances that she believed most or all of other people's problems would be resolved if they turned their lives over to the Lord.[2] On the other hand, Amy—who, along with Rhonda (see chapter 4), was among the least religious mothers involved in this research— was not at all reluctant to proudly take credit for her accomplishments and values.

Alysha's "Leadership Potential"

Annette had high expectations for Alysha prior to the start of her elementary schooling, and although she never said so explicitly, she seemed to believe Alysha was the most promising of her children. During our first interview, Annette praised Alysha's academic skills and apparent aptitude, but she also stressed social skills and personality characteristics that she believed were her daughter's forte. For example, she responded to my request that she "briefly describe Alysha to me, particularly her major strengths or potential problems" by saying: "She's bright. She's kind. I'm noticing that even at a very young age, she's displaying great friendship qualities. She's fun, she's caring, concerned, she's just so—she's just so all-American, she's just a really great girl! She's not having any problems in school—for her age, and you know, school level. And right now I'm not concerned about any problems education-wise. I expect her to do real well. She's peculiar in that she has some extraordinary abilities there, I'm sensing something there. She almost has leadership potential, because she is so sure of herself in so many ways."

Here Annette introduced a particularistic theme that would be reiterated and elaborated throughout this study—that is, Alysha's "leadership potential." Not only did she believe her daughter was inclined toward assertiveness and leadership, she also felt her daughter could possibly influence others to lead more moral, Christian lives. She noted that while "other people might not necessarily have the same values that she has," Alysha might be able to "help them to arrive to her values." It was clear from our first interview, then, that Annette believed her daughter was a strong, principled, and talented child whose potential to achieve in both academic and social arenas was considerable.

The following year, Alysha seemed to be living up to the high expectations Annette had expressed. According to her mother, Alysha was doing well in kindergarten, and Annette again stressed her daughter's leadership potential. When I asked about teacher feedback, Annette laughed as she said, "Alysha's bright, active, alert, and energetic." I reminded her of a comment she'd earlier made on the phone ("You said you thought she was kind of taking a leadership role in the classroom") and Annette quickly interrupted:

A: //Um-hmm, exactly.//[3] As a matter of fact, the teacher has let me know that a lot of times when she is trying to give the class instructions on how to do something, Alysha will beat her to the punch, and instruct the class for her. She'll just blurt out, "Let's do it this way, or that way." [laugh] And sometimes she lets her just go ahead and do it.

K: Well good! 'Cause I know that would bother some teachers, but it's nice that a child would be able to be assertive and to want to help other kids.

A: Um-hmm. So sometimes Ms. Weston allows her that privilege, whereas maybe in another class, they wouldn't. Um-hmm, they would restrict her to being submissive and quiet and—you know. . . . Now the teacher has said that Alysha seems to have stubborn streak, she can get in her moods. And if she feels like she's been done unjustly, she will kind of rebel. She'll kind of sulk, and maybe fold her arms. And they'll just talk her around. And when she comes out, she's all smiles. . . . But if she feels like someone has done her wrong, she will stand her ground. She won't be belligerent or outwardly rebellious or anything like that, but she'll let you know.

K: How do you feel about that?

A: I feel good about that. Because she's not ugly with it, but she will let you know that you've done something wrong and this needs to be cleared up before we go any further. And then when it's cleared up, she's just the same lovable child that she was before.

As I'll discuss at some length below, Ms. Weston's assessment of Alysha's take-charge attitude and her "stubbornness" was somewhat different from Annette's. Annette was convinced her daughter had extraordinary personal characteristics—leadership, assertiveness, and friendliness—that were her "special talent or ability" and should be "cultivated" in order for Alysha "to be the best that she can be." Annette also clearly valued Alysha's independent, autonomous behavior and thinking.

When we met for our third interview in November of Alysha's first-grade year, Annette produced more glowing reports of her daughter's academic progress. Alysha was "doing great," and had received high marks in everything on her report card. Annette described how the first-grade teacher compared Alysha very favorably to her older sister, who "she thought was a good reader," and also good in math, but Alysha impressed the teacher even more. Finally, she noted that Ms. Corbin had begun sending home reading books that were "more advanced than what the rest of the class is doing."

For the first time, however, Annette suggested there were worrisome developments in Alysha's interaction with peers. She said the "girls at this age" were becoming quite "trendy," and occasionally certain girls would "choose not to play with her." Although these snubs were typically forgotten the next day, and they would "want to be friends again," Annette feared these incidents were upsetting Alysha because she is "such a friendly child" who "wants to fit in." Annette was concerned this might negatively affect her daughter's personality, causing her to become less outgoing and self-confident.

During this interview, Annette made no mention of teacher complaints, but did note some general concerns about Alysha's behavior. She noted trying to impress on Alysha "the importance of being trustworthy" and said, "Sometimes when she sees somethin' she likes, I'll have to remind her, if it's not yours, don't bother it." In addition, Annette was concerned that Alysha seemed less open with her than in the past. Now, "if something's troubling her she won't want to talk about it." This "really bother[ed]" Annette, but she characteristically chose to see this in a positive light: "She does have an inner strength, because she must feel like she can handle it." Although Annette did not connect these issues to discussions she'd had with Alysha's teacher, when I later interviewed the teacher, it was clear Ms. Corbin had similar concerns.

My initial concern was that Annette's fundamentalism might

contribute to a rigid and authoritarian parenting style. Before getting to know Annette, I worried that Alysha's opportunities to be assertive, and to develop her own interests and self-confidence, would be restricted in her home environment. However, Annette was pleased with Alysha's ability to "stand her ground" and stick up for herself. While Annette clearly hoped her children's choices would include the strong religious beliefs and practices stressed in her church, she did not believe such things could be forced. And there is considerable additional evidence that Annette made a conscious effort to encourage their independence. During our third interview, I asked how Annette's child-rearing strategies for encouraging academic, social, and moral development might have changed since Alysha was a preschooler. Annette addressed the first two of these areas, then moved on to discuss her approach to the development of morality:

> It's funny. Even though a child might be raised in church, they have to develop their own values. And that's good, because this is not a dictatorship type of thing, or it should not be. . . . I'm noticing that even though she's been raised in church, she's developing her own ideas apart from what she's taught. Sometimes she chooses to do things her way, not the correct way. . . . If she was under a dictatorship, she probably wouldn't feel free enough to develop her own ideas. . . . Even though we are strongly church rooted, she's still herself, and she's still developing what *her* values and morals are. . . . She is expressing some of the values of her peers. She likes to dance. You know, I don't dance. . . . She does choose to listen to some rock and roll and some rhythm and blues, and some of that bebop dancin' music. . . .I allow her those freedoms. . . . Another example, I don't wear pants. . . . She knows I don't, and that ladies should not, that our church admonishes that ladies should not.[4] [Alysha—in the adjacent room—interjected: "I have some blue jeans."] Yeah, I know. But I'm letting her be somewhat free, within herself, to discover herself. . . .

Annette's child-rearing practices did not, therefore, seem to reflect the dogmatism I feared, and that others have warned against.[5] And perhaps even more significant than any of Annette's words on this matter were my observations of Alysha's activities during this interview. Shortly after we began, the four oldest children arrived home from school. After visiting with me briefly, Alysha went into the adjacent room and turned on a radio while her mother and I continued talking. For much of the rest of my visit, Alysha danced quite earnestly and sang along with the songs that played on the popular station. We do not, therefore, need to take at face value Annette's claim that Alysha was granted autonomy from the quite restrictive ideology of the Richys' religion—Alysha's behavior confirmed her mother's assertions, as they were being made.

Choosing Newberry

Like the other mothers, Annette placed high value on her children's education. During our second interview I asked her to "talk a little about how your own family, or grandparents, parents, or people in your community—how you remember them talking about education as you were growing up." Her brief reply revealed the taken-for-granted nature of these values: "In most intelligent homes [laugh] education is stressed. And it was stressed when I was a small girl, and that was just the way it was. I mean, you get a good education, and become self-sufficient. . . . I guess it's just so—it's been so normal for me to know that education's important, I couldn't imagine having any other type of feeling." She seemed to imply my question was at least somewhat ridiculous—in her mind, there really was no other way to be.

Annette routinely attended parent-teacher conferences and extracurricular activities in the evenings, but her younger children made it impossible to visit or help out at the school with any regularity. Alysha's kindergarten teacher, Ms. Weston, did report that Annette visited the classroom shortly before her youngest child was born, but such visits were understandably rare. Annette did, however, keep herself well informed about material covered in Alysha's classrooms, she mentioned working with the children on various subjects as need arose, and she proudly displayed to me several projects Alysha had made at school.

While Annette had less time to devote to routine involvement in Alysha's schoolwork than she would have liked, one action she and Manny took in support of their children's education was particularly impressive and potentially important. During Alysha's Head Start year, Annette heard of a small, experimental public school that would stress language arts education, democracy, and community. Newberry Elementary was scheduled to begin operation in the fall of 1990, and would enroll a limited number of children—during its first year, it would have only one classroom each for kindergarten through third grade. Annette applied to have her three oldest children admitted, and their names were entered in a lottery. Her children were indeed selected, and all three began attending Newberry that fall.

While it may seem that merely enrolling one's children in an alternative public school is a small investment in children's education, this came at no small expense or inconvenience for this family. In order for their children to attend Newberry, parents were required to sign a contract that stipulated that they 1) buy uniforms the children were required to wear each day; 2) provide transportation to and from the school; and 3) attend at least four parent-teacher conferences each year. The first two of these presented significant hardships and expense for the Richy family, and transportation was especially problematic. Annette and Manny had two cars when we first met (two station wagons, both quite old), and initially Annette loaded up the younger children each morning and afternoon to drive Alysha, Melinda, and Michael to the school, which was located on the west side of town about five miles from their home. Remarkably, twice during this study the Richys had a car stolen—once during the first winter the children attended Newberry and then again in November 1992. Both vehicles were damaged beyond repair, and Manny transported the children while Annette was without a car. Fortunately, the school's before- and after-school child-care program made this new arrangement workable.

Providing their own transportation for the children, and the expense involved in fueling and maintaining vehicles and purchasing uniforms, presented major difficulties for this family. Annette rarely complained about finances, but I knew there was very little money to spare.[6] However, Annette felt the potential benefits of enrolling the children at Newberry outweighed the difficulties. For example, she was quite disillusioned with traditional public school classrooms: "My oldest son went through Head Start, and that gave him a wonderful head start in kindergarten, first grade, and second. But I don't believe his strengths were cultivated because I think he was just shoveled along with the rest of the children. . . . In the public schools, he could have almost been a genius at a young age, but they didn't want to take the time to notice that. . . . But there was something there, and it hasn't been cultivated yet. But now . . .[at Newberry] I think they will have an excellent chance to get ahead. . . . And I think that only through a special program they'll ever really get to be what they could be."

Later, in line with the school system's policy of keeping siblings together, the younger children followed their siblings to Newberry, which expanded its program to include fourth- and fifth-grade classrooms. For this Annette was very thankful, because she believed the emphasis on small classrooms, individual attention, and a developmental orientation might give her children a better chance to succeed in public schools.

Other mothers in this study also sought alternatives to traditional arrangements (Tasha, chapter 7, and Denise, chapter 10), and there is evidence such alternatives may indeed contribute to more positive outcomes for low-income black children than is typical for traditional public schools (Slaughter and Epps 1987). Although Annette believed private schools might best cultivate children's unique talents and abilities, her family could not afford such expense. However, they were willing to make real sacrifices in order to give their children what they believed was the best available alternative, given the scarcity of their resources.

ALYSHA'S EXPERIENCES IN EDUCATIONAL SETTINGS

Alysha attended the afternoon Head Start class, where throughout the year the children contended with unusual interruptions in their normal routine. For the last two months of the school year, Ms. Wilcox and Ms. Swanson were the teacher and teacher's aide in the afternoon class, but there had been many changes in personnel earlier in the year. One head teacher's illness led to her resignation, and a teacher's aide also left her position. Prior to Ms. Wilcox's takeover shortly after midyear, a series of substitute teachers had each stayed only briefly. Bill Corsaro often said during this period that he was a more consistent person in the children's lives than were their teachers.

These interruptions in routine contributed to a rather unique situation for the children. They seemed to have greater opportunity to control and shape interaction and routine in this classroom than was true in the morning class. Alysha's classmates included several rather precocious children who were articulate, self-confident, and quite domineering in their interaction with peers (including Zena, chapter 5, and Ramone, chapter 8). Changes in personnel gave the children unusual opportunities to construct a classroom environment that suited their wishes, and the mix of children's personalities encouraged the development of assertiveness among even less extroverted or self-confident children. As Bill said in our later interview with Alysha's kindergarten teacher, children in this class needed to learn "to stand up to" their more forceful classmates in order to participate fully and positively in the peer culture; a somewhat exaggerated assertiveness bordering on bossiness was "actually pretty adaptive" here.

Though she was not a leader in her Head Start classroom, I observed that Alysha was a bright child who spoke up frequently in interaction with peers and teachers, and who participated confidently in the common playful disputes among these children. Alysha did not stand out as particularly popular among her peers or extraordinary in her display of academic ability, but her ability to hold her own within this group of strong personalities was impressive. One episode of peer interaction, captured on videotape, demonstrated Alysha's self-confidence and competence, and also demonstrated how—at the age of five—she was clearly influenced by her family's religiosity in her interaction with peers in the classroom.

Lunchtime in both classrooms often provided the children with opportunity for creative interaction with little interference from teachers. One day in May, Jerald (J) and Ramone (R) were discussing the television show *Hard Copy*, which led to a good-humored argument about what channel the program came on. Alysha (A), several other children (C1 C2 C3 C4), and Corsaro (B) were also seated at the lunch table, while a teacher (T) was nearby (and I videotaped). The transcript picks up as the boys' discussion evolved into competition over who had the "biggest cable."

J to R: It comes on every night.

R to J: We watch that channel and it don't come on our TV. We got eighty channels. And we got that channel, but when we watch that channel, that don't even come on. . . . What channel it come on?

J to R: HBO.

R to J: We watch HBO.

J to R: It comes on cable.

R to J: We have cable.

C1:   We got cable too.

C2:   We do too.

C3:   We do too.

C4:   We do too.

R: I got the biggest cable. I got the biggest cable.

J: I got the little—[holding his hands close together].

T: I thought all cable was the same.

B: [laughs] So did I.

J: (either), My cable's this big [holds one hand under the table and the other above his head].

R: My cable's 'bout this big. [holds hands about a foot apart].

A: Jesus is bigger than everybody.

J: //I'm bigger than Jesus.

A to J: Nah-uh. Jesus is bigger than everybody.

T: You'all got to stop [laughing].

J to A: My cousin's is bigger than Jesus. My cousin's is bigger than Jesus. My cousin's is that big [again holds hands very far apart]. Yeah.

A to J: But he don't—big as this . . . [reaches as far up as she can]. He's this big.

J to A: My cousin's this big [reaches up].

T to A: Alysha, get through so you can drink your milk today.//

A: //He's this big. [holds hand far above table].

J to A: Who? Who?

A to J: Jesus.

This delightful episode captures Alysha's desire to participate in peer interaction and her ability to do so despite her lack of knowledge on the particular topic. Although it seemed most children's families had cable television, Alysha's family certainly did not; this was a luxury they simply could not afford. The exchange continued a longer, quite sophisticated discussion between Ramone and Jerald (which included debate about what kinds of things you can get "in the back of your head"—both words shaved into your hair, and ideas), during which Alysha and the others listened attentively but made no attempt to interject remarks of their own. Ramone and Jerald controlled the interaction for several minutes, and when other children finally attempted to comment that they too had cable television, they were barely noticed by the two boys. Alysha, however, was more skilled and was able to contribute a well-timed new twist on the evolving topic that was then acknowledged and incorporated into the playful dispute. And although she was uninformed on the subject of the boys' conversation, she found a way to make a relevant contribution by introducing a subject she did know a great deal about—Jesus.

Alysha's adaptive ability to hold her own among other, very assertive, children at times seemed to carry over to minor defiance of teachers as well. This, too, was a tendency of the children in the afternoon class, and could conceivably have developed in response to instability of classroom personnel. These were not typically serious incidents of defiance, but rather, usually consisted of children breaking small rules while the teachers' backs were turned (for example, waving forks in the air or blowing bubbles in milk, during lunch), and laughing secretively among themselves about it.

For their parts, when Ms. Wilcox and Ms. Swanson saw a need

to correct the children, they did so in ways that both effectively halted the behavior, and may also have encouraged further independent thinking and the ability to stand up to others. For example, they often disciplined with primarily rhetorical questions (that acted as imperatives) about the appropriateness or motivation for particular behavior: "How you supposed to sit, Ramone?" "Alysha, why are you singing at the table?" (see Corsaro 1994). This style likely contributed to the children's tendency to engage in playful oppositional interaction. In this environment, then, Alysha became a relatively skilled participant in these routine activities in her peer culture.

Alysha's Transition to Newberry

Perhaps predictably, the skills Alysha developed in Head Start were not well suited to her new environment at Newberry, and she began to experience some difficulty in her relationships with peers and her teacher. With its innovative program, Newberry was able to draw children with "a great diversity of socioeconomic backgrounds" including, according to Alysha's first-grade teacher, "some very wealthy children going here." The oppositional style that was so common in the Head Start classroom was rarely apparent when we observed these children briefly during our visits to interview the kindergarten and first-grade teachers. The interaction skills Alysha displayed the year before were unappreciated and seen as inappropriate in her new environment, which now included primarily white classmates and a white teacher.

The teaching style of Alysha's kindergarten teacher, Ms. Weston, seemed to reflect Newberry's emphasis on "democracy." She allowed the children considerable freedom about the classroom, and there was much time for independent activity. At the same time, she placed great value on the children getting along well and developing respect for one another (Ms. Majors, chapter 5, had similar emphases). Unlike half-day kindergarten programs, which necessarily focused on academic skills and knowledge, Newberry's full-day schedule allowed emphasis on interaction and relationship skills as well.

Ms. Weston's interpretation of Alysha's social skills differed considerably from Annette's. Ms. Weston and Annette discussed similar qualities they believed Alysha possessed, but their evaluations of these qualities were quite far apart. I asked Ms. Weston "how you would evaluate Alysha's overall performance" during her kindergarten year, including discussion of her "major strengths, or any weaknesses that you've noticed." She first indicated she was considering how to respond ("Ummmmm"); then there was a long pause. I prodded her, saying, "I don't just mean academically," and she then produced a very lengthy response, including this description:

T: Alysha's like a double-edged sword. She's a challenging child, she's a very bright child. Um, it needs control. I think Alysha, she just lacked a little control when she came in my room. She's a delightful child, very bright, really sharp. Picks up on everything, right away, but is always that first one to shout it out. . . . I found I could easily mold her, with that little hug, that little extra secret. That worked real well. . . . But she's a bit compulsive. I've noticed it about food, I've talked to [her] mother about it . . . She's to the point where she will hide it, kind of like—there's so many children—you know, [her] mother had another baby?

K: Well, yeah. That was gonna be my comment, that I think maybe coming from this large family where everybody's so—all the children are also so young, that she has to do something to stick out. And that's just carrying over into the classroom.

T: Um [laugh]. The other day we went to the post office. . . . We were gonna purchase the stamp, we had x'ed the corner and we had written letters to home. And before we could purchase the stamp, she dropped it in. It was gone! That's Alysha . . . and it's not *wrong*, it's just always a little step ahead. And I hate to stop her all the time, but it is impulsive. . . . So, that's challenging. But she gets along with the other children, bossy kind of get along, but there's no other major problems with her other than that compulsive [behavior]. . . .

Ms. Weston characterized Alysha as bright but impulsive and lacking in control. She had not yet mastered the skill of waiting to be called on, or waiting to receive the "go-ahead," during structured activities, and her lack of interaction skills the teacher valued clearly detracted from credit she received for her knowledge and academic skills. Both Annette and Ms. Weston described Alysha as a bright child, but Annette clearly overestimated the degree to which Alysha's enthusiastic and somewhat domineering classroom participation was appreciated by the teacher. Annette was correct in noting that "a lot of times when [Ms. Weston] is trying to give the class instructions, Alysha will beat her to the punch," and she also correctly stated that Ms. Weston at times "allows her that privilege." However, she never suggested that Ms. Weston considered this a serious problem Alysha needed to control. Instead, Annette felt Alysha's behavior indicated leadership that could, at times, "get the initiative going" among the other children.

In addition, both women noted Alysha's stubbornness, and it was here they seemed most distant in their evaluations. Recall that Annette asserted that Alysha was not "belligerent or outwardly rebellious," but rather, "if she feels she's been done unjustly, she will stand her ground." Annette was pleased with this aspect of her daughter's personality, and she believed that once an incident was resolved, Alysha became "just the same lovable child" as before. This assessment was in contrast to Ms. Weston's remarks about a "very serious incident" in which Alysha had allegedly taken and eaten another child's candy and then refused to admit her transgression:

> Alysha's a really strong-headed child . . . she wouldn't apologize or admit to it, so the only punishment I do use is I separate them. . . . So she went over there and she just pouted. I did everything to try to get her out of it, to give her any way out with a little respect. She wouldn't go for it. . . . I had her mother in here, we had a real serious conversation about it. . . . I gave Mom a blank tape to take home for Alysha to use because I told her it was necessary for her to release that anger somehow. . . . Now that I'm talking about it, even when it's over, she doesn't like to admit to it, or talk about it. And Mother didn't seem to know how to handle that either, and I remember saying to her, "Later on when she's thirteen, this is gonna come flying out of this child with all kinds of fury."

Ms. Weston believed Alysha's "stubborness" was very serious, and unlike Annette, she felt it was a sign of deep-seated anger. Also unlike Annette, Ms. Weston had concerns about Alysha's inability to get past such incidents. Annette, however, maintained her interpretation of Alysha's activities as indicative of high personal standards and leadership qualities.

I also asked Ms. Weston directly about "the role Alysha's parents are playing in her education." She noted that Annette was "cooperative," had visited the classroom before the youngest child was born, and made sure Alysha returned her homework. Then she continued:

> Her mother is always very agreeable, [pause] I'm not sure that she understands. You know, some of the deep stuff I was talking about. . . . [returning to talk about the candy-stealing incident] Alysha wouldn't speak. And it's just like, [pursed lips]. It's that response, and she'd do it for hours . . . and I had her mom come right in and we sat and talked. Nobody else was in the room. And I still couldn't get her to talk. [Ms. Weston makes a sound I associate with a shudder.] And I told her mother, "This is not good, this is not good." But her mother always just smiles kind of nicely and—

usually when I talk to her mother, I try to be specific and I try to tell her exactly what I want her to do. And then wrap it up and say, "Now do you understand?" All that kind of instruction with her mother.

In addition to feeling by this time that the teacher was overreacting to the candy incident, I was startled by Ms. Weston's description of her interaction with Annette. I, too, had found Annette somewhat difficult to talk with, and had often struggled with her minimal response to my questions and comments. However, I had never questioned Annette's intellect, and I bristled when Ms. Weston did so. I attributed some of my difficulties interacting with Annette to my own attitudes and biases, and as I came to know her better, I became accustomed to her mild-mannered, hesitant, and somewhat closed-mouthed style, and to her tendency to carefully consider her words before speaking. I also knew that when our interviews hit upon an issue that piqued Annette's interest, she would reveal an insightfulness not otherwise apparent.

Ms. Weston's remarks suggested another explanation, but one I believed was inaccurate. Clearly Annette's style did not put people at ease and, as my own ruminating over potential explanations for the difficulty suggests, people who interacted with Annette might be prompted to ask themselves, "Just what is the problem here?" Ms. Weston apparently answered this by questioning Annette's mental capabilities, but I offer another possible interpretation at the close of this chapter.

Both Ms. Weston and Alysha's first-grade teacher, Ms. Corbin, pointed out that one of Newberry's strengths was teachers' cooperative sharing of information in order to construct a well-integrated environment for their students. What this meant, in part, was that there was much discussion of individual children among the teachers. Ms. Corbin explained that Ms. Weston had informed her about Alysha's history in her class, and she would do the same for the second-grade teacher next year. "Last year's teacher works with this year's teacher, and everything is building," she said.

Clearly, this cooperation among teachers was facilitated by a small school and small classrooms (there were only eighteen children in Alysha's kindergarten classroom, and seventeen in first grade), and this arrangement was designed to provide a secure and consistent environment for children. No doubt most students benefited a great deal. In fact, the interaction between teachers as students passed from grade to grade, the strong involvement of parents the school required, and the fact that children remained with the same cohort throughout their elementary years—all these features of Newberry mirrored another, very successful program (Follow Through) that I discuss in chapter 4 (also see chapter 10). I wondered, though, how this interaction between teachers might influence perceptions of particular children and parents in potentially negative ways, and I approached the interview with Alysha's first-grade teacher curious about the extent to which her remarks would reflect Ms. Weston's earlier perceptions.

Ms. Corbin was a white woman of about fifty who had been a Montessori teacher prior to coming to Newberry. She noted that the change from a Montessori philosophy to a more developmental orientation had been difficult for her, and she was still struggling with that transition. "Montessori never tackles social skills," she said, and in her own training and experience she had "missed the aspect of social development . . . [which] has been, probably in all my teaching, sadly lacking." Now, at Newberry, she was pressed to consider the "whole child," and this had not come easily. In the past, she'd "never put any credence in social development. I thought, no, academics come first. [But now] I'm working on it! And I'm getting so I really like it."

We saw evidence of Ms. Corbin's efforts in this area during our observations of the class on the day of our interview. After a problem with misbehavior in the Spanish teacher's room, Ms. Corbin conducted a spontaneous behavior lesson about how the children should behave toward one another. Instead of teasing and yelling at a girl who had knocked down a poster, they should say things like: "D., don't take that down. Let me help you put it back." She then had children come up to the front of the room, and she knocked things over and asked them how they should respond. Now they were instructed to say "Don't do that," and "Let me help you move it back." When Ms. Corbin escalated the dispute, the children were to respond with "I'm going to tell the teacher." This lesson got quite tedious, and while Steven was in front roleplaying, he briefly cocked his arm as if to swing at Ms. Corbin while her back was turned.

While some children were attentive during this activity, others seemed to share my own feeling that it was tedious and ineffective. The black children in particular (like Alysha and Steven) seemed to view the instruction with some disdain, and Steven's behavior was reminiscent of the behind-the-back defiance of teachers we observed in Alysha's Head Start class. Ms. Corbin's style was unlike anything

I observed in the Head Start classrooms, and also very unlike the straightforward strategies I saw employed in the black families I knew.

In any case, Ms. Corbin was clearly emphasizing development of social skills, and unfortunately, this was an area where she—like Ms. Weston—believed Alysha was quite sorely lacking. Below she responds to my request for an "overall evaluation of Alysha's performance," and also remarks on Annette's involvement:

> OK. Well, socially, Alysha has some social skills to work on. I think that's because she's one of seven children, and she wants a whole lot of attention. Her mother and I have had a lot of discussions about this, and I really admire her mother. Her mother's really working hard with the children in the home. And Alysha will do anything to get the attention, up to the point of taking things. . . . And I think that's because she's one of seven and sandwiched in the middle. . . . However, along with this taking things you can tie in a little bit of manipulation. . . . Ms. Weston was working on that last year, and I'm working on that this year, and I see improvement, but she's got a long way to go. . . . And I think, again, just not enough attention. . . . But she has good friendships with other children, but there's still that manipulation, that I don't think is healthy. Um, academically, I think of all the [Richy] children I have known, she is the brightest, brighter than Melinda. . . . Melinda's a good, steady, hardworking child. A wonderful child, who has a lot of depth of character. And Alysha I think has that same depth, but you don't see it a lot because she's so busy acting out her need for attention.

Ms. Corbin responded to my question by talking uninterruptedly for several minutes about behavioral problems, and her own interpretation that those problems stemmed from Alysha's place in her large family. When she finally mentioned academic skills, she praised Alysha highly, but then qualified this praise by returning to the theme of "need for attention," which obscured the possible "depth of character" she felt was so apparent in Melinda.

Ms. Corbin did have more to say about Alysha's academic skills. For example, Alysha was "an excellent reader," reading "way above grade level— about mid-second-grade reading." And "her math is good, strong, first grade. And developmentally, she's right on track." But although Ms. Corbin made it clear that Alysha's academic performance was very strong, it was striking that during an interview that lasted over an hour, she had little else to say about this aspect of Alysha's experience in her classroom. Instead, the teacher focused and elaborated on Alysha's behavior. Annette too seemed to place greater emphasis on her daughter's social skills and potential "leadership ability" than on her academic potential. That Annette appeared to share the teachers' stress on social rather than academic aspects of Alysha's educational experience likely made their criticisms all the more disheartening.[7]

As we approached the end of our interview, Ms. Corbin had already expressed much praise for Annette. When I finally asked her specifically to describe Annette's participation, she continued to present Annette in a very positive light. She noted that Annette was "very concerned, very supportive" and "a very good mother." She was amazed at "everything that woman does, she has to have all the energy in the world." She also praised the Richy's choice of Newberry, despite the hardships this entailed. Finally, she concluded: "I see all of those children as high achievers when they mature. They may not go to college, but I see them going to some kind of trade school, and those children will do much better than their parents.[8] And it will not be so much what happened in any classroom, but the ideals and the motivation the parents have instilled in them. And I see that with that mother across the board, in everything she does with those children."

Despite Ms. Corbin's high praise for Annette, I wondered if Ms. Corbin shared Ms. Weston's perceptions about Annette's inability to understand "the deep stuff" concerning her daughter's "problems." Although there's no denying I was fishing, I tried to articulate a question that focused on Annette's behavior rather than on her understanding.

K: Do you—do you find that, you know, if you make suggestions for Annette, things she can do in the home, that she's quite easily able to do them? Or//

T: //No. I find it, I find her—she's very agreeable, and she's very supportive of me, but I find her limited sometimes when I give her suggestions. That's why sometimes I'm so amazed at what she does, what she accomplishes. Sometimes I don't think she quite totally understands me when I'm talking to her.

I was struck by the way Ms. Corbin repeated so closely Ms. Weston's words—Annette was "very agreeable and supportive" but "limited," and did not appear to "quite totally understand" her concerns or suggestions. It was striking, too, that Ms. Corbin maintained this belief in Annette's limitations despite evidence the teacher cited of her great efforts and accomplishments. Ms. Corbin's statement about Annette's "limitations" seemed strangely incompatible with the praise she'd expressed for Annette's activities, and for her consistent good parenting.

Part of the explanation for Ms. Corbin's seemingly incongruous statement may lie in the close communication between Ms. Weston and Ms. Corbin. As children move from grade to grade—and at times, from school to school—throughout their elementary years, communication between former, present, and future teachers can be very beneficial in that it provides for continuity of approach to both children's difficulties and their strengths. At Newberry—as I suspect is true of most smaller schools—children have a history that follows them and that is more in-depth than the contents of the "cumulative files" teachers at other schools identified as their primary source of information about incoming students. Although it's possible to sing the praises of the approach favored at Newberry, there is clearly a darker side as well. Many parents whose children experience difficulties in particular classrooms look forward to their movement into new classes, where they may begin anew with a clean slate. This, however, was not possible at Newberry. By first grade, Alysha had developed a reputation as a problematic child whose need for attention contributed to many behavioral difficulties. By design, this reputation would follow her into second grade and beyond, where these "problems" would likely continue to receive more attention than her considerable academic talents. In addition, it seemed Alysha's mother had also been labeled, and the kindergarten teacher's perception that Annette was incapable of understanding her daughter's difficulties persisted the following year, when Ms. Corbin, too, found her limited in her ability to put suggestions into practice.

Based on my own interaction with her, I suspect Annette did indeed understand the teachers' complaints about Alysha's problematic behavior and their suggestions for its correction. However, it is quite possible Annette simply did not agree, and she was too unassuming or lacking in self-confidence to challenge teachers' assessments of her daughter outright. I thought her tendency to nod and "smile nicely" when teachers noted Alysha's "problems" was likely her way of appearing respectful of their authority without explicitly collaborating with them in a definition of Alysha as attention-starved, dishonest, and manipulative. Such a definition would clearly quash the dreams Annette had for her daughter. My interviews with Annette also suggested she would be unwilling to interfere too forcefully in Alysha's independent discovery of "her own values." Since Annette did not believe her own religion could rightfully impose its values on her children, it is unlikely she would willingly grant the school this privilege. Perhaps the teachers misinterpreted Annette's polite defiance as incomprehension.

CONCLUSION: THE DIRECTIVE FORCE OF STEREOTYPES

I began this chapter by describing my unfortunate biases, which influenced my interaction with Annette, and I want to return to the issue of prejudice against large families like the Richys'. In Head Start, kindergarten, and again in first grade, Alysha's teachers all expressed their negative perceptions of such families' ability to provide their children with adequate attention and support. Alysha's family size became an easy explanation for her difficulties as she made the transition from Head Start to elementary school, and I participated, along with Alysha's teachers, in constructing this derogatory definition of the family. While I bristled at teachers' suggestions that Annette had limited intelligence, I thought nothing of offering the alternative explanation that perhaps she was "just" at times "overwhelmed by all the children." In retrospect, it seems we could have easily credited Alysha's large family for positively influencing her development of independence, self-confidence, and her desire to stand out academically. But such is the nature of stereotypes—we see so clearly whatever confirms our preexisting notions, and we ignore what disconfirms them.

I have noted Annette's belief that Alysha's self-confidence and leadership qualities were special talents that set her daughter apart from other children. Among her children, Annette believed Alysha was unique in that her God-given gifts were identifiable when she was very young. She once lamented that "I'm still looking for that spark" in her other children, and she repeated her convictions that "every child possesses some special quality, that is unique to that individual. It only needs nurturing, paid attention to, and cultivated. It helps when it can be found in elementary school, so that the child can work toward that, and build upon it."

Unfortunately, after Alysha's experiences at Newberry, Annette felt her daughter was in danger of losing "that spark": "Hers might die out, you know; people change." Though Alysha remained a very strong student throughout this study, her early promise was dimming in Annette's eyes after experiences with teachers who recognized her academic talents but downplayed these and focused instead on what they perceived as Alysha's problematic behavior and personality. While Alysha would likely continue to do well academically, Annette was clearly dismayed at the apparent alteration of her daughter's spirit over the course of this study.

At the end of my first interview with Annette. I asked if she would like to add anything before we finished, and she replied: "I'm very concerned about education, especially education of black children. Some of them are highly gifted and talented children, and only because sometimes they're not in the right place at the right time, maybe because they're stereotyped, they'll never probably be what they could be. Somebody had a saying, 'unsung America,'[9] and I think that applies to a lot of black children—there's so many of them that will be unsung. But once they begin to sing, people will see they can sing beautifully, right along with the rest of America."

Spoken in the summer between Alysha's Head Start and kindergarten years, Annette's words here speak of the promise her own and other black children bring with them to elementary classrooms, but promise that all too often goes unrecognized by teachers and schools. Annette also alludes to the power of stereotypes to shape teachers' expectations, and limit their ability to see the beauty of children's potential contributions to society.

Annette's description of the plight of black children in public schools is strikingly similar to arguments of Swadener and Lubeck (1995), who—like Annette—challenge educators to alter their expectations of children "at risk" for school failure, and instead begin to see and to cultivate the promise such children bring with them to school. I return to these authors' arguments in the final chapter. Now, I turn to the experiences of Cymira, another child of promise who stands out as a shining example of the resilience and achievement that are possible in the face of many risk factors.

4

TRADITIONAL STRENGTHS AND NEW CHALLENGES

This chapter is the first of several devoted to young mothers, women who were teenagers when their youngest children were born. As a group, these mothers were poorer, less educated, and considerably less settled than the older mothers. But their lack of resources did not necessarily translate into poor parental practices. In fact, all three young mothers, but especially Rhonda Craft, tend to defy popular conceptions about poor young single mothers raising their children in inner-city environments.

Like Amy and Jeremiah Stevens, Rhonda and her daughter, Cymira, were embedded in a close-knit extended family network. Rhonda's extended family provided much valuable support, but also created considerable stress in her and her children's lives. When this study began, Rhonda—like Amy—lived with her mother and an adult brother in an apartment they had occupied for fifteen years. In addition to her two brothers, Rhonda's network also included many cousins, aunts and uncles, and her grandmother— the latter a strong family head who was a tremendously important figure in Rhonda's life. Her grandmother's folk teachings, and her own and her brothers' struggles with street life, both seemed to have considerable influence on Rhonda's interpretation of the challenges she faced, and on her colorful parenting style. In turn, Rhonda's own impartation of folk wisdom seemed to have a strong impact on her daughter's emerging personality and world view.

Cymira's concern for others, devotion to family, dedication to educational pursuits, and at times her own impressive, colorful style of talk, all reflected her mother's socialization practices.

For all the mothers, their biographies and their reflection upon their experiences mediated the effect of community features on parenting practices. All contended with similar negative features of their communities (especially neighborhood violence, and other crime), but these community features were not directly linked to predictable parenting practices (for example, greater parental monitoring and control). Instead, similar perceptions about neighborhoods and other families were translated into different child-rearing strategies. This is clear when one compares Rhonda and Amy, the two mothers who represent the extremes of parental control in this study. Rhonda's experiences as a teen were very different from Amy's, and her interpretations of those experiences encouraged her to allow her children considerable freedom while she also encouraged high levels of self-reliance, self-esteem, and a firm sense of values. Here, too, her strategies appeared to affect Cymira's behavior in identifiable ways; her teachers praised the same qualities in Cymira that Rhonda attempted to foster, and our observations supported the teachers' assessments.

Readers will see how Rhonda's own adolescent experiences—truancy and "partying," teenaged sex and pregnancy, and her failure to graduate from high school—powerfully influenced her everyday parenting and her prospective thinking about her children's futures. Although Rhonda enacted a variety of purposeful strategies intended to help her children avoid such outcomes, the threat that Cymira might repeat the "mistakes" that plagued her own adolescence loomed large. Mothers' awareness of this threat of social reproductive processes is a theme introduced here, and examined and elaborated in later chapters as well.

RHONDA'S NARRATIVE: "NOT THE ADDAMS FAMILY"

Among those women involved in this study, Rhonda best fit negative stereotypes of black inner-city mothers. She had three children with three different fathers by the age of twenty, and she had never married. She was a high school dropout, a longtime AFDC recipient, living in a public housing project. Gang activity, drugs, and violence were readily apparent in this project, and I experienced considerable fear about entering this neighborhood during the early stages of this research.

My initial telephone conversations with Rhonda were short and uncomfortable. One of my calls was answered by a gruff man who yelled angrily for Rhonda ("Stupid") to come to the phone. She had seemed suspicious, and only reluctantly agreed to an interview. She set and then canceled and rescheduled this first interview, and insisted we meet at a nearby park, claiming her kitchen was being "remodeled." All of this—in addition to the location—contributed to a good deal of anxiety I felt as I waited to meet Rhonda in Davis Park on a June day in 1990. I calmed myself, however, with thoughts of Rhonda's oldest child, Cymira: Surely the mother of this kind, outgoing, and bright child would share some of these qualities.

And in this I was not mistaken. In person, Rhonda was warm and enthusiastic, and like my anxiety, her suspiciousness seemed to fade within minutes of our initial meeting. I quickly learned that Rhonda was a proud and devoted mother, and an intelligent, articulate woman. She spoke with passion, insight, and elegance about the circumstances of her life, and, for reasons that will never be entirely clear, she came to embrace my intrusions into her life as opportunities to be heard, to "show the other side" of inner-city black family life.

Neighborhood Violence and Complex Socialization Resources

Rhonda was twenty-three when we met, and her children—Cymira, Steven, and Keith—were five, four, and three, respectively. Before completing her junior year of high school, Rhonda had dropped out in the spring of 1985. Cymira was born that summer, and Rhonda never returned to school. Although other mothers involved in this study (Marissa, Harriet, and Tasha) also failed to graduate from high school, Rhonda was the only one who also had no formal employment history. She also was the only mother who had continuously relied on AFDC for the support of her family throughout her children's lives. While Rhonda had entered several educational programs (GED classes, and a data entry program), she had not completed any of them.

Not surprisingly, Rhonda repeatedly lamented the conditions in her neighborhood. Her family had been among the first residents of the complex and had lived there since its construction in the mid-1970s. Most other original residents had since moved out ("We're like just about six families left over here from the seventies"). As one of a very few remaining "old-timers," they had witnessed the complex's deterioration from a place where "when I grew up over here, everybody knew everybody," to a place where "we don't know anything about them, those of us that's been here from the beginning. And you don't know who's gonna snap. . . . They are different people who have came from [pause] 'not-so-right' neighborhoods, and it's turnin' this into a 'not-so-right' neighborhood. . . . They're a lot rowdier than we were. I mean, they're packin' guns, there's a woman three doors down whose child packs a knife, and he's seven years old. And I'm not talkin' no little flick it out—I'm talkin' a knife as long as that little boy's leg."

Rhonda was initially reluctant to allow me to observe much of her family's life at home. In February 1991, however, she agreed to meet at her apartment for our second formal interview, midway through Cymira's kindergarten year. When I arrived at noon on a Thursday as arranged, no one was home, and I waited outside for Rhonda's return. As was the case in most of these neighborhoods, I was something of a curiosity to other residents, and many people watched me as they went in and out of apartments, washed cars, conversed with neighbors, and in one case obviously made a drug deal. Though somewhat uncomfortable, I was determined to wait until Rhonda arrived. After half an hour, however, gunshots nearby convinced me it was time to leave. I deposited a quickly scrawled note in Rhonda's mailbox, and made a hasty retreat.

When I phoned that evening, Rhonda apologized for missing our appointment and explained that she'd been helping her grandmother clean a client's home, and they had been delayed by an unexpected large job. We rescheduled, and early in our interview the following week, Rhonda brought up the topic of shootings in the area. I took this opportunity to tell her about the midday gunfire that I had heard while I'd waited the week before, and I asked whether anyone had mentioned the incident to her. She first noted the routine nature of such events ("Every day you'll hear a gunshot"), then described her upset and her thoughts that day as she realized she was not going to be home in time for our interview: "I was like, Oh, my God, I hope she ain't waitin'! Lord! . . . I was so upset and then I thought—and this is Thursday! Thursday over here is like 'O.K, Corral,' everything happens on Thursday. Just everything. . . . It's a sayin' over here: If you don't live over in this area, don't really invite nobody that doesn't know anything about this area. 'Cause it's not homey at all, you know? Well, just somewhere to live, you know, where I'm living. . . . But I was so worried, I was—Oh, my God, I hope she don't set there! On O.K. Corral day, too!"

Probably because I was not used to being around gunfire, I was still curious about the particular incident. I rather foolishly repeated my initial inquiry: "But I just wanted to know, you know, if anybody had said anything about it." Rhonda's reply now was startling:

> About the shot? Over here, hon, a shot fired is like—hmmm, you count your kids, and you know—whew!—wipe the sweat off, and continue walkin'. 'Cause people 'round here, well, male teenagers around here, just come outside and just shoot up in the air, and you'll be like—'Well, what's the purpose? Why do you shoot up in the air? Had somebody been runnin' past and you know, your hand fell, you done hurt somebody?' But over here, gunshots are like wakin' up and lookin' outside the window. That's why I gotta get Cymira outta here. During the school year . . . most of us are out tryin' to find somethin' to do while they're gone, and we might not make it back in time. It's hostile. They wanna be out there, then they can't because of the weather. So, this time of year [when it starts warming up], we are all jumpin', you know what I mean? We don't wanna go to work, or we don't wanna go to school, 'cause we don't know what's happenin' at home. Who's comin' in your back-door, or all kind of stuff like that.

The incessant nature of neighborhood violence in this family's everyday life is clear in this example ("It's like wakin' up and lookin' outside"), and so are the ways such environmental pressures affect other activities that are taken for granted in safer neighborhoods. Rhonda's quotation of "a saying over here. . . . Don't invite nobody that doesn't know anything about this area," and her description of how neighborhood crime contributes to residents' reluctance to seek work or training, illustrate how such environments can impose restrictions on both social and economic activities. Rhonda violated the first of these community norms by repeatedly inviting me into her home, but she had not chosen to violate the second by seeking regular outside employment, which she perceived as potentially dangerous for herself and her family.

Neighborhood violence was more than a potential threat to this family: Rhonda's brother Stretch had twice been shot in their neighborhood, the second time just weeks before our initial interview. Stretch's injuries were serious—he lost substantial hearing, and suffered a partial paralysis—and Rhonda often noted his anger and depression after the second shooting. Since learning of Stretch's injuries, I have assumed it was his angry voice I heard during that early telephone call to Rhonda, and that this, rather than kitchen remodeling, was the reason we met initially in Davis Park.

Although Rhonda claimed that "the area's not scarin' me," she continually described difficulties raising her children in this environment, and problems she encountered negotiating relations with other residents of the complex. She repeatedly claimed she was planning to move, and in January 1993 Rhonda and her children, along with her mother and brother, finally rented a large single-family home in a poor but secluded neighborhood. Rhonda laughingly described their new neighborhood, which consisted of two blocks of primarily single-family homes bounded by an expressway and three major city streets, as "too quiet." When I asked Rhonda if something had happened "that kind of made you say 'All right, now it is time to get out,' " she summed up her motivation to make the move this way: "The situation just became unbearable. I mean, more shootin's, more fightin', was makin' the children in the area grow up faster than they necessarily needed to. It wasn't nothin' really traumatic, you know, no more than I just couldn't take the atmosphere, it got beyond me. You know, it was too much for me."

I have gone into considerable detail about neighborhood violence here in part to convey an important point: Mothers' child-rearing practices were not predictable reflections of either their expressed concern about dangers, or my own observations of the level of violence or other negative features of the neighborhoods. Given this family's residence in the most obviously threatening environment, it might be reasonable to guess that Rhonda would be among the most restrictive mothers. In fact, however, she was perhaps the least restrictive. Unlike Amy (and unlike Annette, as well) Rhonda allowed her children great freedom of movement about their neighborhood, permitting them to maintain numerous friendships in the complex, and to play outside for extended periods with limited supervision. While she recognized the dangers her children were regularly exposed to, she realistically concluded: "Where I live at, the things that are happenin', the only way that I could not show Cymira, I would have to blindfold her and walk her through everything. I would have to walk her through life with this blindfold not to show her."

Rhonda had earlier explained that while she wanted her children to be nonjudgmental ("I want 'em to know that drug addicts and people like that are people too"), at the same time she stressed that "Momma's not like that. I live in that environment, but *we're*

not like that. . . . We can beat this." After Rhonda moved her family
out of the complex, she repeated this theme (of family difference)
once again: "It's not where you live, it's how you live. I am showin'
them that. Just because we lived there doesn't mean we were part
of the program. We were not."

Complex Influences on Daily Practice

Like Amy and Annette, Rhonda relied on claims of family difference both to allay her own fears about the potential negative
impact of her children's environment, and to provide them with a
resource for resisting those influences. But Rhonda has less concrete evidence than other mothers to hang such claims upon.
Unlike Annette and Amy, Rhonda fit the stereotype of the black
inner-city mother, and she clearly recognized the parallels between
her life and the caricature demonized in the popular press. In fact,
in our first interview, Rhonda described how she used her own past
as a warning to young relatives who were getting into trouble or
considering leaving school:

> I was a child who dropped out; I dropped out at sixteen. I always say
> when I speak to a child who's thinkin' about droppin' out, I'm your
> example. . . . I mean, if you get any worse, you'll be a junkie on the
> street. Like I tell my cousins, all of them that's fifteen, sixteen, and
> seventeen years, you have to go to school. There's nothing out here
> in this great earth that won't be here in four years or two years.
> That person that's tellin' you, let's go to this party, wished she
> hadn't went to that party. I'm the person that went to the party. I'm
> the girl that cut, and went to McDonald's. See me. And, let me
> show you my friend who works at Dow, drivin' this ninety [current
> model year]. I could've been in that ninety, I mean, I am the other
> side, I am the example.

Despite regrets about mistakes she'd made, Rhonda described
herself and her family as very different from those that surrounded
her, and she consistently connected this conviction to "family values" she grew up with and was attempting to pass along to her
children. Primary among these values were notions of interdependence and obligation among family members, and fierce family
loyalty. During one of our interviews, an unfortunate minor incident seemed to trigger Rhonda's impassioned expression of these
values.

We had talked for nearly two hours when Rhonda and Stretch
briefly argued about who would walk to pick Steven up at school.

During their exchange, Stretch was somewhat hostile and sarcastic, and Rhonda was noticeably embarrassed that I had witnessed her brother's off-color language, and abrupt and aggressive demeanor. After he left to retrieve Steven, Rhonda conveyed the connectedness of family members while attempting to explain Stretch's gruffness:

R: That's how he is, he's like that. He means no harm, he's just rough, you know.

K: No, I didn't// take offense.

R: //My brother,// he went off into space somewhere, and you know, he's tryin' to get hisself together. But they're fine, we're all fine. We have our problems, you know, I mean we're not Ozzie and Harriet, but we're not the Addams Family either! . . . The family itself, when one is down and goin' through somethin', we all have to go through it. Even though we may not participate in what it is that brought that person there, when you hurt, and you show you hurt, we hurt. And if you havin' a drug problem or a alcohol problem, and you wanna beat somethin', we might as well have took the same thing or been beat the same way. . . . 'Cause when one person's life is off, the whole family stops. We're so close . . . you know, one hurts, the other one calls, and everybody hurts and you try to figure out how we're gonna get this right. . . . Every day it's somethin' new we have to deal with, and we come together and try to deal with it the best way we can.

Rhonda's description of her family's loyalty and cooperative interdependence was borne out by my own observations of interaction among family members. My visits were typically interrupted by numerous phone calls and visitors—almost always relatives—dropping by. For example, I met Rhonda's uncle Gerrod (who Rhonda had described as "a very strong male figure" in her life as she grew up) in February 1991 when he entered the home, greeted Rhonda and me, and headed straight to the refrigerator. That summer, during an observational visit, a cousin's children knocked on Rhonda's door and delivered most of a gallon of milk. I also met Rhonda's somewhat flamboyant and increasingly friendly mother several times over the years, and observed firsthand her devotion to both her daughter and her grandchildren. At various times, I met several female cousins and some of their children, and heard from Rhonda stories of the mutual support and care-taking they provided for one another. Finally, during a visit in the spring of 1993, I gave Rhonda, her children, and the week's laundry a ride to her grandmother's house, dropping Stretch at his girlfriend's along the way. Her grandmother and several aunts, cousins, and their children were all there when we arrived, planning dinner, doing laundry, and styling one another's hair.

Rhonda and her children were an integral part of a close extended family network that—despite many difficulties in recent years and few material resources—regularly provided its members with a great deal of emotional and material support. This network is similar in many respects to the family support network enjoyed by Amy and Jeremiah Stevens. However, while Amy's network was composed almost entirely of her siblings and their children, Rhonda had regular contact with a wider variety of relatives who supported and depended upon one another.

Rhonda claimed that within their family network, the children had a special place, as did the oldest member, Rhonda's grandmother. Rhonda described these priorities: "Granny believes that if you take care of the children, in the long run, they're gonna take care of you. And that's not a financial statement or a selfish statement, it's a statement that has been said and proven in our family. That the children are important as the grown-ups themselves. And Grandma is most important—I don't know about to everybody else, but to me she is the spine of all of us."

In addition to the value placed on children, this excerpt demonstrates Rhonda's respect and admiration for her grandmother. She credited her grandmother with holding the family together through difficult times, and she often prefaced her very colorful statements with "Granny believes . . ." or more typically, "Like my grandmother always says . . .". This was especially true when Rhonda discussed her child-rearing values. Rhonda's grandmother stressed the priority of children's needs, and Rhonda often noted that her children's well-being *must* come first, before her own, and especially before any man's. In her characteristically metaphoric language, Rhonda described how her children's needs and wishes took precedence over all else, saying: "I got one madame and two pimps. If they say 'Go,' [I ask] 'How far am I goin', you'all?' " She explained the origin of this orientation, which she called a "traditional thing," saying, "My mother's like that about us, so I'm like that, [and] my grandmother's about like that with her kids."

Despite the lack of enduring marriages among their members, families like Rhonda's are actually quite stable—and very common among lower-income blacks. Rhonda's family structure did not represent a rejection of marriage, as her frequent disclosures of her desire for a "normal" marriage and family life attested. "I wanted to marry their fathers," she once said, "I wanted the white house with the white picket fence, but that's not what's happenin'." However, she had been strongly socialized to make such concerns secondary, and instead placed priority on her children and other relatives. In doing so, she ensured a high level of stability and continuity in her children's lives, and also was also passing along "traditional" beliefs about the primacy of blood over marriage ties to them.[1]

Encouraging *Excellence through* Metaphor *and* Folk Wisdom

Rhonda's strong convictions about the importance of children, and her desire to place their needs above all else, also contributed to her stance toward their education. Like the other mothers involved in this research, Rhonda believed a good education would put her children on the most likely route into a better life. Also like other mothers, she believed this high valuation of education set her apart from her neighbors.

Rhonda repeatedly stressed that Cymira must make school "her priority of life" and "not let nothin' stop her from doin' what she has to do. Her only job in life right now, until she's eighteen years old, is to go to school." Although her family lacked successful members to point to as role models, during our interviews Rhonda repeatedly and impressively drew on a variety of resources that were available to her in these efforts. Her talk about education was typically peppered with the folk wisdom that was so often apparent in her speech. Rhonda's expressive talents helped her to articulate her emphasis on educational achievement with notions of dignity, self-respect, high valuation of family, and aspirations for a better future for self and society.

In our first interview, Rhonda described talking with Cymira about education in terms of "steps" low-income children must climb in order to become a mainstream American "Charger": "With Cymira I deal with steps. You're the child on the first step tryin' to make it to the third step. . . . And I press Cymira, to get to that second and third step, you're gonna have to learn. . . . We, as low income people, compared to people who have—'Chargers,' that's what I call 'em, 'Chargers.' We can't charge it, we have to buy it with what we got. . . . If you ever want to be one of the Chargers, you gotta learn somethin', it's all learnin'. Like my grandmother always say, 'Ain't a day goes by you don't learn something.' "

The following year, Rhonda elaborated further, describing how education provides not only individual benefit, but also enables positive contribution to family and the larger society: "I want her to be able to tell me how to do trigonometry and algebra. I didn't get a chance to learn that. . . . What you know, come back and teach me. I want her to learn, to become a better person, to become somebody she can be proud of. I want her to understand what life *is*, not only on the streets but all in the mind. You learn something, you can help someone else, you can help this *world*. And if we all come together on this, we can change it."

Finally, she perhaps best summed up her beliefs about education as the foundation for a dignified life when she again evoked her grandmother's words: "Why get on your knees all your life, when you can stand up and make this walk, stand tall and proud to make this walk?"

Rhonda and other mothers routinely drew on such metaphoric imagery when discussing the topic of education with their children. The rich oral tradition that Rhonda apparently grew up with and was passing along to her children was an important resource that helped her both to make sense of her often chaotic world, and to instill values in her children. When Rhonda repeated her grandmother's words, as she did with great conviction, emotion, and regularity, it was clear such folk wisdom was a vital source of inspiration and pride for her. It was also clear when she employed this colorful language that she was attempting to pass on feelings of pride and dignity to her daughter, and inspire Cymira to achieve all she could.

Emerging Fatalistic Beliefs

Rhonda believed there were few limits on what Cymira could accomplish. For example, she said Cymira "wants to be a doctor, a policeman, a lawyer, or a nurse," and she reported this exchange between her and her daughter: "'Can I be president?' I says, 'Well, we still fightin' that issue.' 'Well, I can be that.' I say, 'Yes you can.' 'Can I make furniture?' 'Yes you can.' "

Despite her professed confidence, Rhonda also feared that Cymira would face great pressure from both male and female peers to downplay the importance of schooling. Rhonda viewed her own past experiences as a guide for what *not* to do, and in line with these experiences, she warned Cymira of peers who would tempt her to neglect her schoolwork in favor of having more "fun." During a short visit in June 1993, Rhonda commented emotionally on her recollections of her own past, and how these powerfully informed her thinking about Cymira's future. She'd been an excellent student, but her friends would always say, "All you know is books." She then reportedly swung "three-sixty" (360 degrees) away from her studies, at their urging: "You got to know all these other things. This will change your life." She said that sometimes "I sit up thinkin' about all these wonderful things I see in Cymira, and then sometimes I just cry, because my mother saw all the same things in me."

The rather fatalistic fears that Rhonda expressed here were common among mothers in this study. Such fears reflected awareness of social reproductive processes, as well as the daily struggle that these mothers waged in a battle with their environment for their children. However, although Rhonda at times expressed very fatalistic views, her stance in response to her fears was anything but passive. Rather, she was reflective about the effects she believed peer pressures had on her own life, and she attempted to prepare Cymira for likely future dilemmas. She also attempted to provide her with views and strategies that would help her to resist negative pressures, as this excerpt from our third interview illustrates:

> When I went to see [Cymira's first-grade teacher] at the parent-teacher conference, she said Cymira is more advanced in math than the class. . . . And I explained to her that at home, I tend to teach them more 'cause . . . I don't want them to ever be blindsided by anything as far as education's concerned. . . . And it's not that I want my daughter to be over the class, or the know-it-all. . . . I don't want people to say, Well, you think you know everything. No, because that's what they did to me. I don't want her to have that pressure. 'Cause personally, after hearin' it so long, I did things, I purposely failed tests. I did do that so that I fit in with them. Like I told her, you don't have fit in with no one.

Rhonda's experiences as a young teenager remained painful in her memory, and she feared her own children would succumb—as she had—to the pressures she felt. Rhonda's fears about peer pressures were not translated into the obvious strategy of restricting Cymira's contact and interaction with peers, however. In fact, Rhonda believed that controlling and isolating strategies like Amy's were futile or even worse. She believed it was her own inexperience, naiveté, and lack of self-confidence as a young teenager that most contributed to her many difficulties. Instead of overseeing her children's every move, then, she provided them with knowledge, values, and skills that she hoped would help them to both understand and resist the many negative pressures she felt they would undoubtedly face.

Encouraging self-esteem was an important part of her strategy. In our first interview, she pointed out the importance of self-esteem for children's healthy development, and she drew on her grandmother's words to articulate this belief, saying, "Don't criticize her, don't degrade her, until she's seen a thousand yesterdays." This theme was resumed in our second interview, when Rhonda again quoted her grandmother: "As long as you are positive with yourself, and with them, you'll live a positive life. . . . Don't break her spiritually, and don't break her self-esteem, and she'll be all right." Finally, Rhonda connected her emphasis on self-esteem with her own difficulties in childhood, and in our third interview she said, "I wanna build that self-esteem up way bigger than mine, because I let people break me down."

Independence, Understanding, and Competence in Community Contexts

Rhonda also constantly urged her daughter to use "Cymira's mind and not everybody else's." Rhonda's words were strikingly similar to those of Amy, who lectured Jeremiah about the importance of "using your own head" in interaction with peers. However, while Amy provided Jeremiah with little opportunity to practice and refine independent decision-making skills, these were more than empty words for Rhonda. During our interviews, it was clear that Cymira was granted near-adult status. Her interruptions were treated as relevant and informative contributions. Never did Rhonda ask Cymira not to interrupt, or to leave us alone while we were talking. Occasionally mother and daughter collaborated in telling an event, with Rhonda altering her story at times to reflect Cymira's corrections or elaborations.

Rhonda also pointed out with pride that Cymira "will correct you when you're wrong. . . . If an adult is wrong, she's gonna let you know, no, you're wrong; this is how it go." At one point, she recounted a humorous event in which Cymira confronted a male friend of Rhonda's about behavior the child knew her mother did not condone. Although Rhonda had ignored the behavior and was embarrassed when Cymira questioned him about it, she allowed Cymira to speak her mind, and she concluded: "If there's somethin' that you just have to say, say it. Don't hold nothin' in or back." From every indication, Cymira's intellect, competence, and right to participate in family affairs were fundamentally respected by her mother.

Rhonda also believed that Cymira should be well informed about "adult things," especially about relationships between men and women. It is in this area that Rhonda explicitly said she wanted Cymira to be "streetwise." She drew on her own experiences as a "naive" sixteen-year-old whose innocence was exploited by Cymira's father, and vowed her daughter would be more sophisticated, assertive, and, above all, more certain of her self-worth than she was herself. She laughed when she described the way she'd like to see Cymira approach male-female relationships: "I want you to be loving, caring, understanding. But be smart. Don't let no man tell you, 'Baby, it's greener on the other side.' If it is, why are you over here messin' with me?"

Rhonda's tactics were obviously very different from those of the two mothers discussed earlier. Rather than isolating her children from peers and from others in their neighborhood, Rhonda accepted their exposure to harsh realities of their inner-city environment, and she actively encouraged them to be knowledgeable, competent, and somewhat hardened and cynical actors in this arena. On the other hand, she encouraged Cymira and her brothers to view themselves as set apart from others in their community ("We're not like that"), and to strive for futures as mainstream American "Chargers."

Rhonda in fact articulated these opposing inclinations at times—for example, when she suggested that her "loving, caring, understanding" daughter should be prepared to meet a hypothetical man's suggestion that "it's my way or the highway" with a cutting reply of "See you down that long stretch." The balance of opposites she attempted to encourage in her children was articulated even more clearly when she said: "Like I told my family, I don't want 'em to be rough, but I don't want 'em to be wimpy either. I don't want 'em to be takers, and I don't want 'em giving everything, you know what I mean? This is this side, and this is this side. Try to work yourself in the middle so you have room to tilt over."

It may appear that Rhonda's socialization strategies were essentially contradictory, and such seemingly conflicting emphases suggest great complexity that could be very difficult for Cymira and similar children to interpret and integrate. Yet, as others have noted, managing such contradictions seems to be a special burden and, indeed, a special talent of black families in America. Patricia Hill Collins (1991a), for example, argues that inconsistencies like those apparent in Rhonda's views and practices reflect mothers' efforts to balance the need to ensure children's physical survival on the one hand, while at the same time encouraging them to transcend the many obstacles they face. Similarly, Elijah Anderson's work (1994) suggests that the organization of social life in low-income urban black communities reflects the contradictory pushes and pulls of two distinct value orientations, "decent" and "street." While the majority of homes hold mainstream, "decent" values, because the street-oriented minority is able to dominate public spaces, even parents with a strong decency orientation find it necessary to familiarize their children with the "code of the streets." Even young children must be encouraged to be competent players: Parents in the communities Anderson studied understood that knowledge of the code of honor and respect, and a presentation of self that included exaggerated toughness, were essential if young people hoped to successfully negotiate their volatile neighborhood environments.

In such contexts, Rhonda's practices and goals seemed not inconsistent or contradictory, but rather reasoned responses to the multitude of complex situations and challenges that her children faced or would soon confront. Rhonda's efforts reflected personal knowledge of the pushes and pulls that confront low-income inner-city children. And her belief that children need information and practical experience in order to respond in positive ways to these influences was based in her regret over her own former lack of knowledge and experience.

When Cymira made a smooth and uneventful transition into a new school midway through her second-grade year, Rhonda was clearly proud of her daughter's ability to "adapt to" and take new situations in stride, saying, "I like that she can do that, she adjusts way better than me dealin' with new things." Indications that Cymira was having little difficulty coping with new and challenging situations provided welcome evidence that Rhonda's efforts might well be paying off. I also saw considerable evidence that her mother's beliefs and behaviors were reflected in Cymira's attitudes, achievement, and behavior in the classroom.

CYMIRA'S NARRATIVE: TAKING HEAD START SERIOUSLY

Cymira was, by all accounts, in many ways an exceptional child. A bright and serious student, she always performed well above the average in her classrooms (and typically well above average on nationally normed standardized tests). She was outgoing and well liked by children and adults, and seemed comfortable and confident in various settings with different people. Her middle name,

Solei, appropriately describes the effect she has on others—she did indeed seem to bring sunshine into the lives of people around her. Sounding remarkably like her mother, Cymira answered my question about the origin of her middle name by telling me her mother "named me that when she looked in my eyes on the day I was born."

In Head Start, Cymira excelled in structured learning activities and participated enthusiastically in teacher-directed lessons. Unlike other children, who occasionally got upset if they gave a wrong answer or made mistakes in constructing crafts, Cymira remained unflappably positive in the face of minor failures. Corsaro noted Cymira's mature ability to generalize information and make comparisons among different lessons or events, as well as her appreciation for—and at times production of—the subtle humor enjoyed by adults at the Head Start center. Her maturity was evident in other ways as well, as she linked the "adult" knowledge she possessed with concern for other children's discomfort or upset. For example, once during lunch (fish was the main course) one boy asked another: "Jermaine, do you go fishin' with your daddy?" Jermaine either did not hear or ignored Charles's question, and Cymira quietly said to Charles, "He ain't there. I don't think so." "Oh," Charles said, and dropped the issue. Cymira was also quick to defend children who were being picked on, a quality her mother also noticed and appreciated.

Cymira got along with other children and was well integrated into the classroom peer culture. However, because she typically chose craft activities, puzzles, or writing during free time, she only rarely participated in creative, relatively unsupervised, activities that occurred, for example, at the sand table, housekeeping area, or block area. Lunchtime and group activities, however, provided Cymira with opportunities to display her advanced verbal abilities in frequently complex and animated conversations.

One particular videotaped episode from the Head Start center demonstrates many of these qualities. A teacher read a tale of how the alligator got a bump on his nose, and the children listened attentively to the story of the evil alligator and the eventual revenge taken against him. After the story was finished, the teacher asked the children why another animal had hit the alligator on the nose, and Cymira responded enthusiastically by recounting the main themes of the story. Not only did she display her vivid memory for detail and impressive verbal abilities here, but she also demonstrated compassion for the injured parties, outrage at the alligator's offenses, and a keen sense of fairness ("Because he didn't want the alligator to win because he ate all of them animals' eggs! . . . and then the eagle put a bump on his nose and let the turkey get it and take it to the finish line. . . . I didn't like that alligator!").

From Head Start to Public School

Cymira entered kindergarten in the fall of 1990. Although a nearer school was available, Rhonda sent her daughter to a school a bit farther away, where she could participate in a federally funded program open only to graduates of Head Start. Probably the most important benefit of the Follow Through program was its full-day schedule. Cymira's teacher, Ms. Roth, described other components of the program when I interviewed her in May 1991. Designed to continue the emphases of the Head Start program, Follow Through used a system of positive reinforcement (practiced by this teacher through the use of a token economy), stressed parental involvement, and placed importance on stability and continuity in children's lives. As long as the small group of children remained in the school district, they would stay at this same school, with the same classmates, through the third grade. While they would change teachers each year, all Follow Through teachers worked together to facilitate the children's smooth movement through the early grades.[2] Other benefits of the program included a full-time classroom assistant, small class size, and finally, enrolled kindergartners were provided bus transportation to school if they were not within walking distance, a service not available to other kindergarten students in the city.

Ms. Roth had over twenty years' experience with Follow Through, both in classrooms and in administration. This teacher had devoted much of her life to low-income students, and she spoke with pride of the great benefits she saw in the program. Her experiences with Follow Through, and her long history teaching in schools that served primarily low-income families, had given her a unique view of the "at-risk" children in her classroom. She responded quite dismissively to my inquiry about how children from low-income homes might experience public school differently from children from more affluent families: "I don't really have too much to compare," she said, and refused to speculate further. Although she complained bitterly about excessive paperwork, lack of funding, and cuts in the Follow Through program, her dissatisfaction with her work was never associated with her students or their parents. In fact, among all the kindergarten and first-grade teachers I interviewed, Ms. Roth was the only one who did not at some point complain about the caliber of her students or the dedication and participation of their parents.

Ms. Roth placed importance on the development of social skills, language skills, and on curricular requirements of instruction in basic skills. Using conventional behavior modification techniques, she created a token economy in the classroom, where children were routinely and concretely rewarded for "proper behavior," "following directions," and "adequate responses to questions and comments," while negative or inappropriate behavior was ignored "unless they are just to the point where they are harmful to other children." When I asked Ms. Roth what things "are particularly important that you and the children accomplish during their kindergarten year?" her response clarified her objectives:

> Social skills are important, manners, how to get along with others, understanding feelings of others. Communicating with one another as well as with the teacher. . . . Other skills, we have to kind of work with the system, because there's certain academic skills that they need for the California Achievement Test. . . . And communication I think is important too, oral language. Many of our children in this area fall short in oral language skills, so the more we can get them to communicate orally, it helps for their success. . . . [And] every morning we have a period for free-play, definitely. This is important also, decision-making, I think children need to learn to make a decision. And this is a good time to start.

When the interview progressed to the particular children in Ms. Roth's class (Martin , chapter 10, was also in this class), the teacher had only praise for Cymira's talents:

T: There was no problem with Cymira coming into kindergarten. She just fit right in. She was a mature child for five. She has lots of enthusiasm, a lot of motivation. She's really eager to learn. . . . We did a series, where each week they have an animal. . . . And from time to time we would refer back—how does this animal compare to the one we studied two weeks ago? And Cymira was always the first one to tell us. And even after we left that program, we would be talking about, um, maybe an animal with different characteristics, and she'd say, "Oh! Such-and-such an animal we studied did that." So she has a very vivid memory. She retains much. She can relate it, and compare it real well.

K: Is there anything that sticks out as maybe what you would see as her greatest strength, or anything that is a weakness for her? You know, in terms of her future success?

T: I think she will be very successful in whatever she does. . . . I think she will be very well liked. She has a splendid personality. She's very lovable, very kind, very helpful. She helps other children in the class. . . . She's very compassionate with children. She has very fine qualities.

In light of what Ms. Roth felt was especially important for children to master in kindergarten, her extremely positive evaluation of Cymira—who had already demonstrated both social and academic precociousness in Head Start—was not at all surprising. And while Cymira's mature intellect and her talent in structured activities would likely have garnered praise in any kindergarten setting, Ms. Roth's priorities and the structure of her classroom permitted recognition and reward of her other "fine qualities" as well.

Ms. Roth's values and her classroom organization complemented the emphases and styles of the Head Start teachers from the year before, and those of Cymira's mother. The more obvious parallels between Cymira's Head Start and kindergarten classrooms were clearly purposeful, with the objectives of Follow Through deliberately designed to reinforce and build upon children's Head Start experiences. In addition, Ms. Roth's personality and style were similar to those of Ms. Castle, the head teacher in Cymira's Head Start classroom. Both teachers successfully mixed a no-nonsense, authoritarian teaching style with an affectionate, teasing manner of interacting with children. Ms. Roth was not only kind and positive toward her students—she also had high academic expectations for progressively greater achievement, and after a job well done, she rewarded the children with a variety of interesting activities centered around holidays, other cultures, and cooking. Cymira, well used to such a mix from the year before, adapted easily to Ms. Roth's expectations and overall style.

Rhonda valued many of the same qualities that Ms. Roth believed were important for future success and that she identified in Cymira. That is, in addition to their high valuation of Cymira's obvious academic talents, both women stressed compassion for others and a communal orientation, social maturity, and self-motivation and confidence. The continuity among Cymira's family life, her experiences in Head Start, and her kindergarten classroom clearly contributed to a smooth transition into public schooling, and to the maintenance of the self-confidence and enthusiasm that were so apparent in Cymira.

A month after I interviewed Ms. Roth, my daughter and I attended the kindergarten graduation ceremony she orchestrated.

By the time the ceremony began, all of the approximately thirty-five chairs were filled by parents, siblings, and other relatives of the eighteen graduating children. Mary and I joined several others standing in the doorway and along the wall. Each child was dressed stylishly, and each had at least one family member in attendance (Rhonda and her cousin attended, as did Martin's mother and younger sister). Many parents brought cameras, one videotaped the proceedings, and the scene was much like a high school graduation in miniature, complete with mortarboards and rolled and tied diplomas.

Ms. Roth began the program by praising the group as a whole, then distributed thirteen categories of individual awards—including awards for reading, math, gym, art, homework, attendance, "good rester" and "good cook," and citizenship awards. The citizenship award was given to just one boy and one girl, and I think I was as proud as Rhonda and Denise when Cymira and Martin received these honors. Then Ms. Roth called each child in turn to the front of the room to receive a diploma, the audience applauded, and the teacher made a personal comment about how the child had contributed to the group. This emphasis on individual contributions to the collective mirrored the orientation of Head Start teachers that we had observed the year before (see Corsaro and Rosier 1992).

Ms. Roth then turned her praise to the parents, congratulating them for their children's accomplishments, and their support throughout the year. She urged them to maintain their high level of support, and stressed the importance of high school graduation for future success in adult life. This comment met with many nods of agreement from parents (but I was struck by how unlikely such comments would be were these middle-class kids, and by Ms. Roth's failure to mention postsecondary education). To conclude the ceremony, Ms. Roth informed the audience that this would be the last year for Follow Through, and she noted that their children—many of whom were already reading—were lucky to have had the benefit of a full-day kindergarten program. In obvious distress, she then invited everyone to have cookies and punch.

Afterward, Ms. Roth told me the Follow Through program was being completely eliminated. She had known this for several weeks, and had not said more during the program because she "didn't want to start crying." That afternoon, Rhonda and Denise both said they were disappointed they would be unable to enroll their younger children in Follow Through. Rhonda somewhat angrily complained about money spent on the space program, defense, and "'cross seas,'" but, she said, "what do they do for us?" When I visited Rhonda later that summer, she complained that a very wealthy nearby suburb was planning construction of a new, multimillion-dollar high school. She argued that while deteriorating inner-city schools were losing badly needed funding, the people who already had superior facilities and resources would now receive even more.[3]

Follow Through Teachers Continue Its Emphasis

Although the elimination of Follow Through threatened the continuity that had served these students so well, Cymira continued to excel in first grade. She remained in the same school and, along with only one other classmate from Ms. Roth's class, entered the class taught by the former first-grade Follow Through teacher. Ms. Nelbert had taught the Follow Through first-grade class for over ten years, and during Cymira's year in her class she was adjusting to changes that came along with the elimination of the program. Specifically, Ms. Nelbert had a larger class (twenty-three students) than in the past, and her students' preschool and kindergarten experiences ranged from no preschool and only one week of kindergarten, to a full year of Head Start and a year of full-day kindergarten. Their skills and knowledge varied accordingly. In addition, Ms. Nelbert no longer had a full-time classroom aide. Instead, this larger, less homogenous class benefited from an assistant only in the afternoons.

Before interviewing Ms. Nelbert in April 1992, Bill Corsaro and I observed her classroom during the afternoon session. When we arrived, Ms. Nelbert (a white woman in her mid-forties), her aide, Ms. Kallas (a slightly older black woman), and the children were returning from lunch. Ms. Nelbert invited us into the classroom and told us where to sit, but made no special introduction to the class. Cymira was pleased with our presence, but she was not distracted and attended conscientiously to her business. Throughout the math and social studies lessons, and a visit from the librarian, Cymira displayed the academic skills and precocious participation that we had come to expect. For example, while Ms. Nelbert discussed directions for completing a page in the math workbook, Cymira finished the page and moved on to the next. As she continued to work ahead, however, she kept a finger marking the earlier page, and flipped back to it repeatedly when the teacher asked questions about the children's work.

During their discussion of kilograms, Ms. Nelbert asked what would happen if she and one of the children sat on opposite ends of a teeter-totter. All children knew that they would go up and Ms. Nelbert would go down. She then asked how they could make her go up. The room was quiet, and after a moment Ms. Nelbert called on Cymira, whose hand was raised high. "Put about seven of us on!" Cymira said, and everyone—adults included—laughed at this humorous prospect.

A bit later, Cymira was again the only child who appeared to know the answer to a question, but this time she kept it to herself. The children were asked to match various objects with their approximate weights (for example, match 4K with a watermelon and 1K with a bunch of bananas), and this ignited a discussion of bananas. Ms. Nelbert asked the children, "Who eats bananas without peeling them?" and although many replied, "I do!" or "S/he does!" pointing to a classmate, none offered the response the teacher was looking for. Ms. Nelbert then told the children to "go home and ask Mom, or Dad, or Grandma, or Auntie, or your cousin: Who eats bananas without peeling them?" At this point, Cymira leaned over and whispered quietly to me: "Gorillas. Gorillas and monkeys," but she did not share this with the class.

Cymira seemed to monitor herself so as not to appear the "know-it-all" of the class, and this restraint was apparent throughout the afternoon. She often looked about the classroom when Ms. Nelbert asked a question, sometimes raising her hand only if no one else did. She never called out answers before being recognized, and she never appeared disappointed if she was not called upon. She clearly understood the question-answer routine and the teacher's preference that other children answer, and this was one of many indications of her social maturity (other children did call out answers, or rose excitedly out of their chairs with hands held high when they knew answers, or appeared distraught when they were not called on to give them). As I watched her, I was reminded of Rhonda's concerns that Cymira not be seen by peers as someone who "think[s] you know everything," and then be pressured to downplay her intelligence to fit in. It was striking that Cymira's self-restraint seemed to reflect her mother's concerns.

Cymira's attitude in the classroom was also remarkable in that, while she clearly enjoyed school, she approached it in a very serious and businesslike manner. She participated enthusiastically throughout the afternoon, and spoke occasionally to me, but she did not engage in off-task conversation with her classmates. A couple of girls watched Cymira closely and occasionally attempted to get her attention, but she paid them no mind and instead concentrated on the tasks at hand. These classmates included Felicia, who I knew was a neighbor and close friend who often visited Cymira's home to watch television, play school, or play Barbies. Rhonda reported that Cymira at times grew impatient with Felicia: "Cymira thinks Felicia doesn't listen enough, she's too busy tryin' to see what the boys are doin'." Ms. Nelbert noted that Cymira was respected and liked by her classmates, but she was not "extremely buddy-buddy or chummy" with anyone. Instead, she "knows that she's supposed to do certain things, and she takes her schoolwork pretty serious."

Cymira's relationships with peers in this classroom were reminiscent of a similar situation two years earlier in Head Start. A girl named Mystic was in the same class, and although the two interacted occasionally, there was no indication of more than a casual relationship. However, Cymira made a rather startling announcement during the final week of class: "Mystic's my cousin," she said matter-of-factly to me and the teaching assistant, Ms. Murdock. "What?" we said, laughing. "Why didn't you ever tell us?" "I just didn't want no one to know till the end of the year" was the gist of her reply. Even more so than Felicia, Cymira was very close to Mystic, and their families interacted almost daily. But, as Ms. Nelbert perceived and as Rhonda stressed repeatedly, Cymira had a job to do at school, and she managed her relationships with peers in a way that would not interfere with her "on-the-job" performance.

As was true in kindergarten, Cymira's intelligence, hard work, and maturity were noted and appreciated by her first-grade teacher. The general evaluation of Cymira that Ms. Nelbert offered echoed many of Ms. Roth's earlier comments, and also confirmed my own observations and Rhonda's reports to me:

> Cymira is a well-rounded little girl. She's a delight. She's a good student, a strong student, she works very hard, and she's very conscientious about her schoolwork. But she also is a little more mature than the other children. Because, like . . . joking? She seems to sense a little more about it's time to stop, and she can draw herself back, and control herself. And I've noticed that she'll pick up on what you mean, more subtle things, in speech and everything. She can read that, she's very perceptive to what's goin' on. . . . She also makes mistakes, and she doesn't get upset about it. She's like, that's OK, now she did it, now all right, let's go on. So she's a great little girl.

A bit later, I asked her to describe the role Rhonda seemed to play in Cymira's education, and she continued to offer nothing but praise. Rhonda was, according to Ms. Nelbert, "very encouraging towards her." The teacher speculated on the mother and daughter's relationship, concluding that they "have a good relationship. . . . I feel her mom has spent a lot of time doin' the right things for Cymira." Finally, she noted the kinds of questions and concerns Rhonda brought into their conversations, which impressed Ms. Nelbert a great deal. Rhonda wanted to know about "not just her grades, but the overall picture. She asks about that, and most parents don't ask about those kinds of things: How are they getting along with the other children? How are they doing with the other teachers? What's their outlook, what's their attitude? She asks those kinds of things. To me, that says she has a wide picture of what Cymira needs."

I was particularly pleased to hear that Ms. Nelbert believed Rhonda had an appropriately "wide picture" of Cymira's needs. I knew very well that Rhonda put much effort into preparing her daughter for the myriad of future experiences and challenges, "not only on the streets but all in the mind." The teacher's words were also gratifying because I knew Rhonda felt considerable ambivalence about her methods and competence as a parent, despite her efforts, which seemed skilled and monumental to me. When she sought out her mother's or grandmother's advice on child-rearing, her confidence was shored up tremendously if she received her grandmother's approval ("my grandma's the one I always want to do good for"). She also once said, at the close of our second interview, that talking with me made her feel as if "it's really a lot I should be doin', a lot more" for her children. I replied, "Well, I think you're doin' wonderful," and the interview tape concludes with her words: "Oh, good, I hope so. Lord knows I'm tryin', I'm really tryin'." Despite the self-doubts Rhonda expressed, she sustained remarkable effort to encourage her children's success, and I was pleased that this was appreciated by Ms. Nelbert.

These teachers' recognition and appreciation of Rhonda's concern and involvement in Cymira's academic, social, and moral development underscored the success of her parenting. It also suggested that Ms. Roth and Ms. Nelbert were especially sensitive to the challenges facing inner-city black parents, which was likely heightened by their training and involvement in the Head Start and Follow Through programs. Other teachers, for example Jeremiah's kindergarten and first-grade teachers (chapter 2; also see chapters 8 and 10), were also sensitive to these families' challenges, but Head Start and Follow Through teachers consistently demonstrated the greatest appreciation for the complexity of parents' situations and the socialization tasks they faced. Although both these federal programs were founded upon a model of family deprivation, individual teachers demonstrated keen understanding of inner-city parents, and a heightened compassion for both children and parents, that was unmatched by other teachers I interviewed.

Head Start and Follow Through teachers also seemed careful to acknowledge and lend legitimacy to the experiences of their students. For example, Ms. Nelbert's request that her students go home and ask "Mom, Dad, Grandma, Auntie, cousin" the answer to her question about bananas, was a somewhat subtle but nonetheless clear acknowledgment of the variety of family settings that are normal for these children. Other teachers purposefully avoided references to family members or personal questions that might provoke children's revelations of their families' deviance from conventional norms (see chapter 5). Such avoidance may make some teachers more comfortable, but it can do little to make children feel secure and confident in school settings.

We cannot know for certain how much of Cymira's apparent self-confidence and sense of belonging in school was due to teachers' sensitivity to the complexity of life in inner-city black families. However, her excellent performance in early elementary classrooms seemed to be encouraged by the continuity she experienced between her family, Head Start, and kindergarten and first-grade settings. With this foundation, when major changes did occur in Cymira's life during her second-grade year, she coped with them quite easily. She took her family's departure from the only neighborhood she had known, and her midyear transfer to a new school, in stride. As Rhonda reported at the end of Cymira's second-grade year, she had "no problems. . . . She just went on about it as if 'Hey, it's a new school. OK, so it's new people, I can deal with new people.' She dealt with 'em. She came right in, and her attitude never changed as far as her work. You know, if anything, she wanted to do more."

According to Rhonda, Cymira also "made a very good first impression on her teacher" at the new school, who complimented her intelligence, cooperativeness, and helpfulness. Finally, Rhonda proudly showed me results from Cymira's California Achievement Test, taken just weeks after the mid-year transfer. Although Rhonda had "worried about how she was gonna take them tests, bein' in a new school around new people," Cymira did very well. She scored in the 70th percentile for second-graders nationwide on the Total Battery, and her math scores, and scores for language use and mechanics, were all above the 85th percentile.

CONCLUSION

Shortly after our fourth interview in June 1993, Rhonda and her children moved again and Cymira entered another new school in the fall. Although I know no details of Cymira's experiences in third grade and beyond, Rhonda felt that once again her daughter's transition into a new environment went remarkably smoothly, and Cymira continued to do well and enjoy school. She also continued to demonstrate unselfish caring and concern for others, and clear devotion to her family. Late in December 1994, I received a short note from her thanking me for the small gift (McDonald's certificates) I had sent for Christmas. She wrote in part: "How are you? I hope you like your new home. How is Mary? Is she playing any sports? Hope you have a Merry Christmas and all your wishes come true. Don't forget Keith's birthday on the 4th of March and Steven's birthday on the 4th of January. I will write you another time. PUT ON YOUR GLASSES!!"

Before I received this delightful letter, I did not know her brothers' birthdays, and I laughed at her not-so-subtle hint that I might remember their birthdays as I routinely did her own. Her concern for them was touching, as was her interest in and best wishes for Mary. But best of all was her bold command (accompanied by a smiley face) to "PUT ON YOUR GLASSES!" This was an inside joke Cymira and I had shared in the past. Both she and I were supposed to wear glasses, but we both disliked them and rarely did—although we laughingly insisted that the other must do so. I had not seen Cymira for nearly a year and a half, and this intimate joke brought tears to my eyes, as I felt certain she knew how much pleasure this would give me. I also felt growing confidence that Cymira might indeed overcome the many factors that put her "at risk" for school failure, and fulfill the promise that Rhonda saw so clearly in her. In the following two chapters, however, the children of the other young mothers experience considerably more problematic transitions into schooling, and inspire less optimistic outlooks for their futures.

5

PARENT AND TEACHER
EXPECTATIONS

In this narrative, we will meet one of the most clearly troubled families involved in this study. Despite their many problems, however, Zena's parents' determined attempts to provide a better life for their children were quite impressive. Zena Worthy and her two younger siblings (Duane Jr. and Dominique) are the children of Marissa Dunbar and Duane Worthy, who were seventeen and eighteen when Zena was born. The chapter details how the family struggled with joblessness, poverty, homelessness, and relationship difficulties throughout the study years. In addition, Marissa's support network was clearly inadequate to meet her needs. She complained of the minimal and sporadic assistance she received from her extended family, and this—together with her decidedly negative memories of her childhood—seemed to powerfully influence both her parenting objectives and her prospective thinking about her children's futures.

Marissa hoped to raise her children very differently from the way she had been raised. Her desire to produce an entirely new parenting style was much different from Amy's purposefully reproductive strategies, and different also from Rhonda's attempts to mix innovative tactics with a stress on "traditional" strengths her family exhibited. While Amy (and to a lesser extent, Rhonda) had a blueprint of sorts for her parenting strategies, the image Marissa drew on provided her with little constructive knowledge or experience. Rather, her childhood taught her only what not to do, and she was left to her own devices to create a more positive family life for her children. I often felt Marissa was clutching at straws in this endeavor, as it was painfully clear that, unlike other mothers, she had so few resources to draw upon.

In addition to Marissa's bitterness about her extended family, I also noticed a growing sense of fatalism apparent in her talk about her children's futures. For example, Marissa remarked several times on her children's apparent unwillingness to listen to and learn from her attempts to assist them with schoolwork. On these occasions, her dependence on teachers and her frustration over her own felt impotence was clear. A sense of fatalism was also apparent when Marissa anticipated the likely ineffectiveness of her attempts at parental guidance once her children reached adolescence. Here readers will recognize parallels with Rhonda's fears about Cymira's negotiation of the pressures of adolescence. Finally, Marissa at times seemed painfully aware of social reproductive processes that might affect her children's lives; she recognized the parallels between her own situation and her mother's experiences as a young woman, and she matter-of-factly anticipated her children would face similar difficulties.

Despite such evidence of fatalistic attitudes and feelings of powerlessness, I stress that Marissa did not respond with passivity. This is perhaps the critical point this narrative introduces—when Marissa and other mothers perceived their own likely powerlessness to control children's outcomes, they reacted with active resistance to processes they feared might nonetheless be inevitable. When expressing fatalistic views, Marissa was not attempting to justify a decision to give up on efforts to alter her children's likely outcomes. Rather, she seemed to prepare herself for the possibility that her continuing efforts might be to no avail. This, however, did not convince her that the struggle was not worth the effort.

Predictably, the narrative demonstrates how Zena's transition into the early years of schooling was marked by ups and downs much like the material and interpersonal difficulties experienced by her family. Zena's experiences in educational settings at times helped her to contend with family difficulties, and at other times seemed to exacerbate existing problems or even disturb a temporarily tranquil and stable home life. Zena's classrooms at the Head Start center and at the neighborhood school offered her comfortable environments in which she felt secure and self-confident despite a home life that was at times chaotic and potentially unsettling. And in these settings, she did very well. On the other hand, her adjustment and performance were threatened when she was bused to a primarily white school for first grade. As was true for Alysha, Zena struggled with the challenges presented by the move to a culturally dissimilar environment. And like Alysha's mother's, Marissa's frustration with this situation was clear. Also like Annette, Marissa's originally high expectations for her daughter's success were adjusted downward, and in this chapter I look closely at the role of teacher expectations in this process.

MARISSA'S NARRATIVE: HIGH HOPES AND FEW RESOURCES

Marissa and Duane began their relationship when they were "thirteen or fourteen," and although they never married and never "lived together," they had maintained their relationship through many hard times and were cooperating in raising their children. Duane's sincere concern for and investment in his children was clear, and he, in fact, was the only father who became actively involved in this research (Duane participated in both our first and second interviews). Neither parent was a high school graduate, and they had both been sporadically employed in low-paying jobs throughout their adult lives.

Marissa left high school after her sophomore year, shortly before Zena's birth. She relied on AFDC for brief periods after each of her children were born, and when not receiving this assistance, she typically remained eligible for food stamps and Medicaid. Unlike Rhonda, Marissa had considerable work experience in a variety of low-level service positions. She had previously been employed, for example, at a fast food franchise, and had begun but not completed a nursing-assistance program (she had attempted this training while also working full-time). At the time of our first interview, however, Marissa was without income or welfare assistance of any kind, having just days before lost the housekeeping position with a national hotel chain she'd held for two years. Throughout these years, Duane was employed only occasionally and part-time, primarily in construction. Although he rarely made significant financial contributions to the family, his more consistent support had come in the form of reliable and loving child care.

Marissa was the most difficult mother to initially contact, but I finally reached her after several calls to several relatives, and she reluctantly agreed to an interview. We arranged to meet at Duane's mother's home, which Mrs. Worthy shared with Duane and two other sons. When I arrived at the appointed hour, Marissa cleared away several overflowing suitcases to make room at the table for herself and Duane and me. When we began to talk, Marissa quickly explained her living situation. She and her children were literally living out of suitcases: "I don't really stay here; we don't have a place now," she said. She described staying with her grandmother at times, and "stayin' anywhere we can," while waiting and hoping for assistance in finding shelter for her family. This was the first indication of the severe problems this family faced, and as our acquaintance progressed, I learned more about their troubled history.

Marissa told of how they had become homeless, their movement "from shelter to homes to shelter to homes," and her eventual success in finding a home for the family. Zena was absent from the Head Start center for much of the winter, and during our second interview, Marissa explained that she had been unable to keep up the bills where she was living, and had moved with the children to a homeless shelter and transferred Zena to another center. When Marissa left the shelter several months later to stay with her grandmother, Zena returned to her original classroom. The elderly woman soon lost patience with the children, however, and at the close of the 1989–90 school year (the point of our first interview), the family was moving between the homes of relatives—Marissa's grandmother, her brother, and Duane's mother.

Finally, in November 1990—after spending several more months in a different shelter—Marissa rented a duplex with the aid of a Section VIII housing grant (she had been on the waiting list for several years). This latter period in a shelter had been especially traumatic for the family. Marissa had attempted to end her ten-year relationship with Duane and "just break away and make a new life for the kids and me." However, once settled in her new home, she gave in to pressure from the children, from Duane, and from her own lingering desires to "get married, and really be a family," and agreed to a reconciliation. Marissa soon secured employment as a housekeeper in a nursing home, and Duane resumed his practice of caring for the children while Marissa worked. Although he was present in the home on a nearly daily basis, Duane continued to live with his mother.

Such were this family's circumstances as Zena negotiated the critical transition into formal schooling. Given their difficulties, it is easy to suppose Zena's parents had little time or energy for concerns about their children's schooling, and it was true these issues at times took a backseat to more pressing problems of poverty and homelessness, unemployment, lack of transportation, and personal traumas that plagued the family. However, both parents maintained concern for Zena's education throughout this period, and they acted on these concerns as best they could. This was apparent first in the mere fact that Zena consistently attended Head Start, albeit in two different centers, throughout the 1989–90 school year.

Beyond enrolling Zena and her brother in Head Start, Marissa's and Duane's strategies for helping the children were much less focused and specific than those of other mothers. However, they clearly valued education and did what they could when they could. For example, during our first interview, Marissa said she'd missed opportunities to work with Zena because of her work. But, she said, Duane would "teach her things when he can, when she's over here." And, she continued, "now I don't have a job, we do that a lot, we sit down and have her learn things, and she's really anxious to learn. She'll cry if we don't sit down with her and teach her."

That Zena was "really anxious to learn" was a quality both parents recognized and valued in their daughter. During our first interview, I asked Marissa and Duane, "What do you expect her experiences in public school will be like?" Marissa began to respond, but Duane interrupted:

M: I think she'll be all right in school, she's willing to learn and she's//
D: //When she grow up, she's gonna be the type to, um, experience a lot and want to do a lot of different things. That's the way she really is, she like to experience everything, try to learn how to do everything. So, no tellin' what Ze' might [laugh], you know, do. I think she'll be pretty bright. 'Cause she's willing to learn and just go out there and try learnin' everything, as best she can.

Both Zena's parents felt she was bright and motivated, and they had high expectations for her future. I was impressed by the way Marissa and Duane valued Zena's apparent intense desire to learn and her curiosity, and by the emphasis they placed on experiential learning. Although neither Marissa or Duane had spent a great deal of time working with Zena on readiness skills, they felt their daughter had personal characteristics that would contribute to her eventual success. "No tellin' what Zena might do" seemed a perfect summary of the "sky's-the-limit" expectations Marissa and Duane seemed to hold for Zena prior to the beginning of her elementary schooling.

Marissa also reported visiting the Head Start center "when I had the chance" (Bill Corsaro met both parents at the center on one occasion), and described her interaction with teachers there: "We set down and we talked about what she had learned and what she needed to learn, what I think she needed to learn and stuff like that. And like I told 'em, her colors, she needs to really practice on her colors and on her shapes. And to this day, since she got in school, she knows those colors and she knows those shapes. They tell you to work with her at home when you can. And they will work with her in school, and you put it together and it stays up there."

Marissa had followed the teachers' urgings to work with Zena to reinforce classroom learning, and she embraced the notion of partnership with Zena's teachers. During this and other interviews, Marissa conveyed both her sense of obligation to assist her children in their schooling, and self-doubts she had concerning her ability to do so effectively. For example, she noted that while she and Duane "sit down and help her a lot," Zena often resisted their efforts. Marissa concluded that while parents' efforts are important, "we can't really do it, it takes someone else to do it." She appeared genuinely grateful for teachers' suggestions about what to do at home, and she relied heavily on teachers to tell her how to assist her children.

As our first interview neared its end, the theme of parent/teacher partnership was again apparent. Marissa again spoke of hopeful expectations for Zena's future, but now her words were tempered by a pessimism that seemed to emerge from memories of her own educational career. After she noted her satisfaction with the Head Start program, I asked Marissa, "What do you think public schools are like as far as offering opportunities for Zena and for your other kids?" Her reply betrayed enduring bitterness about her own youthful experiences:

M: If public school is like when I was growin' up, it's nothin'. Well, but, I just want to see them stay in school, 'cause I think school is the best thing for 'em. I don't want to see them drop out like I did, 'cause you don't have anything. I want to see them go on, but when they get to a certain age, it's really hard to keep a child in school. But I would like for them to stay in school, we're gonna help 'em as much as possible. We probably don't know everything, we probably don't know that much, but what we do know we'll teach them so they'll know. And someone else will come along like the teachers, and teach them more. And put all that together, it could be a smart kid.

D: The public schools really didn't have that much to offer.

M: They don't. They sit down and they tell you things one time, it's like if you don't catch on, then you won't.

Marissa's Biography: New Parental Practices

Unlike other mothers involved in this study, Marissa rarely mentioned childhood experiences in school or in her family during our interviews, but when she did her recollections were primarily negative. Both Marissa and Duane had perceived school as unstimulating and unsupportive. Although their parents had urged them to stay in school, as teenagers they made their own decisions. As Marissa said during our second interview: "My mother thought education was best for all of us. I mean, we was up there, with a broken leg or whatever, we was in school. But as we got older—I didn't graduate, and [Duane] didn't either. . . . When they get to a certain age, and they think they know it all, and they're out of your control, you can't really do nothin' but tell 'em, you know, sit down and tell 'em that school will help you get through life."

Here, as Marissa drew on memories from her own youth to think about the future, she anticipated a loss of parental control that she viewed as inevitable when children moved into the adolescent years. Marissa mentioned such concerns and beliefs in several interviews, and when she did, she evoked a theme of early independence of teenagers that emerged in interviews with many mothers. For example, Rhonda also noted that she was granted freedom to make her own decisions about schooling at an early age, saying that "when I started in high school, that's when it was more or less up on you, what you do." Nearly all the mothers—both graduates and nongraduates alike—at times expressed concerns about their children's coming adolescence and the rebelliousness that so often accompanies it. As Marissa and Rhonda did, other mothers also incorporated many of their experiences growing up into their prospective thinking—and worries—about their children's future choices about schooling.

Marissa described a chaotic childhood very much like her own children's early years. She had "lived a lot of places," and attended many different schools. Her mother, she said, was "goin' through the same thing I have just went through" (homelessness), and had also moved her family between the homes of various relatives. Although Marissa could not undo the upheavals her children had experienced to date, her own childhood impressed upon her the need for stability and predictability in their lives, and she and Duane were working hard to achieve that.

In addition, Marissa also wanted desperately to be a better mother than her own. She complained about the lack of support and assistance she received from her family, especially her mother and grandmother, during particularly difficult times in her life. When she'd needed them most, they declined to help, and Marissa recalled such remarks as "Well, we got somethin' to do," or "I can't help you, I'm busy fillin' my jars with jelly," and noted that "my mother, she's got every excuse in the world." Later, she commented that her own children would likely experiences similar difficult times, and said that "I just hope that I'm there to help 'em pick up the pieces. 'Cause my mother wasn't there, so I want to be there for them."

Marissa also hoped to allow Zena, Duane Jr., and Dominique greater freedom to "be children," and she wanted to be less authoritarian than her mother had been. During our third interview, as Marissa talked of her efforts to help Zena deal with problems with her first-grade peers, she compared her tactics to her mother's: "I try, but I'm not gonna try too hard, 'cause that's what my mother did to me. She tried too hard, you know. Instead of sittin' down and talkin' to us, 'Is there a problem in school? Is there someone you're not gettin' on with? Is it your teacher?' Instead of that, [it was] 'You're goin' to school today!' And so you learn off things like that. I look back on what she did to me and I want to be totally different for them. I want to have that special relationship with them, not just as a mother, but also as a friend."

Marissa was, therefore, a concerned and caring mother who tried hard to raise her children to avoid the many problems she had experienced as a child and young adult. Although she seemed to have only negative memories of her own childhood and education, she was convinced success in school would be her children's ticket out of poverty: "It's best to get a education to get a better job. You know, sit behind somebody's desk, be important." Despite her best intentions, and in stark contrast to mothers considered in earlier chapters, Marissa's experiences had provided her with few tools to work with toward this goal. She and Duane relied on teachers' advice when available, but otherwise employed rather unfocused and less than routine strategies such as occasionally overseeing and trying to assist with homework, providing Zena with small amounts of money to spend on books, and at times monitoring and discussing her television viewing.

Continual stress and changing family circumstances also exacerbated this family's difficulties. Marissa's values and goals were clear, but translating these into concrete action was more problematic. Her struggle, fatigue, and confusion were often apparent, and these at times were manifested in a growing sense of fatalism concerning her ability to make a positive difference in her children's lives. But Marissa resisted the sense of powerlessness she clearly felt. She continued to strive for her children's betterment, despite the many obstacles she faced. Unfortunately, Zena's experiences in educational settings presented even further obstacles.

ZENA'S TRANSITION INTO SCHOOLING

Perhaps more than is true of the other children, a brief description of Zena's appearance may help readers better understand her experiences as she moved through the early years of schooling. Marissa once remarked that Zena "favored" her father's side of the family, and indeed, Zena resembled her mother very little, and was clearly her father's daughter. Duane was an imposing man, very tall, muscular and dark skinned. In Head Start, Zena was larger than all but one male classmate, and in coming years she remained taller and heavier than most children her age. Also like her father's, Zena's face was large and full, her skin and hair were very dark, and she always appeared older than her age. Coupled with her assertive interactive style, Zena's physical characteristics made her a rather imposing member of the Head Start peer culture, who clearly inspired respect in her classmates. Later, these characteristics likely contributed to difficulties she had getting along with less culturally similar classmates in first grade.

Perhaps in response to her family's difficulties, Zena exhibited rather precocious social maturity and independence. This was apparent in her behavior at home as well as her interaction with peers. As early as kindergarten, Zena was washing dishes, sweeping, and helping with the cooking and laundry. She also took full responsibility for self-care activities such as bathing, picking out her clothes, and even fixing her own hair in braids and barrettes. In addition, she was quite active in teaching her younger brother and sister letters, numbers, and songs she learned at school, and she often initiated "school" role play where she was the teacher and they were her students. Marissa appreciated these activities a great deal, and felt Zena was a great help to her. However, when Marissa at times complained about Zena's bossiness or her unwillingness to accept her parents' help or guidance, she did not seem to consider that these characteristics were likely also manifestations of Zena's advanced independence and self-reliance.

From Head Start to Kindergarten

Given her family's multiple problems, Zena easily fit the category of a child "at risk" for educational failure. However, her entry into Head Start was quite smooth, and she competently and confidently adjusted to classroom routines. She quickly integrated herself into the classroom and peer culture, and easily reestablished her position when she returned after spending time in both a homeless shelter and another Head Start center.

Zena was a popular and respected member of the peer culture who seemed more socially mature and sophisticated than many of her classmates. She was somewhat reserved in structured activities, but when called upon proved herself to be among the brighter children in the class. It was, however, in the area of peer relations that Zena excelled, and she was especially adept at initiating and engaging in fantasy play with other children. For example, she frequently introduced monster characters such as "Nightmare Freddy" into peer play, initiating chase sequences that are popular with most children this age. Bill Corsaro once commented to Zena and Ramone (chapter 8) on their knowledge of such frightening movies and characters, saying he didn't think they should watch such shows because they are "too scary." Both children laughed at his concern, noting that these shows were "not scary" because they are "not real." Ramone explained to Bill that Freddy has "just got on a costume that makes people scared." When Bill persisted and asked if these programs didn't give them bad dreams, Zena dismissed the notion by explaining that her bad dreams related to real-life concerns: She didn't have bad dreams about Freddy, she had bad dreams about a dog that chased and tried to bite her. Zena and Ramone left little doubt about their ability to distinguish make-believe from feasible threats, and they displayed here mature and sophisticated reasoning that was quite stunning for children their age.

Zena also excelled and often took the lead in fantasy play centered around the enactment of family roles. She had a flamboyant, exaggerated style the other children admired, and she demonstrated much skill in the oppositional, argumentative discourse enjoyed by many of these children. She often took the role of a harried mother of several children who struggled to meet her children's wants and needs in the face of challenging circumstances. In an episode recorded in field notes, Zena hurried to meet an appointment for her sick baby doll at "the clinic." When her two other children (two boys who also participated in this role play) dallied getting ready to leave, she exclaimed: "Come on! You gonna get left in a minute, you hear me?" At other times, Zena took the role of mother in telephone play, and she once pretended to watch from her window as a neighbor's house went up in flames. She reported the ongoing events to her telephone partner as emergency personnel arrived and rescued the family, and she shook her head sorrowfully as she noted that children upstairs in the house had been hurt in the fire.

The issues and concerns Zena expressed and enacted in family role play were based in her awareness of real-life problems that mothers, especially those raising children in poverty, at times confronted. A final example of family role/telephone play demonstrates her awareness of these pressures and her ability to address troubling aspects of her own life through play with peers. In an episode captured on videotape, Zena and Debra collaborated in a long telephone conversation in which each girl pretended to be a mother caring for several young children. Each complained of the difficulty they had meeting their children's requests to go to the store, and to the park, when they had no private transportation. The girls noted how time-consuming it was to walk to bus stops, wait for buses, and transfer from one route to another. Zena's feigned exasperation was clear when she said at one point, "Guess where my kids told me to take them? To the store. When the bus comes by, my kids waitin' for it. I don't got time to do that!"

Other topics introduced in this telephone drama included constant need to discipline the unruly children, and their remarkable ability to create never-ending work for the mothers. As the episode neared its end, Debra began to complain about her "man" rather than her children.

D: My man start in on me.
Z: [Jumps up] I don't have one!
D: He's been hittin' on me, he's been hittin' on me for ten minutes.
Z: You got one and I don't have one. My kids been askin' for "my daddy." I say—they say "I want my daddy, I want my daddy," all day.

This episode was a fascinating display of the girls' awareness of the problems and pressures that can accompany raising children in poverty. Debra's introduction of the issue of domestic violence was striking, but since she was not among the children followed in this study, I have no data that would shed light on questions about her own exposure to incidents like the one she depicted here. We were unaware, at the time this episode was recorded, of parallels between Zena's family life and her family role enactment. However, as I later began to learn of Zena's family's circumstances and history, this episode became especially intriguing. Her parents were indeed physically separated while Marissa and the children stayed in a homeless shelter. In fact, during our third interview (the first at which Duane was not present), Marissa described her children's distress over the separation from their father during these periods using almost identical words: "It was just them and me. And they was goin' through a lot of changes, 'cause it was like always 'Where's Daddy? Where's Daddy?' "

Zena's year in Head Start, then, had provided her not only with opportunities to prepare academically for kindergarten, but also opportunities to work through and develop understanding of family problems with a group of similar peers and sympathetic teachers who could relate to the issues that were so important to Zena. That she succeeded and in fact excelled in both academic and social areas evidenced the effectiveness of this Head Start classroom in providing an environment where children like Zena could feel confident, competent, and secure. In the midst of family problems that might easily have overwhelmed her, Zena's success here gave her a sound foundation to build on as she entered kindergarten and the public schools.

Further Family Uncertainty and Another Helpful School

Unfortunately, Zena did not begin kindergarten until well over two months into the fall semester. After a very uncertain period rocked by homelessness, unemployment, and unstable relationships, Zena's family finally moved into their own home, Marissa secured a new job working days, and she and Duane reconciled after their breakup. At this point, in mid-November, Zena entered a neighborhood school about four blocks from her new home.

Zena had missed considerable class time and was far behind, and Marissa visited Zena's teacher to learn how she could help her daughter catch up. Ms. Hill gave Marissa materials to work with, and she and Zena regularly complied with the teacher's suggestion—especially on weekends when there was no assigned homework. Marissa soon saw evidence these efforts were paying off. In February she reported that while Zena's first report card "wasn't bad, but it wasn't good neither," her second report "was outstanding, she had improved on just about everything."

Continuity between certain features of Zena's Head Start and kindergarten classroom seemed important for helping Zena recover from her late entry into kindergarten. As was true in Head Start, all of Zena's kindergarten classmates were black, and Zena again attended the afternoon session, which allowed her to begin her day at a leisurely pace. The class size was also almost identical, and Zena was one of only thirteen students. Finally, Zena again had a black teacher.

Ms. Hill was a woman in her thirties who had taught at this school for eight years. She clearly enjoyed working with the economically disadvantaged children and families in this neighborhood. However, although she demonstrated understanding and concern for her students, she was unlike other teachers who placed high value on developing close and motherly relations with them. Rather, Ms. Hill had a no-nonsense style (again, similar to that of Head Start teachers) and was a strict disciplinarian who responded to the constraints of the half-day kindergarten schedule by allowing almost no free, unstructured activities. She believed students should instead utilize every moment preparing for the academic emphasis of first grade. When we interviewed Ms. Hill early in May, she'd already completed the kindergarten curriculum and was now "really treating [the students] as beginning first-graders." For example, she assigned vocabulary lists, had introduced addition and subtraction, and was working on sentence construction. Ms. Hill's expectations for her students were high, and it seemed they would be well prepared for even the most challenging first-grade programs.[1]

Ms. Hill's assessment of Zena's performance during the year essentially confirmed Marissa's reports: She was impressed with Zena's progress, and described her as an attentive student who was good at listening and following directions. She also believed Zena was "very capable of doing good work," and she was impressed with Zena's determination to "catch up" with the other students. And she was especially pleased with the motivation Zena displayed: "I've never gotten an 'I can't do,' OK? She will try, and put forth the effort, and that . . . tells me 'Yes, I want to do.' That in itself says so much."

Ms. Hill also said Zena was one of her quieter students. While Zena had shown a flair for peer interaction the year before, this characterization did fit with our observations from the Head Start center, where Zena was somewhat hesitant during structured activities and rarely volunteered answers. Since the structure and pace of Ms. Hill's classroom gave little time for social activities and interaction with peers, it was not surprising that Zena was subdued in this setting.

Finally, when I asked about Zena's parents, Ms. Hill said simply: "They're concerned, I know her mom is. She has asked me, you know, 'How is she doing, what can I do to help her?' She's very supportive also." The teacher was uncritical of Marissa's level of involvement, and although her comments were brief, they were meaningful in light of earlier remarks she had made about expectations of her students' parents. As was true in interviews with several other teachers, Ms. Hill had not waited for my questions about parent involvement, but rather had introduced this topic in the context of other discussions. My queries about teaching philosophy and classroom procedures had elicited this answer: "You know, parental support means so much. I tell my parents at the beginning of the school year, I can't do it alone, it's a team effort. That's what I expect, I have expectations for parents as well as for the children. And it makes a big difference, at the end of the year I can really tell those students whose parents have been supportive during the year."

This was not a teacher who was satisfied with perfunctory participation, and Ms. Hill's characterization of Marissa as "concerned," "very supportive," and someone who asked, "What can I do to help her?" indicated Marissa had met the high expectations Ms. Hill held not only for her students, but for their parents as well.

First Grade: New and Difficult Challenges

As was true of Zena's experiences the previous year in Head Start, during her kindergarten year she appeared to have overcome significant family-related problems. Her parents and her teacher were pleased with her progress and anticipated a smooth transition into first grade and continued achievement. As the year ended, however, Marissa was disappointed to learn that Zena would have to participate in the mandatory busing program. In the fall of 1991, Zena began first grade at a new school miles from her home. Like other children in this study (see especially Sheila and Tamera, chapters 6 and 7), Zena had some difficulty adjusting to a full-day schedule, and the thirty-minute bus ride each way further lengthened her day. Other aspects of the classroom presented new challenges as well; Zena was one of only a handful of black children among the twenty-two children in the classroom, and for the first time she had a white teacher.

In addition to our interview with Ms. Majors in March 1991, we also observed this classroom throughout the afternoon session that day. I was especially pleased with Ms. Majors's invitation to do so since earlier conversations with both her and Marissa indicated that Zena was having considerable difficulty. Each had suggested that Zena's difficulties arose primarily from "attitude" problems and problems getting along with classmates, and I welcomed the opportunity to observe interaction among members of this class.

Ms. Majors had taught for nine years in another IPS school, and was completing her fourth year in her current position. She described the school neighborhood as a very low-income, "very transient" white neighborhood where "some of our red-necked families" held racist attitudes toward children who were bused in from the city's central district.

Ms. Majors was one of several teachers who mentioned parents' lack of concern when I asked about the least pleasing aspects of their work, and her comments were the most impassioned expression of this downside of teaching. Her concerns went beyond parental neglect of children's schooling to include a more general neglect she thought common among her students' parents:

T: . . . It's very rewarding; the children are the best part. The worst part is dealing with parents.

K: Well, actually, that's my next question. [In addition to] the things about your work that you find the most rewarding or pleasing, what do you find the least// pleasing?

T: //because you want to slap some of them. You just wanna slap 'em. You just wanna say, "Why don't you feed your kid, why don't you love 'em, why don't you dress them right, and why don't you reinforce things?" And you just can't say what you really think. And you also [want to] say, "Well, why did you have this child if you're not gonna take care of him?" You know, and I always think, I could do a better job. That's the worst moments, when I start thinking bitter things like that. . . . I take better care of my dog than some of these children are taken care of.

She went on to describe various ways she felt many of her students were neglected, noting that most "don't have book bags . . . they don't have crayons, they don't have scissors. They don't have the things that we take for granted—glue and paint, and magazines."

Perhaps in part because she felt many students were severely deprived, Ms. Majors placed much emphasis on developing close and caring relationships with the children. She described herself as a "physical person," who "enjoy[ed] the hugs and the love I receive from the children," and she added that "there are days when they need that."

Ms. Majors's teaching style was decidedly more flexible than the no-nonsense styles of Zena's kindergarten and Head Start teachers. While students were granted much freedom, they were also expected to interact together in cooperative and kind ways, and Ms. Majors hoped they would come to feel that "we're a family here." It was apparent from our observations that many of the children responded well to Ms. Majors's loving and freedom-granting style, but none of this fit with Zena's past experiences or her personality. Not surprisingly then, Ms. Majors reported that Zena was having many problems. She described Zena as an "outsider" who didn't fit in with the other "sweet and innocent" girls. She complained about Zena's "attitude," saying Zena was often "so moody," "unhappy," and "she kind of fusses, pouts and slides her feet around . . . it's a little belligerence, a little chip on her shoulder." In addition, Ms. Majors said that Zena "has said things to the other kids like 'You're white and I don't like you.' I've never heard her say that, but the other kids tell me that." In fact, two white girls approached us during our visit and complained that Zena "thinks she knows it all" and is "always telling us what to do."

Although Zena had previously excelled in peer relations, her skills did not easily transfer to her new environment, and the take-charge, dramatic, and confrontational style that had served her well was now quite problematic and unappreciated. Zena also seemed uncomfortable with Ms. Majors's affectionate style. The teacher reported that although "I do have a relationship with her, she will hug me," Zena remained somewhat standoffish. In addition, for the first time Zena's academic performance failed to meet her parents' expectations. Although Ms. Majors believed Zena was a "solid" student, she said behavioral problems had hampered Zena's ability to complete work conscientiously and on time.

My several conversations with Marissa earlier in the year had prepared me to expect such reports. Marissa had not attended the fall parent-teacher conference, but had reportedly "had the conference over the phone with her." During this and other phone conversations, Ms. Majors had complained to Marissa about Zena's "attitude." There had also been notes on the back of Zena's report cards. All the communications Marissa described seemed basically the same—they focused on Zena's negative behavior and attitude. For example, Marissa reported that in both a phone call and a note Ms. Majors said essentially the same thing: "Zena's a terrific student but behavior in school—she likes to mess with the other kids. And she say bad things, bad words [quiet laugh], to the other kids." Marissa also said the teacher had questioned whether Zena was getting enough sleep.

I knew from our interview that Marissa had taken the teacher's comments quite seriously. She complained about Zena's attitude—especially her bossiness—several times before we spoke specifically about school. She said, for example, that Zena "has a attitude sometimes, if she's not gettin' enough rest." In response to complaints from the teacher, Marissa had taken several concrete actions. First, she began enforcing an earlier bedtime, and all three children now were in bed by 8:00 P.M. Second, to allay problems Zena had forgetting her homework, Marissa placed a large bowl on a table near the front door, and Zena deposited her completed homework there each evening (this would apparently be the last thing Zena saw as she left for school in the morning).

In addition, Marissa began to talk with Zena about controlling her anger. Marissa related Zena's difficulties getting along with her classmates to problems she had in the workplace. She said that "Zena's got a bad temper, you make her mad and she'll just blow. I used to be like that." Marissa noted she had "had people come up to me and call me nigger," and said she used to "just snap," but had taught herself to think, "I need this job. So, I can't nothin' but take this. And you just keep smilin'. . . . " The crux of the matter for Marissa was that "it's all about self-control." I asked if she wanted Zena to learn "to put up with that," and she replied:

M: Yes. Yes. You have to learn how to control your temper. Walk on off. Forget it. Words ain't hurt nobody. Just go ahead about your business. Yes, I'm teachin' her that. . . .

K: So is that something that you have just recently started emphasizing, or have you//

M: //Yes, ever since her teacher sent me a note about her attitude, that's what did it. 'Cause see, I don't never get up there to the school, so I don't know what's goin' on, so I'm glad she did write that down, so I know what's goin' on.

Although Marissa was disappointed with Zena's behavior, she believed her daughter was doing excellent work in school. "Especially in math," she said, "only papers she brings home is a happy face with a A." Prior to the end of the first marking period, Marissa had anxiously waited to see if Zena would make the honor roll, but when we met for our interview, I learned that she had not. Marissa said, however, that "the report card was outstanding. I don't know why she didn't; I can't get out to Zena's school to talk to her teacher, it's so far out." Later she noted Zena had received "two Cs, the rest As and Bs," and she didn't understand why such marks did not earn honors (Marissa apparently did not understand the precise GPA requirements for honor roll: no more than one C in academic subjects). However, Marissa had concluded that "if you're gonna make honor roll, it's more than gettin' As on all your papers, it's got somethin' to do with your personality, how you act toward other kids."

The concern Marissa communicated to me was clear, as were the seriousness she attached to Ms. Majors's complaints and the steps she'd taken to address them. Ms. Majors, however, had perceived her much differently. As the teacher discussed Zena's various behavioral and attitudinal problems, she introduced the topic of her communication with Marissa:

T: . . . As a child, how do you get out of being an angry child? They don't know how. I've called her mother a few times about it, and her mother's just "Well, that's the way she is at home." And I don't know where to go from there. I've never met the mother. She's never been in, for conferences or open house or anything like that. It's a real loss when I don't meet a parent. I always think: "Wouldn't they want to meet me, to see what kind of ogre is teaching their child all day?" That bothers me, when I don't know all the parents.

K: Yeah, I was gonna ask you about how you felt about the role Zena's parents were playing in her education. We may as well talk about this now. Um, what kind of contact have you had with Zena's mom over the last year?

T: The school system provides a day where the children are released, and it gives you all day to have parent conferences, and she did not respond to that. I don't know what more I can do. I realize with our bused children live on the other side of town, and if they don't have transportation, it's hard. But I always think: I'd hitch a ride somehow. I mean, I can't believe they wouldn't want to meet me and just size me up. Anyways, to me it's a signal when they don't even come for that. I know there are reasons sometimes, but we usually get a pretty good turnout. I really can't sing the benefits of integration wholeheartedly. There's a lot of pluses, but I don't know if it's worth it, losing the neighborhood schools. Because maybe it would be a different story if she was still at school [PS#X].

Ms. Majors had made similar remarks during our earlier phone conversation to arrange the interview. At that time, she'd commented on Zena's attitude, said Marissa was uncommunicative, and she had "basically given up on getting help from the family." Importantly, during this call she also suggested that both Zena's behavior and the lack of support she perceived from Marissa had contributed to a decision she had made concerning tactics she would use with Zena. She had concluded, she said, "that it's best not to push Zena into something that she doesn't want to do, because she is just not going to do it."

I'd approached this interview, then, hoping to share my own knowledge of Marissa's concern and activities, and this point in the interview provided that opportunity. When Ms. Majors wondered if things would be different were Zena not bused, I told her Marissa had indeed met with both Zena's Head Start and kindergarten teachers, especially during Zena's kindergarten year. Now Ms. Majors noted that she spoke with neighborhood parents each day as she walked out with students at dismissal. Just that afternoon, she had talked with three parents.

From this point in the interview, Ms. Majors seemed to reconsider her earlier appraisals of both Marissa and Zena, and she commented that the interview was "helping me think of more positive things about Zena." Other comments suggested alterations in her thinking about Marissa:

> The mother has responded on the report card. I try to write a comment on everybody's report card, every time. And the mother usually will write back. And that's good. And that's a rarity here; most of my parents don't.

> And when Zena's out, I'll usually get a note, too. And I don't always get that from all of the kids; usually I don't. And I have called her when Zena went on one of her little spells of bein' fussy for days, and she said she would talk to her. So I really guess I can't complain, you know; she said, "Well, she's like that at home." In a way that makes me feel better that she's not acting up just at school.

> Zena brings a [book] bag every day, bless her heart. So she doesn't lose it, so that's a really good thing she does. . . . So that's another plus about her mother that I hadn't even thought about. Because I know that bags don't come out of the air. The parents are providing them.

At the end of the interview, as we discussed Zena's academic performance, Ms. Majors noted that Zena's grades were sometimes "marked down" when she did not turn papers in on time. I mentioned Marissa was surprised Zena had not made the honor roll the first marking period, and Ms. Majors responded: "Oh, wonderful! I'm glad her mother wanted her to! That's neat." (Her clear surprise suggested that she had suspected Zena's mother did not care about such matters). And finally, Ms. Majors concluded: "Zena's a good, solid student, but there are some that are better than her, and those are the ones that are on the honor roll. And it can't be for everybody."

During the last several minutes of our interview, then, Ms. Majors clearly questioned her own attitudes toward this mother she had previously "given up on getting help from." She mentioned that school can be an intimidating place for parents, especially if their children have difficulties and they receive only negative reports from school personnel. She seemed surprised at herself when she observed: "The only time I have contacted Zena's mother has been negative, now that I think of it, and how awful of me."

My portrayal of Ms. Majors may suggest I am wholly critical of her, but this is not the case. During our observations in her classroom, I was impressed with the rapport and genuine affection between Ms. Majors and most of her students. The children's excitement during activities and their eagerness to please their teacher were clear. There was also no doubting Ms. Majors's sincere concern for all her students, including Zena, and her devotion to the children was revealed by the emotion she communicated during our interview. Unfortunately, Ms. Majors's teaching style and her emphasis on close relationships among members of her classroom were so contrary to Zena's past experience and personality that they seemed to exacerbate difficulties Zena had coping with a set of peers so radically different from those to whom she was accustomed.

On the other hand, Ms. Majors's communications with Marissa had indeed been wholly negative. For parents like Marissa, whose own experiences as students were so negative, withdrawal from contact with teachers is a common reaction to consistently bad reports about their children (see, for example, Comer and Haynes 1991; Lareau 1989; Toomey 1989). While this suggests Marissa's past experiences could have contributed to a reluctance to participate in Zena's schooling, she did not interpret her behavior as withdrawal. Rather, she believed the school's distant location, coupled with her own lack of resources to overcome this obstacle, precluded her physical presence at school. At the same time, her activities at home demonstrated that she remained concerned and involved in Zena's education.

But Ms. Majors could hardly be faulted for failing to incorporate information to which she had no access into her definition of the situation; she had no way to know, for example, about strategies Marissa enacted at home such as the earlier bedtime, the routine placement of homework, and the conversations aimed at helping Zena control her temper. Other evidence of Marissa's concern to which Ms. Majors was privy, however, went unnoticed or was discounted. By her own admission, Ms. Majors placed great importance on parents' presence at school as a symbolic indicator of parents' educational values ("To me it's a signal when they don't come"), and this symbol was apparently powerful enough to overshadow contradictory evidence.

Although Ms. Majors did not perceive her this way, it was clear to me that Marissa took the teacher's complaints about Zena very seriously, and she attempted to combat the problems through actions at home as best she could. However, despite her sincere desire to help her daughter, Marissa always seemed quite dependent on teachers to direct her in specific strategies to encourage Zena's success and development at school. When Ms. Majors "basically gave up on getting help from the family," Marissa was left seemingly clutching at straws and remarking that "I don't know what's goin' on" at the school. Both teacher and mother were clearly frustrated with their apparent inability to help Zena remedy her problems and with the lack of communication between them. Although the responsibility for their failures must be shared by the two women, it was striking to observe how readily Ms. Majors seemed to "give up," despite her professed "understanding" of the difficulties parents like Marissa may have finding transportation, and interacting with school personnel they find intimidating, in environments reminiscent of their own not-so-distant failures.

Return to the Neighborhood School

As Zena's first-grade year ended, Marissa remained pleased with the work Zena brought home, confused as to why the As and happy faces she saw on these papers did not translate into higher report card grades, and frustrated with continuing reports of bad behavior. She did eventually meet Ms. Majors on two occasions, once accompanying Zena's class on an end-of-the-year field trip to a downtown museum. This occasion is important to note—the museum, like the school Zena had attended for kindergarten, was within easy walking distance from Marissa's home. When the field trip fell on a day off from work, Marissa readily volunteered to go with the class.

With the first-grade year's end came other developments in the family. Marissa and Duane again separated, and this time Marissa believed the separation would be permanent. Earlier in the year, Duane had secured a full-time job with the city, and he had increased pressure on Marissa to get married. She had resisted, preferring to continue to wait until she, too, had attained some job security and was more personally settled. Eventually, Duane tired of this situation and began to see another woman, and the two decided to end their lengthy but often difficult relationship.

On a more clearly positive note, I learned that Zena would return the following fall to the neighborhood school for second grade. Marissa had found a sitter who lived within the district boundaries of the neighborhood school, and IPS permitted parents to use day-care providers' addresses to determine school attendance. She was pleased with this development and looked forward to having all three children enrolled in the nearby school.

When I interviewed Marissa the following December, I learned of her new part-time job at a resale shop, where she was happy with her work and friendships she'd developed with co-workers. She was feeling quite financially secure with her combination of wages, a small AFDC check, food stamps, Medicaid, a child-care allowance, and a small child support payment.[2] This was a very chatty interview, and both Marissa's mood and appearance suggested a happiness and relative contentment with her life that were delightful to observe. She was clearly moving toward the stability and the independence that she had always so obviously desired for her family. Though the family remained far from secure by objective standards, I perceived relief, relative contentment, and a real sense of pride in her accomplishments in Marissa that day.

During the interview, it quickly became apparent that Marissa's contact with Zena's teacher, and her active involvement in Zena's schooling, had—predictably—increased considerably. Early in the school year, she had visited the classroom quite frequently: "I used to go up there every Friday before I started workin', just to see how she did the whole week." In a reversal of roles of sorts, this year it was Marissa who complained that the teacher was uncommunicative during these visits. She also described limited interaction when she attended the parent-teacher conference, which Marissa felt provided her with little information about Zena's performance. Despite the teacher's lack of communicativeness, Marissa felt Zena's problems had greatly lessened. Marissa was also considerably more aware of specifics of Zena's academic work than she'd been in years past.

Zena had received one D on her report card, and otherwise Bs and C's. Marissa reported that Zena excelled in math and spelling, but struggled with language mechanics and had begun receiving Chapter I tutoring in this subject. When I asked whether she was satisfied with Zena's grades, Marissa suggested that although she still wished for the excellent academic performance she had expected prior to Zena's entry into formal schooling, she had modified her expectations somewhat. She continued to hope Zena would raise her grades high enough to earn honors, but Marissa seemed somewhat embarrassed, now, when she suggested this optimistic prospect. When I asked about her satisfaction with Zena's current schoolwork, she replied that "that's a hard question. Because I'm satisfied, but I'm not. That's any mother, she wants to see straight As." With a small laugh, she added that "we're still workin' on those As."

A few moments later, when Marissa talked of encouraging Zena to take extracurricular activities classes related to science and reading because "them are the classes that you need, if you wanna make the honor roll," she again concluded her remarks with a small, embarrassed laugh. I felt, at these moments, that Marissa feared I would think her foolish for maintaining such high expectations and aspirations for her daughter in the face of consistent contrary information from the schools. But in fact, I too perceived in Zena a good deal of unrealized potential. In light of her quick-wittedness, self-confidence, and maturity, I shared to some degree Marissa's frustration and disappointment with Zena's somewhat mediocre performance.

It also seemed Marissa had stepped up her in-home school-related activities with Zena. For the first time, Marissa got out a folder that contained samples of Zena's work, and she occasionally referred to these papers as we talked.[3] Also for the first time, she described a daily routine: She would relax in a rocking chair after work while she and Zena told one another about their day. She also began to purchase workbooks for the children, and gave Zena several pages to complete each weekend. During the week, Marissa supervised the completion of the "piles and piles" of homework Zena was assigned each night. Finally, after Zena forgot her homework on several occasions early in the year, Marissa again designated a spot near the front door for completed homework not to be forgotten in the morning. These routine activities linking Zena's school and home life, as well as Marissa's continued insistence on an early bedtime, added needed structure and predictability to Zena's daily life that I felt had been lacking in the past.

During Zena's second-grade year, the behavioral difficulties that had so concerned her first-grade teacher ceased to be a problem. According to Marissa, the one consistent complaint registered by Zena's new teacher was that "she talks a lot in school. But her teachers really haven't been tellin' me about this attitude that she had at [PS#X]." While I did not know how Zena's teacher felt about her relationship with peers that year, repeated reports of talkativeness suggested that her assertive, expressive style of interacting with peers—which had gained her respect and popularity in Head Start—may have again served her well in second grade. Marissa reported that Zena had made several friends who occasionally phoned in the evenings. After a trying first-grade year, it seemed Zena's return to the neighborhood school not only had positive effects on Marissa's involvement in Zena's schooling; it also provided Zena with an environment where her expressive talents were likely once again appreciated and admired by the primarily black classmates who lived in the surrounding neighborhoods. Both Zena and her mother experienced renewed connection with and belonging to the school community, and were clearly more comfortable in their interactions there.

CONCLUSION: TWO COMPARISONS

Two comparisons between this and earlier narratives require attention here. The first comparison concerns Zena's and Jeremiah's contrasting experiences in school and with teachers; the second draws attention to the different economic situations of Zena's and Cymira's families.

In first grade, Zena was viewed by her teacher as a "bright enough," "average" student who had serious attitude problems and an unconcerned mother. There was no indication from my interview with Ms. Majors or observations of her classroom that she was dissatisfied in any way with Zena's academic performance;

nor did this teacher suggest that she thought Zena's work could or should improve. I have noted Ms. Majors's remark that other students were just "better" than Zena, and "those are the ones that are on the honor roll." Yet Marissa was very disappointed with Zena's grades throughout the year, and she believed her daughter was much more capable than her grades suggested.

Jeremiah, on the other hand, received grades virtually identical to Zena's, yet his teachers were as convinced as his mother that his level of achievement in school failed to reflect his true abilities or potential. I believe the explanation for this difference lies in part in teachers' apparent tendency to base their expectations for students on their perceptions of the students' parents. This might not be altogether unwise if there were some certainty that teachers' perceptions of parents were accurate. However, when someone like Marissa is labeled by her child's teacher as unconcerned, there is set into motion the potential for an unfortunate self-fulfilling prophecy cycle whereby: 1) A teacher falsely defines a parent as unconcerned; 2) in line with belief that parents who are unconcerned have children who are unmotivated, the teacher's behavior toward the child reflects diminished expectations; and 3) the child responds with lower levels of achievement. While this study cannot offer conclusive evidence that such processes occur, Jeremiah's and Zena's cases are provocative and suggestive of this possibility.

Another theme of Marissa's story is her determined attempts to provide her children with a better life than their parents', and her persistence in this goal despite the other pressing demands she faced. Marissa also persisted in working toward her own personal goals of self-reliance and self-sufficiency, and was never satisfied to resign herself to long-term dependence on AFDC. Instead, she drew on assistance from welfare programs when necessary, but seemed driven to employment by both a strong work ethic and a high energy level that made her uncomfortable with too much time spent in the confines of her home. In short, she exhibited personal qualities portrayed in popular culture as desirable (and supposedly too often lacking) for low-income single mothers, and she did what she was supposed to do—that is, she strove toward self-sufficiency and independence from the welfare system.

However, Marissa's low wages and lack of job security often placed her family in precarious situations. This family often went without basic necessities when Marissa found herself unsupported by any safety net; they weathered many periods when they lacked money, transportation, medical insurance, and, of course, shelter.

Despite the social desirability of Marissa's efforts to be self-support-
ing, it is ironic that Rhonda Craft was better able to maintain a stable and consistent home life as a long-term AFDC recipient who
never seriously attempted to join the labor force during our
acquaintance. While Rhonda certainly also struggled to make ends
meet, those ends remained consistent, and her family's well-being
was not jeopardized by an unpredictable low-wage labor market
and abrupt termination of employment that more than once left
Marissa in dire straits. In the next and final chapter devoted to the
young mothers, I examine the experiences of Harriet, whose continual struggle to support her family on extremely low and uncertain wages took a heavy toll on both her own and her daughter
Sheila's well-being.

WORK, ILLNESS, AND INADEQUATE SUPPORT

This last chapter devoted to the young mothers is somewhat unusual among the narratives that comprise this book. Its difference reflects a marked difference in the tone and content of my interviews and other conversations with Harriet. Much more than was the case in my talks with other mothers, our conversations were dominated by discussion of the mounting financial pressures, health-related concerns, and other constraints that hampered Harriet's ability to support and encourage her daughter, Sheila. Although material presented certainly speaks to general themes developed elsewhere (including, for example, claims of family difference, awareness of social reproductive processes, and the encouragement of children's early independence), these are elaborated less in this chapter than in others. Instead, I focus more on financial deprivation and the social policy environment that seemed to dramatically affect Harriet's health, her ability to maintain her family at a reasonable level of comfort, and her daughter's educational opportunities and experiences.

As was the case with Marissa (chapter 5), Harriet's strong work ethic and her dislike of AFDC and caseworkers kept her in the labor force whenever possible. Also like Marissa, Harriet earned extremely low wages that even in the best of times could barely sustain her family. When circumstances left Harriet without a sorely needed paycheck, keeping the family afloat proved impossible, and this family too found themselves homeless. Harriet contended with additional problems presented by her extremely poor health, and the family's lack of medical insurance exacerbated their problems, as did the absence of income support when Harriet was physically unable to work. In addition, lack of access to affordable, accessible, and quality child care threatened Sheila's and her young brother's well-being as well. Although Harriet had the support of numerous caring individuals who made enormous contributions to the family, her great needs routinely overwhelmed their generosity.

HARRIET'S NARRATIVE: CONTINUAL STRUGGLES AND SETBACKS

Before I conducted any interviews, I spent a day locating each of the nine homes I would visit in the coming weeks, accustoming myself to the areas where the children and their families lived. Harriet and Sheila's neighborhood was one that put me at ease; the homes on their street were modest but well kept, and this was certainly among the "better" neighborhoods I visited.

When I returned for my first interview, Sheila sat on the large porch of their duplex, watching for me to arrive. She took me inside the small but nicely furnished home to meet her mother, and I was immediately surprised to see Harriet had an infant son. She had not mentioned this on the phone, but I did know she was working, and we had scheduled the interview for her day off. I was pleased and somewhat amazed that despite the now obvious other demands on her time, she had agreed to meet with me.

I began this interview by asking Harriet the names and ages of her children. In addition to five-year-old Sheila and four-month-old Jermaine, Harriet had two older daughters, then aged eight and six. When I next asked Harriet's own age, it was all I could do to disguise my surprise to learn she was just twenty-five years old. Harriet looked like a much older woman, and it was primarily her very tired face and extremely large and sad eyes that created this impression. Over the years of our acquaintence, Harriet's appearance, and her health, declined at an alarming pace.

When we met, Harriet, Sheila, and the baby, Jermaine, shared their home with Jennette, the older woman who owned the duplex. Harriet's family had lived across the street for many years, and Harriet had known Jennette since she was in elementary school. In the past, Jennette's daughter had been Harriet's best friend—they attended high school together, and later shared an apartment. Although the friends no longer socialized, Jennette remained an extremely important person in Harriet's life. She had periodically provided Harriet with inexpensive rent and child care since before Sheila's birth, and at the time of our first interview, Jennette was caring for both Sheila and Jermaine while Harriet worked full-time.

Harriet completed a nine-month training program and was certified as a nursing assistant. She had believed her training would translate into higher wages, but this did not occur. For example, only a month before our first interview, she took a job working nights in a nursing home, after receiving AFDC for several months before and after Jermaine's birth. Once Harriet resumed full-time work, her wages exceeded AFDC eligibility, and she immediately lost both her AFDC grant and food stamps. Despite her training and her willingness to work nights, she was paid only $5 an hour. At this rate (then $1.20 over the minimum wage), Harriet's earnings for full-time work fell well below the poverty level for a family of three (92 percent). Throughout our acquaintance, Harriet worked all the overtime she could, sometimes working as many as sixty hours per week. The demanding work schedule Harriet expected of herself not only contributed to her declining health but also prevented her from securing basic opportunities for her daughter, including on-time enrollment in kindergarten.

Harriet realistically saw herself as little better off financially than if she had remained on welfare, and she offered this impression of the prospects of welfare recipients like herself who attempted to gain financial independence: "When you go to the welfare office, they say, 'Go get a job.' True enough, there's jobs out here, [but] they're hard to get. And for people that have small kids, it's hard to get a sitter. Say, for instance, you go to McDonald's and make eighty dollars for a week. You got two kids, and somebody wants forty-five dollars or fifty dollars a week to keep those two kids. There's no need of you workin'. . . . That's why a lot of people stay on welfare because if you're on welfare, once you start workin' and you go a penny over their limit, everything's cut off."

Harriet was insightful in her analysis of reasons that other AFDC recipients might choose not to seek employment. Although AFDC grants are meager, mothers who leave welfare for unstable low-wage employment can put their families at risk of losing everything if they subsequently lose their jobs and have little or no accumulated savings to tide them over while they seek new employment or reapply for benefits.[1] A similar scenario had led to

Marissa's family's homelessness that I noted in chapter 5. Although the service jobs typically available to women leaving welfare sometimes raise a family's earnings over the poverty level, such jobs rarely provide medical insurance. If parents' earnings make them ineligible for Medicaid, families frequently go without adequate medical care, or amass huge debts if a serious illness or injury occurs.[2] In addition, the costs of child care, transportation, and other work-related expenses severely deflate already insufficient incomes. Harriet's conclusion—that limited chances for AFDC recipients to better their situations through employment meant "there's no need of you workin' "—was therefore quite accurate. But despite the very real costs of choosing work over welfare, Harriet's choice reflected a strong work ethnic, belief she would eventually get ahead, and extreme dislike of sharing details of her life with unsympathetic caseworkers. "I hate for them to stay in my business, 'cause they meddle so much," she said.

Baby Jermaine's father, James Mathews, was deeply involved with the family, and I quickly got the impression that Harriet and James were planning a life together. He was employed as a waiter in a small restaurant owned by one of Harriet's aunts, where he earned even less than Harriet. Sheila's father was "an older man" who had died several years earlier. Although he had agreed to establish his paternity legally, this was not accomplished before his death, and Harriet was unable to do so without his assistance. This unfortunate circumstance effectively deprived Sheila of Social Security survivors' benefits that would have otherwise substantially increased this family's well-being.

Soon after the younger one's birth, both of Harriet's other daughters began living with Harriet's mother and stepfather, who were their legal guardians.[3] Harriet's parents moved to a middle-class area far to the north of the city's traditionally black neighborhoods shortly after Sheila was born. Harriet played a very limited role in these children's lives, seeing them on some weekends, and contributing little to their upkeep. Despite infrequent contact, Harriet spoke of her older two daughters' accomplishments in school during each of our interviews, and she clearly kept up-to-date on happenings in their lives. Although she often talked vaguely of reuniting with her older children sometime in the future "when things get better," this never seemed a realistic possibility.

Changing Circumstances

There were many changes for Harriet's family between our first and fourth interviews. Harriet made frequent job changes, always looking for more convenient hours or a bit more money. Although she constantly checked ads and followed up leads, she never earned more than $5 per hour. In the fall of 1990, as the other children in this study entered kindergarten, Harriet's employment situation prevented Sheila from doing the same. Harriet was then using public transportation to get to her job—she worked an early morning shift (6:00 A.M. to 2:00 P.M.) in a retirement home and left home long before it was time to get Sheila off to kindergarten. While nearly 90 percent of children in this state attend kindergarten, it was not mandatory, and IPS did not provide transportation. Jennette suffered serious health problems that prevented her from taking Sheila to school, and since their home was not within walking distance, Sheila did not begin kindergarten that fall. Thereafter she was one year behind the other children involved in this study.

Harriet and James Mathews married in February 1991. For six months Harriet continued to live with Jennette, while staying only occasionally in James's nearby apartment. By July, they'd saved enough for a security deposit and first month's rent on a small but comfortable and affordable home. They stayed there only one month, however, before they felt forced to move again because of neighborhood conditions. Harriet described events preceding this second move:

> The house we was livin' in was a real nice house, but it was the neighborhood. My kids couldn't go outside to play . . . because that neighborhood was really bad. And Sheila had never, never been in a neighborhood where people fight all day, and shoot their guns. And they sold drugs over there, and she was like "Mommy, all we see is police cars all day long." You know, and "Why we never get to go outside? It's too hot to stay in the house." . . . It was [laugh] like all of us were scared. Sometimes we'd have to get out of our beds and get on the floor at night. One time we had 'em standin' right on our doorstep, shootin' back and forth on the street. And the police would come, but they would wait till it was over because they were scared, too.

In response to these frightening conditions, the family moved to a duplex where the rent was higher and they paid more of their own utilities. Each month Harriet and James struggled to meet their financial responsibilities, and during their first winter together, they were without heat for more than a week when they were unable to pay the gas bill. In addition, they were now at quite a distance from Jennette and since James's car was often not running, the family suffered from their lack of access to this important source of assistance. In this new neighborhood, however, Harriet felt she could safely allow Sheila and Jermaine to play outside, although she limited their play to the yard and sidewalk immediately in front of their home.

James continued to work in Harriet's aunt's restaurant, and his hours and income declined as this business floundered. Although Harriet often urged him to seek other employment, James did not look for another job until the business eventually folded. When Harriet and I met for our fourth interview (in December 1992), James had been unemployed for several months.

During Sheila's kindergarten year (1991–92), Harriet continued to rely on Jennette for child care for Jermaine, paying just $20 weekly for full-time care. Harriet made new arrangements for Sheila, however. The new sitter was an elderly woman who lived across the street from the school Sheila now attended. "Miz" Jones cared for over a dozen children each day, including several toddlers. James had known Miz Jones since he was a young boy, and she had cared for him while his own mother worked. Like Jennette, this sitter had been a "godsend" for the family. In the fall of 1991, Harriet had faced a situation very similar to that of the year before, with conflicting work and school schedules and lack of transportation for Sheila again threatening to be insurmountable. Miz Jones proposed that Harriet misrepresent to school administrators the nature of Sheila's relationship to the sitter (they said she was Sheila's grandmother) in order to circumvent residency requirements to enroll Sheila in this school.

Miz Jones's proposal made it possible for Harriet to take advantage of this convenient child-care arrangement, which proved quite inexpensive as well. The sitter told Harriet to "give whatever your pocket can give," and she originally paid "fifteen or twenty dollars a week." Eventually, Miz Jones made an unusual request. Harriet explained that "she knew Sheila needed some more school clothes, so she told me, 'Harriet, the money you been givin to me, you take that and put Sheila's clothes in layaway and [keep paying] until you get 'em out.' "[4]

Both Miz Jones and Jennette demonstrated remarkable kindness and concern for this family. The two women contributed a great deal to their well-being, and Harriet and James's financial burdens were considerably eased by these sitters' generosity. However, while Harriet never mentioned it, the quality of the care her children received was quite low—there were far too many children at Sheila's sitter for one elderly woman to tend to adequately, and Jennette's ill health meant that there was always a danger of her needing emergency medical care when she was alone with Jermaine. This had in fact happened once when both Sheila and Jermaine were present; when Jennette lost consciousness, Sheila had competently phoned for an ambulance. This kind of capability, however, was clearly beyond Jermaine, and the child-care arrangement was dangerous for both sitter and child.

The circumstances of Harriet's life to me seemed dismal, but she considered herself quite fortunate to have the constant support of others. She repeatedly described her gratitude for both Jennette and her parents, saying: "It's hard to find people like that, that'll just take your kids like they were theirs. . . . I really thank God for Jennette. . . . If anything happens to her, I don't know what I'd do, I'd be lost. . . . And I thank God for my mother too, 'cause if it wasn't for her I'd have all four of them. And that would be extra hard."

It is indeed hard to imagine how Harriet could have managed without the assistance she received from her parents, from Jennette, and from others like Miz Jones. Although Harriet's case was perhaps extreme among the mothers in this study, nearly all were part of complex networks of support known to be common among African American families.[5] And like Harriet, others also had parents or friends take in their children, and these temporary or permanent arrangements were often crucial to the parents' ability to provide adequate care for their children.[6]

Harriet's network included other fictive kin who, like Jennette, provided her with tremendous support and assistance. One such person was Constance, who was a member of the Apostolic church Harriet sporadically attended.[7] During the later stages of this research, when Jennette was repeatedly hospitalized, it was Constance who typically provided Harriet with much needed help. It was also Constance whose phone number and address Harriet gave me, in case her phone was disconnected or she moved unexpectedly—"She will always know how to get in touch with me." I did, indeed, call Constance several times, and once sent Sheila a small birthday gift care of her when Harriet had no other address. At that time, Harriet knew of no one with enough space in their home (and heart) to take in herself and her two children, so Sheila and

Jermaine stayed with Constance, while Harriet lived with an elderly aunt.

But I am getting ahead of myself. To explain how Harriet came to be homeless and separated from her husband and children, I must consider long-past events in Harriet's life that seemed impossible to overcome despite her concerted efforts.

Early Missteps Prove Insurmountable

While Harriet was forthcoming about her family's recent circumstances during formal interviews, much of my knowledge about her past came from two conversations that were not recorded. The first and most revealing of these took place just after we completed our third interview in December 1991. The second was during a visit to Harriet while she was hospitalized about one year later, in November 1992.

Our third interview was a lengthy one, lasting fully two hours. After we'd finished, I commented that the more I learned about the families' circumstances and practices, the more curious I became about the mothers' pasts. But, I told her, I worried about being perceived as prying when talk turned away from the children. Harriet apparently took this as an invitation to talk about her past in a more revealing and personal way than she had done before. She began by assuring me, "I have not had an easy life, and I don't mind talking about it—I even talk to my kids about it. I don't want them to make the same mistakes that I did." Then, without further prompting, she talked uninterrupted for ten or fifteen minutes about those "mistakes."

She began by telling of quite extreme abuse of alcohol ("a half gallon of Jack Daniels would not last us for one day") and some drugs, which began in her teens and lasted until well after Sheila's birth. She and Jennette's daughter Linda had partied, dropped out of school, worked at fast food places, briefly rented an apartment, and mostly, drank together for several years. They spent much time and money at night clubs, and both young women had many boyfriends. When Harriet's oldest child was born, they moved in with Jennette.

Motherhood did little to change Harriet's ways, and Jennette cared for her daughter while Harriet continued to work, drink, and abuse drugs, while paying Jennette modestly for both rent and child care. A second daughter born soon after was more than Jennette could handle, and—since there was little change in Harriet's behavior—Harriet's parents took both girls in. Finally, the birth of a third child in four years seemed to be the jolt Harriet needed to begin to take steps to change her lifestyle. After Sheila was born, Jennette agreed to care for her while Harriet worked and completed a nine-month nursing assistant program. At the same time, Harriet also gradually began to deal with her drug and alcohol problems, eventually becoming completely sober by the time Sheila began Head Start and Harriet became pregnant once again.

Throughout these disclosures, Harriet repeatedly expressed gratitude toward her parents and Jennette, recalling Jennette's later comment: "Just because you were out on the street, doin' what you were doin', didn't mean we could just let your kids go." She told of the faith and trust she had developed in God during recent years: "God did this for me; I couldn't have done it by myself." Finally, she described her experiences in parenting Jermaine. "I have four children and have never toilet trained a child, or got 'em off the bottle." Biological motherhood was nothing new for Harriet, but actually parenting her youngest child through the demanding periods of infancy and toddlerhood was an unfamiliar challenge, and an additional stressor in Harriet's life.

This account of changes in Harriet's life cleared up many questions I had previously wondered about. Primarily, I'd been curious why the older children lived with their grandparents, but had feared this was too painful a topic to broach. Harriet also answered unasked questions I had about earlier comments she'd made about her isolation from same-aged peers. For example, near the end of our first interview, Harriet answered my query about friends with whom she discussed child-rearing concerns: "I'll be honest with you. Most people my age, they don't even seem concerned about education. Seems to me they're concerned about other things. Which, I don't have any friends anymore, because I don't drink anymore, I don't smoke reefer anyore . . . I'm over that—after my two youngest kids came along, it was time for me to start a different life, in a different environment. . . . Now, older people—yes."[8]

Apparent evidence suggested Harriet had indeed left her earlier, irresponsible lifestyle and was working hard to construct a more secure and wholesome life for her family. And the story Harriet told helped explain her avoidance of same-aged peers who did not share her newfound values and motivation to provide a more stable life for her children.

Nearly a year later, Harriet was hospitalized in November 1992, complaining of shortness of breath and chest pains. I visited her there on the tenth day of her stay.[9] During this visit, Harriet told me of events in her childhood. Her parents had divorced while she was in elementary school, and her mother soon married a World War II veteran who had difficulties with posttraumatic stress ("He used to get to thinkin' about all the things that happened over there, would get to thinking that he was there, and he used to even shoot in the house"). Her stepfather rather routinely beat her mother, and in one battering that included being thrown down a flight of stairs, her mother's ear was completely severed.

During a later telephone conversation, Harriet resumed this topic, now indicating that both her stepfather and father had beaten her mother while she was growing up. She noted this as she told of difficulties in her relationship with James. He was drinking, he'd not visited her while she was in the hospital, and Sheila and Jermaine had stayed with Constance throughout her hospitalization despite the fact that James was now unemployed. He was unoccupied during Harriet's absence, and she was quite frustrated that he'd done nothing to look for a new job. She repeated what she'd told me while she was hospitalized: She was considering telling James to leave the home. "He's still here," she said, "but not for long, I don't think. He had one of his tantrums last night." She then explained: "He never hits me, but he goes around throwin' things, breakin' stuff. When I got up this morning, the living room looked like somebody had broke in and tore everything up. . . . And Sheila was cryin' and real nervous, and all. And I swore my kids would never go through that. You know, all the fightin' and yellin' and stuff. I went through that with both my father and my stepfather, and my kids will not go through that."

Though Harriet and James's relationship had been strained by financial difficulties from the beginning, it appeared fairly solid until Harriet began to experience serious health problems. Many of her past comments had suggested she was the more responsible spouse (for example, her earnings were used to pay rent and all utility bills, while James contributed to groceries and made payments on the rent-to-own furniture and appliances he insisted they needed; he frequently socialized with friends in the evenings while Harriet rarely went out; Harriet arranged child care and was responsible for finding alternatives when arrangements fell through or transportation was not available, but James only occasionally cared for Sheila and Jermaine in Harriet's absence, and Harriet often had others care for the children even when James was available). When Harriet's health was relatively good, she often lamented the family's financial difficulties but complained only mildly about the unequal burden she shouldered. It was not until severe illness threatened both her personal well-being and her ability to keep the family afloat that she became much less tolerant of James's ineffectiveness, and she began to speak of a separation.[10]

In February 1993, Harriet did indeed leave both James and their home of one and a half years. When they were forced to give up the duplex after getting further and further behind in their bills, she made a break from James as well. She moved with her children into the home of a friend, but this arrangement quickly fell apart, and she soon moved in with an elderly aunt, while Sheila and Jermaine stayed with Constance. As a result, Sheila's education again suffered from interruptions and dislocations.

After they separated, James got both a new job working in a factory and his own apartment. Harriet occasionally visited him there, but when we spoke in June 1993 she remained extremely critical of him. Despite ongoing problems in their relationship, a month later Harriet and the children moved into James's apartment. Although she had serious misgivings about their reconciliation, Harriet could not afford her own place, and she was distressed over her separation from the children. As she prepared to reunite the family, she first wrote a check to James's landlord to cover one and a half months' rent; he was already delinquent in his payments.

Harriet's health also remained problematic. Her doctor was opposed to her continued work, and he recommended that she apply for Social Security because of her complete disability. Harriet, however, did not follow these recommendations. Although Supplemental Social Security benefits could provide her with adequate income, she felt her family could not survive the "few months" it would take for these payments to begin once she quit work. AFDC in the meantime was apparently not an option—a caseworker informed her she would be ineligible for benefits for several months as a penalty for quitting her job. In this catch-22 situation, Harriet predictably continued to work, and she hoped for the best where her health was concerned. Her health was even further endangered, however, by the lack of medical insurance to cover the expense of three prescriptions she had been ordered to take. She therefore often went without this needed medication.

Harriet's situation, then, was clearly quite dismal. Although Sheila's transition into schooling did reflect the chaotic nature of her family life, she experienced a good deal more success than might have been expected.

SHEILA'S STORY: EARLY INDEPENDENCE AND RESPONSIBILITIES

Harriet's many difficulties left her both physically and mentally exhausted, and it was clear she often had few personal resources reserved to see to Sheila's needs. Like several of the other children involved in this study, Sheila was allowed little freedom of movement in the several neighborhoods where she lived over the course of this study. However, inside the home she had few restrictions and was often responsible for both entertaining and caring for herself. Depending on Harriet's shift and days off, she often put herself to bed at night, or woke herself in the morning and prepared for school with little assistance. She also took much responsibility for Jermaine's care, and from an early age was quite skilled at bathing, dressing, and tending to other needs of her brother.

During our third interview, for example, Harriet's description of her daughter's typical day included many examples of Sheila's early independence and responsibility. Harriet was working evening shifts during most of Sheila's kindergarten year, and Sheila arose on her own each morning at 5:30 A.M. "Just like one of us when we're so used to gettin' up at a certain time," Harriet said, Sheila woke without the aid of an alarm, and each morning prepared herself for the day with little or no assistance. Harriet felt it was too early to force Sheila to eat, but "if she feels like she's hungry in the morning, she knows to get her a bowl of cereal." Sheila dressed herself, collected her things for school and the sitter, and did "everything but comb her hair." James also came to rely on Sheila to wake him, then he and Sheila left the house at 6:30 A.M. while Harriet slept until Jermaine awakened.

Although Sheila was somewhat jealous of the attention Jermaine received from others, she also gave him a great deal of care and attention. According to Harriet: "Sheila changes his Pampers, she fixes his bottle, she's been doin' this ever since he was born. And she gives him a bath, she just now started lettin' him get in the bathtub with her. She gives him a bath and when they get out, she lays him on her bed and she lotions him down, and she puts powder all over him, and she combs his hair."

Compared to other children in this study, then, Sheila had very early responsibility for her own self-care, as well as the care of her younger brother. Her adultlike activities at home were both appreciated and necessary. Harriet's demanding work schedule required that Sheila grow up "fast," and Harriet was clearly proud of and highly valued her daughter's competence in this area.

After Head Start, a Year at Home

Sheila attended Ms. Castle's morning Head Start class, and I observed that she was shy and quiet, although she occasionally expressed her pleasure with a quick, expansive, and endearing smile. Judging from the rarity of mention of her in Bill Corsaro's field notes, she was not a particularly active member of the children's peer culture. Each of the four times she was mentioned in Bill's notes (once each in the months of November, December, January, and March), however, her activities involved some sort of family role play. She was observed, for example, joining in with other children who were preparing and serving food, cleaning, caring for babies, and talking on the telephone. The housekeeping area of the classroom provided a comfortable context within which Sheila could display her skills and knowledge of family tasks while also gaining competence in interacting with other children despite her shyness.

Although Sheila attended Head Start throughout the year, she was frequently absent, and I have relatively little information on her experiences at the center. Given Bill's interest in children's peer cultures and activities, no effort was made to assure that each individual child was a separate focus of the observations. It is likely that Sheila was often present despite her absence from field notes, but remarkably, she was absent on each of the four days we videotaped children's activities during the final weeks of the school year. Given the chaotic nature of Sheila's family life, there were likely many times she did not make it to the center for a variety of reasons.[11]

Sheila also did not attend kindergarten during the 1990–91 school year. Harriet was frustrated by this situation, and during our interview in February, she reported working with Sheila each day on such basic skills as printing, writing numbers, and simple word recognition. Harriet pointed out the workbooks she had purchased at a nearby drugstore, and she noted that educational toys were the only gifts Sheila had received for Christmas. While we talked, Sheila played nearby with a new toy clock Harriet said was helping her learn to tell time. Sheila also received a "Speak and Spell" and a "Math computer thing" for Christmas (it is likely such expensive gifts came from Harriet's parents, although this was not acknowledged). Harriet said Sheila had "learned all her ABCs . . . and learned her colors and her numbers." Harriet was clear about her motivation for spending time on Sheila's basic skills. IPS personnel had encouraged Harriet to enroll her daughter in kindergarten the following fall, but she hoped her daughter could begin first grade. "I try to work with her at home, so that most of the things they learn in kindergarten, she'll know when she go to first grade."

Harriet seemed confident her activities would adequately prepare Sheila for first grade, and when the 1991–92 school year began, Sheila was indeed enrolled in first grade. She was in this class for less than a week, however, before the teacher strongly recommended she attend kindergarten. Harriet eventually and reluctantly agreed. Although she was disappointed with this development, Harriet's work with Sheila did not go entirely unrewarded. Her kindergarten teacher thought her exceptionally well prepared, and she believed Sheila's experiences as a top student accustomed her to success and laid the foundation for future educational achievement.

Sheila's Kindergarten Year: A Chance to Blossom

Sheila's kindergarten teacher, Ms. Fulton, was a white woman in her mid- to late thirties whose teaching degree included certification to teach mentally and emotionally handicapped children. After college, she worked briefly with the Follow Through program (see chapter 4), then spent several years as a "resource teacher" for mainstreamed special needs children in grades K through 8 within the IPS system. She then taught several different grades at different schools before taking her current position, which she had held for five years.

Ms. Fulton described her approach to teaching kindergarten as "traditional"; she did not believe in teaching kindergarten children to read, and compared to other kindergarten teachers, she had minimal requirements in other areas as well. For example, she required number recognition only through 20, and said "it would be nice" if children recognized "their color words and number words," but "that's not a requirement." For one hour each day, Ms. Fulton combined her class with that of an older, more experienced teacher who was the source of many of Ms. Fulton's beliefs about kindergarten teaching. With the older teacher's guidance, Ms. Fulton emphasized music, thematic units (such as learning about whales), and encouragement of the attitude that "school is a fun place," a place where children experience success and "feel good about themselves." Ms. Fulton did not believe kindergarten children should have homework, so she met IPS requirements for homework for all children by assigning it on Mondays only.

Somewhat remarkably in light of comments by all the other

teachers I interviewed, Ms. Fulton was very clear about her dislike of regular parental involvement in the classroom. When I asked that she "talk briefly about your philosophy regarding parental participation in schooling," Ms. Fulton first described her practice of sending weekly notes to parents. These notes provided information about what was covered in the classroom, and also always included a positive comment about what the particular child had done well that week. She then continued: "I find I really don't want parents to help me in the room. Because then they get really upset that I, perhaps, have neglected their child that day, so I kind of have the philosophy that the less they see, the happier they are. I have had parents in the room, and they were saying, 'Well Sally— well Sally—well Sally.' And I'm like, 'I've already talked to Sally, more than anyone else today.' And I just found that it was a real problem. . . . Sometimes it doesn't turn out to be a positive experience; they come away with a negative feeling."

While Ms. Fulton actively resisted the routine presence of parents in her classroom, she instead invested her efforts on regular written communications with parents, and also noted opportunities for parents to come in for Open House, parent-teacher conferences, and several special events scheduled each year. When asked to evaluate her overall relationships with parents, Ms. Fulton responded positively, saying, "I've been very satisfied with the parents. They just could not be any lovelier."

Certainly this positive evaluation of parents, which differed so radically from Ms. Majors's and other teachers' feelings, was related to Ms. Fulton's desire that parents not be involved in the classroom. She seemed to value parents' input, just not on her turf. And she clearly shared with other teachers strong beliefs about the positive impact of parent involvement on young children. As she said, "many times if there's not a caring parent in the family, they don't do as well. But children whose parents care, they do great in here."

Ms. Fulton's perspective on parental involvement fit well with what Harriet was able to do and provide for Sheila. The teacher expected parents to care about their children, and demonstrate high valuation of education in the home. She also expected parents to see that the small amount of homework she required was completed and returned. Harriet clearly did these things, though she would have been hard pressed to meet more stringent demands.

Ms. Fulton was also unique among the teachers I interviewed in that she did not even remember meeting Harriet at the parent-teacher conference, again suggesting the minimal importance she placed on in-person contact with parents. While trying to recall meeting Harriet personally, she asked "Is she Grandma?" implying that she perhaps remembered an older-looking woman. Although she was unsure whether Harriet had attended a conference, she did receive notes and calls from Harriet, especially if Sheila missed class for illness or other reasons. Ms. Fulton noted that Sheila faithfully returned her homework, and she concluded that "I think she is concerned about Sheila; I've not ever had that impression that she wasn't." Ms. Fulton, then, was satisfied with Harriet's rather minimal participation, and perhaps in part because her expectations matched what both Harriet and Sheila were able to do, Sheila thrived in this classroom.

Given the teacher's uncertainty whether she had met Harriet at the parent-teacher conference, it might be unwise to accept at face value Harriet's statement that she had indeed attended. However, Harriet recounted their meeting in some detail. When Harriet and I met earlier in the year (November) for our third interview, I asked her to describe Sheila's experiences in school so far that year, and she replied:

H: So far this year it's great, she loves it. I went to [the parent-teacher conference], and her teacher said she's one of the best students that she has. She said Sheila follows directions real well with her (but she don't at home). She says she hasn't had any problems from Sheila. . . . She says she don't see why they didn't let her stay in first grade.

K: Tell me more about how that came about. She did start out in the first-grade class?

H: She stayed in first grade for three days, and the teacher said that she wasn't comprehending the way she should. She was trying to get Sheila to write her numbers, to say her numbers, write her alphabet, say her alphabet, write her name. Sheila knows how to do all this, but she told me, "Mama, I woulda done it in first grade but that teacher's not like this teacher. That teacher was mean. This teacher's not mean." . . . So the teacher she has now said that it's good that she's been in kindergarten, but she sees no reason why they didn't let her stay in first grade.[12]

The teacher's reports concerning Sheila's performance in her room is very similar. When we began to talk specifically about Sheila, Ms. Fulton immediately mentioned the fact that Sheila was initially placed in first grade, but "within three days," had been moved into her class. Because of this, Ms. Fulton at first expected to find that Sheila was "slow." However, she "was kinda surprised when Sheila arrived from first grade . . . [she was] as good as many of what I consider top students that are just arriving in kindergarten." Sheila entered knowing all her letters and had "pretty much been one of the leaders on sounds since the beginning of the year." She also was able to count to 100 when she entered, which Ms. Fulton considered "very good." Despite the considerable skills she had demonstrated at the beginning of the year, Ms. Fulton felt it had been good for Sheila to attend kindergarten rather than first grade, because she experienced great success, which "gave her a lot of confidence, that maybe she wouldn't've gotten in first grade."

The teacher's only apparent concern with Sheila's behavior was that she was "very shy," which she mentioned twice. In addition, she noted that unlike many of the girls who came to school looking like "little baby dolls," Sheila at times arrived in ill-fitting clothes and looking somewhat "unkept." Sheila also occasionally said she was hungry, but Ms. Fulton was careful not to make too much of this; it "might be that she's growing too much that day, or whatever." As we concluded our hour-and-a-half interview, Ms. Fulton described her expectations for the coming year: "I think she'll do great next year, I really do. Because she seems to have developed certainly all her skills necessary for first grade . . . I think she'll really blossom next year, that she'll be near the top."

The Transition into First Grade: A Terrible Beginning

In part because of the kindergarten teacher's praise and high expectations for Sheila, Harriet too expected Sheila to excel in first grade. However, Sheila began the year experiencing many difficulties. Like Jeremiah and Zena (chapters 2 and 5), Sheila was subject to mandatory busing, and she attended a school in a mixed-race, lower-middle-class neighborhood on the city's west side. As was true for Zena, Sheila had problems adjusting to the full-day schedule of first grade (Sheila's school day lasted nearly eight hours—she boarded the bus at 8:05 A.M. and did not arrive home until 3:45 P.M.). Ms. Jackson, Sheila's teacher, noted that "Sheila seemed like she could handle the morning session, but was just sort of burnt out by afternoon." According to Ms. Jackson, Sheila expressed her frustrations and problems handling the long day through "negative behavior," and "acting up." The teacher's report confirmed what Harriet had told me much earlier during a phone conversation while she was hospitalized in November. At that time, Harriet said she had received numerous notes and phone calls from Ms. Jackson because Sheila's "behavior was so bad, but her problems never started until after lunch."

During that lengthy call, Harriet had much to say about Sheila's performance in school, and about her impressions of Sheila's teacher. I was surprised to learn that Sheila's marks on her first report card had been very poor—in fact, she received all Ds and Fs. Harriet had been surprised with this report as well. During the early weeks of the school year, Harriet knew all too well that her daughter's behavior had been very problematic (Sheila's desk had been placed facing a corner in the front of the room for "a month and a half"). However, the papers Sheila brought home from school were marked with either "checks" or "check-plusses," and Harriet was therefore stunned when she saw the dreadful grades on the report card. She was angry as well. Like Marissa when Zena's report card grades did not seem to reflect the marks on daily work, Harriet believed Sheila's academic work was being downgraded because of her poor behavior. "And that's not right," she complained. "How she behaves is not what she knows."

Harriet's frustration and disappointment were clear, and as our conversation continued, she hesitated before offering an explanation for the problems Sheila was experiencing. "No offense, and please don't take it the wrong way," she began, "but the teacher's prejudiced." I assured her no offense was taken, then asked why she believed that. She then described attending the parent-teacher conference, and waiting long past her own appointed time while the teacher met with "two white couples" ahead of her for nearly thirty minutes. Then, she said, "the teacher would only talk to me for about five minutes, but she did say one nice thing to me—she said that of all the kids that she has from our part of town, I was the only one who really showed an interest in and cared about their kid."[13]

Unfortunately, Sheila shared her mother's belief about the teacher's racial bias. According to Harriet, one day at school Sheila had angrily called Ms. Jackson "a prejudiced bitch." Harriet had "whupped her for that . . . [even though] it is true. But she's got to know that she can't do that." It was, I thought, quite likely that Harriet had shared her impressions of Ms. Jackson with Sheila, or that Sheila had heard Harriet complaining about the treatment she'd received at the conference. In any case, it was hard to imagine how Sheila could have had a worse start in her first-grade year—her grades and her behavior were dismal, both mother and daughter felt animosity toward her teacher, and Harriet's poor health worsened matters. Each time Harriet was hospitalized during the year, Sheila stayed with friends and relatives who could rarely arrange for her transportation, and her absences mounted quickly. Harriet's illness also likely frightened her daughter and contributed to the considerable stress to her life. In addition, Harriet and James's relationship was quite strained as well, and Harriet believed her husband's angry displays upset Sheila a great deal.

Several weeks later, when we met for our fourth interview in December, Sheila's situation had surprisingly improved quite markedly, and Harriet attributed the change to her hospitalization. "She was so worried about me," Harriet said, that "when I got home she had done all her schoolwork just perfect, had all stars on all her papers." The job Harriet took immediately after her release from the hospital was only five hours a day, 9:00 A.M. to 2:00 P.M., seven days a week. She therefore was able to spend evenings with Sheila, and she oversaw homework and insisted Sheila spend extra time reading. This new routine likely contributed to Sheila's improving performance, and the second report card reflected these new efforts: the Ds and Fs rose to As, Bs, and Cs. Although Sheila had not made the honor roll, her teacher thought this was a strong future possibility.

Perhaps in part because of such dramatic improvement in Sheila's performance, Harriet had revised her opinion of Ms. Jackson. Harriet and I picked Sheila up from school before our interview, and we went inside and briefly chatted with Ms. Jackson. Later, I mentioned that the teacher "seemed pretty pleasant," and "not like she disliked Sheila, which I was afraid of." Harriet agreed, then again noted that "Sheila feels like the teacher is prejudiced, like the teacher don't like little black kids." She, however, had had a change of heart. "At first I had that impression too. But now it seems like she's concerned about all her children."

By the first-grade year, each child in this study had at least one white teacher, and for most children and mothers, this created no particular difficulties. Prior to the 1992–93 school year, none of the mothers mentioned suspicions of teachers' racial bias against black children. However, Harriet was one of three mothers who expressed such perceptions during our fourth round of interviews (also see Tasha, chapter 7, and Evelyn, chapter 9). These other mothers withdrew from interaction with teachers they believed were prejudiced. Unlike Tasha and Evelyn, however, Harriet demonstrated a willingness to work with the teacher to help Sheila maintain her new, more acceptable level of achievement, as well as her somewhat improved behavior. She spoke with Ms. Jackson often, keeping up-to-date on Sheila's activities in the classroom.

She followed through on the teacher's recommendations for in-home activities to improve Sheila's reading, and Ms. Jackson also put into practice some of Harriet's advice on how to best deal with Sheila's behavior. For example, Harriet suggested that Sheila rest inside during the noon recess, and Ms. Jackson agreed. In the course of their cooperative interaction, Harriet apparently came to see Ms. Jackson differently.

During Sheila's first-grade year I was not routinely conducting interviews with teachers; this was the second-grade year for the other children. I did, however, arrange a twenty-minute telephone interview with Ms. Jackson at the end of the school year. Sheila had unfortunately left Ms. Jackson's classroom in late February, and in fact attended two subsequent schools before the year ended. Although she had had no recent contact with Sheila, Ms. Jackson was able to provide much valuable information.

The teacher mentioned Sheila's "negative behavior" almost immediately, noting that she seemed to do things designed to "get attention," like "falling off her chair, bothering other students." Sheila "could be very argumentative." Her comments were some-what vague and she certainly never mentioned Sheila's "prejudiced bitch" accusation, but later in the call she added that some of Sheila's remarks were "pretty hateful."

Despite this, and despite the poor grades Sheila earned ini-tially, Ms. Jackson confirmed Harriet's reports of dramatic improve-ment in Sheila's academic performance. When she left the class in late February, she had a "B average," with Cs in handwriting and art. Ms. Jackson described Sheila's performance in the critical sub-jects of math and reading: "Sheila did real well in math, she could really get into math, especially when she realized she was good at it. Adding and subtraction. Sometimes I would have little contests up at the board, and she was very good and loved that. And oral reading, too. She was taken out of the slower group and moved into a more advanced group."

Although I did not speak with her long, I felt Ms. Jackson attributed much of Sheila's success to her mother's concern and persistence. Near the end of our interview, I asked her to "describe Harriet's overall participation in Sheila's schooling." Her reply emphasized Harriet's sincere concern about her daughter, and her attempts to stay informed despite both her often very demanding work schedule ("two jobs sometimes") and her precarious health: "She seemed very concerned, and it made me feel good. Because of health reasons, I didn't want to burden her. When there was a problem, we would just try to deal with it here. But Mom kind of sensed when something was up and would call. She would check in from time to time. She even called one time when she was in the hospital. Sometimes I would try to make light of some things. And I would have a talk with Sheila, and she would seem real concerned and remorseful."

I asked the teacher how "Harriet's behavior compared with other parents," and Ms. Jackson again praised Harriet highly: "Right up there at the top, as far as the children that do well. And it's because the parental support is there. With so many of the others, it's just not consistent."

Like Zena's, Sheila's performance in her first two years of public school was inconsistent, and it seemed likely that both girls' sporadic performance to some extent reflected instability in their home lives. Despite many family problems, however, and unlike Marissa, Harriet succeeded in conveying her concern to Sheila's teachers. Throughout this research I often felt teachers' perceptions of parental concern had significant impact on their expectations for children. Ms. Jackson had quite high expectations for Sheila despite her early performance, and she concluded our interview by suggesting that, like Ms. Fulton the year before, she also saw great potential in Sheila. "The sky's the limit," she said. "Sheila is so strong willed, if she finds something she really wants, she can do it, she can go for it."

My formal data collection ended at the close of Sheila's first-grade year, but I do have some information about Sheila's experiences in second and third grade. Despite the family's continuing housing instability, Sheila remained in the same second-grade classroom throughout the following year. Harriet reported that Sheila had again begun the year with a "bad attitude," but that had improved somewhat. Although her first report card included an F in behavior, a D in reading, and all other grades of Cs or higher, Harriet believed that with hard work and further attitude improvement, Sheila could achieve the coveted honor roll status.

Just after Christmas of 1994, I spoke with Harriet again. She and James had been living together with Sheila and Jermaine in yet another apartment for about six months. They seemed to be doing relatively well, and both were working regularly. The family had, in fact, been doing so unusually well that they briefly enrolled Sheila in Our Redeemer Catholic School (see chapter 10) at the beginning of her third-grade year. After only two months, however, they were unable to afford the tuition, and Sheila was transferred to her sixth public school in four years.

While Harriet seemed to me overoptimistic about her family's financial situation that fall, I was more than a little surprised they could even consider this option. My surprise, however, was perhaps unfounded: Harriet often commented that private schools seemed to provide a better education, and she had apparently acted on this belief as soon as she saw an opportunity to do so. It turned out Harriet was unable to meet the tuition along with her other obligations, but her action demonstrated continuing high valuation of education and motivation to take actions reflecting these values, despite her difficult circumstances. Although Harriet and her family faced monumental struggles, their attempt to provide Sheila with a private school education underscores the importance of these values for this very troubled, but remarkably resilient, family.

CONCLUSION: WHEN SAFETY NETS FAIL

Harriet's efforts to overcome earlier failings and build a better life continually fell short of success. Her story can be read as an indictment of U.S. social policy, which too often ignores the needs of the growing number of working poor families and children. Like Marissa, Harriet did what poor mothers are increasingly pressed to do; she worked long and hard, strove for independence from the welfare system, and gave high priority to feelings of self-confidence and sufficiency. She made choices in this regard that effectively locked her in to working when this seemed so clearly detrimental to her own and her children's well-being. When she could not work, no safety net caught her family before they fell into homelessness. And no safety net provided the kind of medical care Harriet so desperately needed in order to continue her quest for independence. And as her family struggled to stay together despite repeated upheavals, Sheila's schooling clearly suffered as well. Excessive absences and many school changes added to the great stress this child experienced as her mother tried and repeatedly failed to construct a stable environment for her children.

The inadequacy of the public social safety net is clear, but so too is the critical importance of Harriet's informal support network. Harriet relied on many generous individuals, without whose support her family's circumstances would have been unimaginably worse. Although Harriet's kin and friends were extremely supportive, in the worst of times her network resources were nearing exhaustion. This was painfully demonstrated by Harriet's remorseful admission to me that the $5 I had sent Sheila in a card for her seventh birthday had "bought dinner, some nights there hasn't been no dinner." She explained that others had recently paid the family's rent, and also made a car payment. Harriet was unwilling to ask for additional money for food, and the family was instead at times going without. This call prompted me to send Harriet an unsolicited check for $40, something I never did for any other family.

Despite the extreme hardships she suffered, Harriet survived, although she explained quite bluntly to me at one point: "right now, life is just miserable for me." Sheila seemed to fare somewhat better than her mother. She at times did quite well in school, and seemed generally confident and happy when I saw her. But she'd clearly developed "an attitude," and I feared future outbursts of anger like those she exhibited in first grade would earn her the label of a "problem child." Her early years had provided a foundation of high valuation of schooling and achievement on the one hand, and chaotic deprivation and constant upheavals on the other. How she would ultimately build upon this beginning remained to be seen.

7

INTERRUPTING SOCIAL
REPRODUCTIVE
PROCESSES

With this chapter, I begin to examine the experiences of the older mothers and their children. These mothers are a diverse group, and Tasha stands out among them as the only one who did not graduate from high school, and the only one who had never experienced periods of relative material comfort in her life. Not surprisingly, then, she seemed the most conscious among these mothers of social processes that help to reproduce repeated generations of poverty.

Active resistance of such processes dominated Tasha's child-rearing practice as well as her interviews with me. However, Tasha cast a critical eye not only on the upbringing she had received; she also attempted to learn from earlier missteps she'd taken in her own parenting. At age thirty-four when this study began, Tasha was considerably younger than the other older mothers (who were aged thirty-eight to forty), but her placement among them seemed appropriate given her status as the only grandmother. Her seventeen-year-old daughter, Desiree, already had two children when this research began, and another was born before it concluded. Tasha often lamented this state of affairs, and she was driven to improve her parenting to help her younger children avoid such outcomes.

This suggests an added bonus of sorts of these final four narratives; they include discussion of the older siblings of the focus children, who exerted considerable influence on the mothers' interpretations and strategies. As was true for Tasha, these older siblings at times brought into sharp relief the uncertainty of children's outcomes, and contributed to more than one mother's fatalistic thinking. The older children also both enriched and complicated their younger siblings' lives, and five-year-old Tamera Mitchell certainly benefited both from the involvement of her brothers and sisters in her life, and from her mother's gradually improving parenting.

Tamera's transition into schooling was in many ways similar to that of Zena and Sheila. She too seemed to suffer from a change in schools after her kindergarten year, and Tamera's change in performance between kindergarten and first-grade was the most dramatic of any child in the study. Like Harriet, Tasha attributed her daughter's precipitous decline to the racial attitudes of the first-grade teacher, although Tamera's problems were certainly more complex and included family disharmony. Tasha's subsequent actions were quite different from Harriet's, however, and in this and one later narrative I consider some unfortunate implications of mothers' suspicions of teachers' racial bias.

TASHA'S NARRATIVE

Tasha had six children, three older and two younger than Tamera. Among the children in this study, Tamera was one of only two who lived in the home with her married biological parents (Alysha Richy was the other). Warren Mitchell, Tasha's second husband and the father of her four youngest children, lived with the family in a large, older, rented single-family home in a poor-to-working-class neighborhood just two blocks from the elementary school all of the Mitchell children had attended (and just four blocks from Evelyn and Charles Widel, chapter 9). Their house was in disrepair, and Tasha complained of the landlord's unwillingness to fix the many things that seemed to continuously go wrong. The home was sparsely furnished, and all the floors were bare. This was the only home I visited where the television was apparently left on continuously, though Tasha paid it no attention during our interviews.

In June 1990, both Tasha and her husband worked part-time: Warren and his father worked as private contractors in carpentry, which provided about twenty hours of work per week; Tasha had taken a part-time job working for the Department of the Census that summer, and worked in a school lunchroom when school was in session. Tasha had received AFDC in the past, before she and

Warren were married.[1] In the summer of 1990, her family was receiving only a small amount of food stamps, although Tasha felt certain they also qualified for Medicaid at least during some months. However, she found the process of applying for assistance and dealing with caseworkers so frustrating that she would not put herself through it: "I said forget it, I just take them to Public Health, and if they get real sick, I take 'em to the emergency room." Later, after Medicaid eligibility rules changed in 1991, Tasha's three youngest children became eligible, but the older two were not. Although Tasha understood the changes and knew she could get Medicaid for Tamera and her two younger brothers, she chose not to do so. She explained her decision by arguing that it was not fair to the older children, and she continued to take all of them to the free clinic, or hospital emergency rooms, when necessary.

Tasha had dropped out of high school during her junior year, but she later tested for her GED, and often took college classes in social work hoping to eventually earn a degree. She was the only mother in this study to report that her own parents had not placed much emphasis on schooling. During our third interview, she commented: "It's good for parents to get involved with children in school and stuff. Because my mother didn't take a interest in it, and I didn't either. And I was always a top student, I always made good grades. And then, after a while, I just got bored and just dropped out."

Shortly afterward, she became pregnant with Desiree, who was born when Tasha was seventeen. She was briefly married to Desiree's father, but this marriage lasted only a year before the couple separated and later divorced. Six years later, she had a second child, Nicole, with a man she lived with but did not marry. While Nicole was still a baby, her father was diagnosed with cancer and died soon afterward. Three years later, Tasha married Warren Mitchell, and they had four children in the next six years—Trevor, Tamera, William, and Jonathan, aged seven, five, four, and two when this study began.

Tasha is a fascinating, good-hearted, and very large woman, quite tall and overweight. Although she once told me she was shy, I never saw this; she seemed to me outgoing and friendly, and she took a special liking and was very kind to my daughter. I was impressed with all she did, but felt she always seemed to take on a bit more than she could realistically handle. She wanted and needed to work, and was always employed over the course of this study. She very much wanted to earn a college degree. She twice enrolled in college full-time, but each time could sustain this for only one semester.

She had many plans for things she hoped to do with and for her children, but had neither the time or money to act on those plans. For example, she talked of taking all the children on a short trip to Chicago or to Ohio to visit her sister, but never did so. In fact, when I brought Tamera and Cymira Griffin to Bloomington for a day (an hour's drive from Indianapolis), this was Tamera's first time outside the city. Tasha also spoke of beginning a regular Saturday activity like going to the library, but although they occasionally visited the library, this activity was irregular and often set aside because Saturday was the one day available for housecleaning. Likewise, although she believed it was important that they all attend the large Apostolic church she belonged to on a regular basis, this, too, was an activity the family did in spurts and lapses. She did, however, manage to keep the two older children involved in community activities like doing volunteer work and learning African dance, and all the children attended summer recreation or school programs. She also, at times, noted things she did for herself, such as beginning an exercise program and attempting to spend more time with her mother. But again, she would always find herself too busy to follow through on her plans for more than a short while.

Tasha seemed almost driven by an intense desire for self-improvement. Though she never seemed depressed or morose, her talk clearly betrayed dissatisfaction with her life, and she was determined to make it better. Even more so, she was determined to provide her children with the chance for a better life than her own.

Constructing a New Parental Role

One of the most prevalent themes in my interviews with Tasha was her attempts to improve her parenting style. She was gravely disappointed with her daughter Desiree's early parenthood and failure to finish high school, and she seemed to attribute much of her oldest child's difficulties to her own failures as a parent. During our first interview, for example, Tasha's talk of Tamera's experiences in Head Start led to just such an attribution. She described how Tamera had "excelled" in Head Start, learning how to print her letters, and often bringing home "beautiful artwork," which Tasha routinely hung in the kitchen. She noted that Tamara's work was "very detailed," and then continued: "I think all of that's gonna be a plus for her, and I'm really tryin' to do a little more with them because I don't want them to follow in the same footsteps as their older sister. She got involved with guys, and ended up havin' children at fifteen and sixteen years old. . . . So, I'm really trying to do things different with the other girls, tryin' to keep them out of trouble. . . . I try to keep them busy. Like Tamera, she wanted to go to summer school.[2] I take her to the library. I have her enrolled in the reading program, we're tryin' to teach her to read. But, I'm just sort of really try to keep her busy, keep her motivated."

Twenty minutes later, as Tasha described failings she observed among more affluent parents, she suggested that in addition to keeping her younger children busy, she hoped she could encourage their ability to make independent decisions that reflected their own interests and desires.

> You know, these people so push, they want their children to play the violin, the piano. I think it's more the parents who want it than the child. And my children are—like my eleven-year-old, she works for the museum, she's a volunteer, and I asked her what she wanted to do [there]. . . . And I so wanted her to pick computer because she's so good on the computer. I said, "Well, why don't you take computer?" And I was really—and then I looked at her, and I looked at the expression on her face, and I thought, oh, well, I'm gonna shut up and let her pick what she wants to do. And she picked natural science. So . . . she works with the animals at the museum, and she really likes it. I think, bein' a parent, you have to kinda stand back, and watch, you know? Instead of what we want 'em to do, I think that we oughta give 'em some guidelines, but let them pick. So I'm—I'm learnin' [laugh]."

In our third interview, Tasha repeated the idea that she should encourage her children's independent decision-making, and this time she seemed to connect this emphasis to helping her younger children avoid their older sister's mistakes. I was trying to ascertain how parents' strategies changed in response to their children's growing maturity, but Tasha's response focused on the maturation of her own general parenting style over time. Tasha first spoke about the values stressed by her Apostolic faith (for example, "They're taught not to lie and not to steal"). Like Annette she also noted the "dress code" for Apostolic women, and said she was "lettin' [Nicole and Tamera] make that decision, if they want to follow, they can." We then had the following exchange:

K: As far as these kinds of things that you do with her to encourage values, is there anything that you do with her now that you wouldn't have done a couple years ago?

T: Well, the way I have changed is that I used to not even let them have a choice, I would scream at them and say "You better do like I say." And now, you can't hardly do kids that way no more, so that's where I've changed. I kind of make them think, instead of me dictatin' it to 'em— "Here, you gotta do this, you gotta do that"—I let them think about it. . . . So that's where I have changed, I let them make their own decisions, and kind of try to steer 'em along.

K: So would you say that when Desiree was about Tamera's age, that you were very dictatorial//and

T: //Um hmm,// Yeah, I was, but I've changed. You know, that's just like when I started with Desiree, she always had to wear dresses. Now, I'm lettin' Nicole wear pants. . . . And I always didn't want them to talk to boys on the telephone. And now I let Nicole talk to boys on the telephone. . . . Nowadays you have to handle 'em so different. 'Cause it is not like what it was when I was comin' up.

K: Why?

T: I don't know. When I was their age, if I hadn't listened to my mother and I thought I had a opinion, you might get a beatin'. I mean, just for—they called that talkin' back. . . . Now, if [my children] start goin' off and shakin' their finger at me and puttin' their hands on their hips, now I won't allow that. But if they have somethin' to say, say it.

Tasha had formerly been a quite authoritarian parent, but had gradually moved toward allowing her children greater autonomy and independence. Instead of insisting the children obey her unquestioningly, Tasha now tried to just "steer them along" while they made decisions about their lives. She also claimed to allow respectful disagreement from her children, and encouraged them to express opinions. Her oldest daughter, however, had not bene-fited from this alteration in parenting style, and Tasha implied she'd been wrong in the way she had tried to raise Desiree. But, as the excerpt above suggests, Tasha's earliest parenting strategies were reflections of those used by her own mother. As Tasha became more experienced and thoughtful, those strategies began to change.

Once, when Tasha talked about her reading activities with Tamera, she noted that "I can't ever remember my mother readin' to me," and she quickly added, "I try to do a lot of things with my children that my mother didn't do." Tasha remembered her mother as a "bitter" woman, who allowed her children little free-dom. Tasha also often suggested she had received frequent "beatings" from her mother. And in three of our four interviews, Tasha remarked on her mother's tendency to downplay the importance of education, especially college. For example, in our second interview (February 1991) she said: "The way my mother raised me, she always taught us, go to school and get your diploma, but that was it. You know, high school diploma and get out and get a job. I found out that workin' on jobs, they'll work you to death and don't want to pay you anything. And I really don't want my children to have to go through that. . . . Whatever they do, I want them to like whatever they're doin'."

In many ways, then, Tasha attempted to do things differently with her own children; allow greater freedom and autonomy, limit physical punishments, and emphasize the importance of a college education. Her hope was clearly that her different parenting style would produce different results—that her children would achieve more positive outcomes than she, or Desiree, had experienced.

The Childhood She Never Had

Tasha was the oldest of her own parents' six children. Although her parents had children together for several years afterward, Tasha reported that her father was rarely in the home after he "had ran off with some woman" when she was about five years old. After that, her mother received welfare until she got a job waiting tables when Tasha was eleven. While working as a waitress, she went to night school to earn her high school diploma, then began to work as a nurse's aide, her occupation from that time forward. Tasha's mother worked a 3:00 to 11:00 P.M. shift for several years, then switched to a night shift. In our fourth interview (December 1992), Tasha explained that once her mother began to work, she was responsible for the care of her younger siblings. That responsibility weighed heavily on her, and she sadly noted:

T: I guess I feel like I've always been a grown person. [laugh] And I won't never work the night shift! I won't do it, because I won't leave my kids all night. I prefer workin' while they're at school, so that when they're home, I'm home. So I think out of goin' through that, I guess I learned that. You know, I don't want my kids to have to go through it, that's too much responsibility.

K: Yeah, I'll say. That's striking that you say "I feel like I've always been a grown person."

T: Yeah. I don't think I've ever been a child. And I think maybe that's one reason why I like bein' by myself now, do what I wanna do.

Tasha really did like being by herself, and this had a clear effect on her support network. Of all the mothers in this study, Tasha seemed to have the least extensive and interdependent network of family and friends. She had many relatives in the city including her mother, father, and most siblings, but she saw them rarely and liked it that way. She seemed to have many friends, but only once mentioned receiving instrumental support or assistance of any kind from them (a girl friend sold her a bedroom set at a good price and insisted she pay only small amounts as she could afford it). She clearly liked to keep to herself, and among the households in this study, hers was the least tightly tied to a support network.

Tasha's statement that she felt "like I've always been a grown person" was truly striking, and it was easy to understand why she wanted to be sure her own children never experienced the kind of responsibility that had so burdened her. But, in wanting to encourage independence on the one hand, while trying not to force early responsibilities, Tasha placed somewhat contradictory demands upon herself and her children—in some ways similar to the seemingly contradictory socialization tactics Rhonda employed (chapter 4; also see chapter 8).

In her practice of these socialization goals, Tasha seemed more successful at encouraging her children's independence than at limiting their responsibility. These were children who did indeed seem to have much say in how they spent their time, and Tasha tended to give them great autonomy in choosing their activities, as she did with Nicole concerning her volunteer activities at the museum. Like Cymira, the Mitchell children were also granted considerable freedom to move about the neighborhood. By first grade, Tamera could travel anywhere on their block, as long as she informed her mother of her whereabouts. A year later, Tasha noted that Tamera was able to cross the street on her own so she could now visit a nearby store by herself. The Mitchell children were permitted these freedoms despite what Tasha viewed as the declining nature of their neighborhood.[3] In the year prior to our fourth interview, several incidents had cemented this impression in Tasha's mind. People had broken into and begun staying in a vacant house directly across the street from the Mitchells, and Tasha worried about their presence on her block. Nicole was hit by a car as she walked to school one morning during the 1991–92 school year, suffering moderate injuries. The driver did not stop and was never identified. And during the fall of 1992, then nine-year-old Trevor witnessed a (nonfatal) drive-by shooting in the neighborhood. In addition, near Christmas of 1992, I took Trevor and Tamera in my car to see some Christmas lights, and as we drove past homes on their street, he pointed out several, saying, "That's a crack house," and "That's a crack house." Tasha later just shook her head in disgust when I told her of his remarks. Instead of increasing her children's restrictions, however, Tasha responded by stepping up her search for a suitable home in another neighborhood. She talked of moving for over two years before the family finally did so, in the spring of 1994.

While it was clear the Mitchell children were granted much independence and autonomy, they also had plenty of responsibilities. Tasha did not work nights or evenings as her own mother had, and she therefore saved her children—especially Nicole, since Desiree had her own apartment—from the most burdensome responsibilities she'd shouldered as a child. However, on two occasions when my daughter and I visited their home and had dinner with the family, I saw that the three older children (Nicole, Trevor, and Tamera) were expected to help out a great deal with household work. In the summer of 1992, for example, Nicole—then thirteen—was asked to get dinner on the table and also run to the store for a last-minute item, and seven-year-old Tamera in particular seemed responsible for keeping an eye on her youngest brother as the children played outside after dinner. While Tasha and I sat on the porch and visited, Trevor was told to go inside to fetch several things for his mother. I also knew the girls were regularly expected to do the washing, sweep the floors, and complete other routine household tasks. None of this seemed particularly out of the ordinary or excessive, but it is worth noting, because the children were indeed given responsibilities that exceeded many other families' expectations. But one incidence I knew of was more extreme, and suggested that necessity played a role in Tasha's ability to shield her children from excessive responsibility at young ages.

In telephone conversations prior to our third interview (midway through Tamera's first-grade year), I learned that Tasha had recently secured what seemed to be a dream job: a full-time position doing hands-on nutrition and food preparation training in the homes of low-income mothers. This position paid a better salary than anything she'd had before and included medical benefits for herself and her family. We arranged to meet at Tasha's home during her lunch break from her new job, but I arrived at noon to find no cars parked in front. I knocked on the door to make certain no one was home, and to my surprise, Tamera first opened the door a crack, then let me inside to wait for her mother (she had been sweeping the floor). I knew all the children had lately been ill with pinkeye, and I could see this was why Tamera was home—her eyes were clearly runny and red. I had previously given no thought to what Tasha might be doing for child care if her various children were ill, but now the answer was apparent. Before Tasha arrived ten or fifteen minutes later, Jonathan—who also was not feeling well—emerged from upstairs, and Tamera's commands to him showed clearly that she was in charge.[4]

Once Tasha arrived, we quickly began our interview so as to finish in time for her next appointment. Not a word was said between us about Tamera and Jonathan being home alone, and when we were finished, Tasha and I left the house together, again leaving the children home, now apparently for the afternoon until Trevor would be the first to arrive at about 3:30.

This was the only incidence I witnessed throughout the course of this research that I knew would be considered child neglect in the eyes of the law. I was uncomfortable with my knowledge of it, especially when I later learned that Child Protective Services were briefly involved in this family's life. However, certain information made the situation more understandable for me. I knew that unlike nearly all other mothers involved in this study, Tasha was uncomfortable calling on friends or relatives for assistance. I knew, too, that Tasha was thrilled with her new job and would not have wanted to jeopardize it so soon with absenteeism. Finally, I knew I myself had also on occasion reluctantly left my own daughter alone at a similar age, when her school was not in session and I attended classes. All this led me to feel that although Tasha's decision to leave the children home alone was perhaps regrettable and potentially dangerous, given the circumstances it was at least understandable, and relatively safe as well. On the other hand, I knew many other people would see this differently. In addition, it seemed to clearly go against Tasha's fervent wish that her children avoid the weight of responsibility that she felt had deprived her of her own childhood.

Weeding Out the Negative

During this same interview, I learned that Tasha and Warren had separated nearly three months earlier, in the fall of 1991. We spent considerable time talking of the children's adjustment to this occurrence, and Tamera's initial rebelliousness in its wake. Tasha described this: "Any time I told her to do something, she would say 'no,' she'd rebel, she wouldn't do anything I asked her to do." According to Tasha, Tamera was "Daddy's little girl," and she seemed hardest hit by the separation. Tasha also noted that at first, Tamera and the other children seemed to feel they needed to take sides with one parent or the other. To combat this, she and Warren decided that "if we had anything ugly to say about each other, we weren't gonna say it in front of them." She then elaborated, and connected this decision to her own early experiences:

> When we were comin' up and my mother and father were sepa-
> rated . . . and my mother constantly talked about him, bad-
> mouthed him the whole time. Till, you know, it has to have some
> effect on—I have five sisters, and I've got one sister that's married
> and has been married for about twelve years, but the rest of them,
> they can't stay with a man long. And I figured, well, since my
> mother talked about my father and men in general that whole time,
> it had to plant somethin'. And I was thinkin', whatever's gonna hap-
> pen in my marriage, I probably just can't trust men. That had to
> come from my mother. So now, I'm makin' sure I don't do that in
> front of my kids, so they won't have the same experience.

Tasha's comments here indicated she actively monitored her own behavior in an effort to shield the children from unpleasantness in their parents' relationship (for a similar example, see Denise, chapter 10). In addition, this excerpt underscores that, as Tasha explained her present child-rearing strategies—in this case, that she and Warren should not say "anything ugly" about each other in front of the children—she connected these strategies to memories of her negative experiences as a child. In this example (as in earlier ones), Tasha displayed considerable insight into the reproductive processes she felt had profoundly affected her own life, and, armed with this insight, she arrived at a strategy for helping her children cope with their parents' separation. This example is especially striking because of the metaphor of "planting" that Tasha used. When she concluded "it had to plant something," the clear implication was that what is "planted" must be purposefully weeded out or it will continue to grow and reproduce.

This, I believe, is the essence of Tasha's parenting—attempting to weed out the negative effects of her mother's—her model's—poor parenting habits from her own interaction with her children. This seemed a monumental task, and one Tasha often indicated was far from finished. When she told of the new, creative, productive strategies she devised that differed radically from her mother's tactics, she regularly interspersed phrases such as "I'm learnin'," and "I'm tryin' " throughout her talk. She never claimed to have achieved success, only that she was "getting there." It is also important to note that on this journey, Tasha occasionally sought out "expert advice" on how to best deal with her children. For example, she once went to Ms. Castle, Tamera's Head Start teacher, for advice on how to effectively discipline Tamera's older brother Trevor. She also reported that the Head Start social worker had on occasion been quite helpful. In addition, in 1990 she took a parenting course (called "Participating Parents for Progress") that included suggestions for disciplining children as well as increasing children's enthusiasm for schooling, and the following year attended a program that "taught you how to make games for your children." Both programs were offered at the neighborhood school. This was another way Tasha demonstrated her awareness of her lack of parenting skills and knowledge, and her great desire to improve.

In many ways, Tasha's situation was much like Marissa's (chapter 5), whose childhood also provided her with little constructive knowledge or experience and instead taught her merely what not to do. However, although Marissa recognized and commented on her negative upbringing, and although she saw the potential for certain patterns to repeat in the next generation, she seemed much less hopeful about breaking this cycle, and less deliberate and assured in her strategies. Similarly, Rhonda also worried a great deal about the social reproductive processes that she believed threatened her children, and unlike Marissa, she was deliberate and somewhat confident her strategies could help her children avoid negative outcomes. But Rhonda's focus was on peer relations, and she did not acknowledge or scrutinize the family processes and practices that may have contributed to her own youthful "mistakes." Tasha's keen awareness of reproductive processes was—like Marissa's—family-focused, and her purposeful attempts to undermine these processes were unparalleled in this study.

Before examining of Tamera's experiences in school, it is important to describe Tasha's perceptions of her daughter's personality. In my initial interview with her, I asked her to describe Tamera's strengths or potential problems. As she noted her daughter's apparent ability to stand her ground, her reply again suggested the value she placed on independence: "The thing that really stands out with Tamera is I don't have a problem with her lettin' people run over her. My eleven-year-old, she's real shy. She let people run over her. Tamera, she doesn't, so I think that's gonna be a plus for her. She stands up for herself, I don't have that to worry about."

A moment later, Tasha noted that Tamera had not always been this way. Though she (like her sister) had formerly been quite shy, "she's just made this tremendous turn-about since she's been in school" (Head Start). Later, I also asked what Tasha expected of Tamera's educational career. In addition to noting that "I don't think Tamera's gonna have too many problems at all, I can't think of any problems that she would have," she speculated on how her daughter's personal qualities might translate into eventual occupational outcomes: "Tamera probably won't have a secretary job, she may be a scientist or whatever, because she has a lot of determination. She's real quiet and thinks things out before she actually carries it out."

Despite Tasha's praise for her daughter and high expectations for her future, the issue of shyness and quietness was a persistent theme in interviews both with Tasha and with Tamera's teachers. Tasha seemed always hopeful that her daughter was "coming out of it," although, as she suggested in our second interview, she felt Tamera was naturally "a private person." During this interview, Tasha also noted that Tamera's kindergarten teacher had commented on her shyness with adults. Similarly, in the third interview, Tasha remarked that "Tamera has never been the type to just be real outgoing . . . and she's extremely shy at this time . . . I guess she's gonna be a private person." Finally in our fourth interview, Tasha remarked that "we try to get Tamera involved in different things, to get her out of this shyness." This suggested some concern on Tasha's part, but she continued to believe "she's comin' out of it gradually herself," and "I'm not worried about it."

My observations suggested that Tamera did indeed seem to become gradually less shy as she got older. In Head Start she seemed quite timid and had limited interaction with others. In the coming years, however, she gradually warmed up to me, and by the time I found her home alone in first grade, she and I were able to have a playful and informative conversation after only a few awkward moments. In the summer of 1992, she announced to Mary and me that she wanted to visit our house, and one year later, she did indeed come confidently to Bloomington with Cymira and us. During that visit, she seemed to enjoy herself greatly and was quite verbal and engaging throughout the day as we swam, visited the IU campus, and went to Mary's softball game.

However, her tendency to be quiet and shy seemed to contribute to major problems in her early years of schooling.[5]

TAMERA'S UP-AND-DOWN SCHOOL EXPERIENCES

Tasha's frequent comments about her daughter's shyness were consistent with remarks of her teachers and with our observations in Ms. Castle's morning Head Start class. Like Cymira, Tamera preferred creative arts projects, puzzles, writing exercises, and more structured activities over unstructured peer play in the block, family, or sand-play areas. However, unlike Cymira, she seemed to rarely involve herself in lunchtime conversations with peers and, although she participated deftly when called upon, she seldom volunteered answers or comments during structured group activities.

Tamera seemed truly shy and self-conscious with adults and most children, yet she did not appear unhappy at the Head Start center. As is true for Sheila (chapter 6), there are but few mentions of Tamera in Corsaro's field notes. These included notation of Tamera's involvement in four activities: drawing pictures with three other girls (Corsaro noted little sustained talk, but Tamera was the most verbal of the four girls); putting puzzles together at the table; building with blocks and other materials at the table (including Tamera's initiation of a playful dispute over materials with one other girl); and writing letters and her name on the chalk board. Bill also noted that Tamera stood out among the other children in her Head Start class in that "she really has an interest in the purpose of academic kinds of activities" and would occasionally ask questions like "Why are we doing this?" On the one day she was present during videotaping, a smile was often visible on her face as she joined the group in a bouncing ball game in the gym, and answered quietly and correctly when called upon during circle time.

Quiet Excellence: A Kindergarten Star

When Tamera moved on to kindergarten, this pattern of shyness and quiet but competent participation in educational activities apparently continued. Tamera was one of three children involved in this study (along with Zena, chapter 5, and Charles, chapter 9) whose kindergarten teacher was Ms. Hill. Ms. Hill was a no-nonsense teacher with high academic expectations for her students. Since this was a half-day class, she allowed little socializing or free play, and she prided herself on providing her students with an excellent preparation for first grade. Ms. Hill was pleased with the performance and progress of all three of these children, but she reserved her highest praise for Tamera. She began by noting that Tamera "is one of my star students," who "just masters everything, she really does." After telling us Tamera had participated in her summer program for incoming kindergartners, Ms. Hill reported that Tamera was already very skilled when she entered in the fall, at which time she:

> Knew her address, telephone, could say her birthday, the days of the week, her right and her left hand. And this was done in September. [And] she knew her colors in September, she knew her shapes, she knew her numbers, when she counted for me she was able to count to ten, and then in October, she counted up to twenty-nine. Then here, December, she counted up to seventy-nine, and I'm sure when I sent home the report card, she was able to count to one hundred. She tied her shoes . . . and, you know, fine motor skills, like her coloring, everything is fine. She was one, because she did well with the Early Prevention Screening, who did not have to be posttested. . . . Yeah, she's great, she's fantastic, I mean, that's everything. So yes, a star student. I told her mom, I wish I could keep her back another year just so I could have her again. . . . I talked to her mother just yesterday, and I told her. I mean, some of them you just want to keep!

Although Ms. Hill did not comment on Tamera's shyness to us, during my interview with Tasha that year, she reported Ms. Hill had told her that "Tamera was real shy around the teachers, she's real shy around adults. But she wasn't that way around the children." Her shyness notwithstanding, however, she had clearly excelled in kindergarten, and both her teacher and her mother had high expectations as she began the transition into first grade.

Tasha had a thorough knowledge of the school system, the Head Start program, and social service agencies and programs. Her knowledge about such matters seemed considerably more extensive and refined than that of most mothers in this study. In the fall of 1991, she translated her knowledge of the schools and her moderate dissatisfaction with her son Trevor's experiences in their neighborhood school into a deliberate action intended to secure a better education for Tamera and her brother William. Like Annette and Harriet, Tasha enrolled her children in an alternative program, in hopes of better outcomes. She entered a lottery system, made it through that selection round, and enrolled Tamera and William in first grade and kindergarten in a Special Option program within the IPS system. Both children were then bused, voluntarily, to a school in another neighborhood. Although William did well in his kindergarten classroom in this environment, Tamera's experiences in first grade were quite different.

Tamera's Troubles Begin

Like Zena and Sheila—the two other girls bused during their first-grade year—Tamera experienced many problems in both academic and social areas. Also like others in this study, Tamera's adjustment from a half-day kindergarten to a full-day in first grade was difficult, and she had to make an additional adjustment from a highly structured and traditional classroom in kindergarten to a more innovative and less predictable first-grade classroom. She also had a white teacher for the first time, and classmates who included children quite different from her both racially and in terms of socioeconomic class (the makeup of the student population in this special program was much like that at Newberry, the alternative program Alysha attended). These changes proved too much for Tamera, and within the span of one year, she went from being described as "great," "fantastic," "a star student," to being recommended for retention in first grade.

Tamera's first-grade teacher's evaluation of her indicated she was "working below first-grade level," and "probably next year would continue working at first-grade level." A combination of factors likely contributed to the rapid and dramatic decline of Tamera's school performance, including her problems adjusting to a full-day program after two years attending half-day; being bused out of familiar surroundings; her parents' separation just prior to the beginning of the school year; a number of illnesses in the first half of the year that kept her away from school; and teacher and curriculum characteristics that seemed to impede her ability to achieve at her established level.

When I interviewed Tasha in December of Tamera's first-grade year, she reported no serious problems. Tasha had attended a parent-teacher conference, and the teacher's comments satisfied her that Tamera was continuing to do well. She noted, however, that Ms. Kemp was "concerned" about two problems—that Tamera was "extremely quiet," and there had been an incident in which Tamera was bullied by another child but had made no attempt to either stop the child or complain to a teacher. But Tasha's overall assessment of the teacher's comments to that point was that "she said that Tamera was doin' real well."

Several months later, in the early spring, I began to make arrangements to interview first-grade teachers. As was my practice, I first called Tasha to enlist her aid in gaining Ms. Kemp's permission to call her at home to arrange for an interview. At that time, I found the relationship between Tasha and Ms Kemp had so deteriorated I was unwilling to ask for Tasha's assistance, and I made initial contact with the teacher myself by phoning her at the school. Over the phone, Tasha told me that "I don't like that woman!" and then said, "I'll tell you, I have had nothing but problems with that woman. You know what she did? She called the Welfare on me!" Apparently, Ms. Kemp had called Child Protective Services to report that, because of Tamera's repeated absences, illnesses, and especially a long bout with pinkeye, she suspected Tamera was being neglected. In addition, Tasha noted that the teacher then "had the nerve" to phone and inform Tasha she was considering holding Tamera back for another year in first grade because "she doesn't think she has enough confidence with her reading." Before we hung up, Tasha also reported she had "put [Tamera] in this after-school tutoring program, and she seems to be reading good here at home."

In her interview with me, Ms. Kemp indirectly suggested she placed much of the blame for Tamera's social and academic difficulties on problems in the home. When I asked her to describe Tamera's "overall performance over the last year," Ms. Kemp first noted that "when she came to us, she was extremely quiet." She then continued: "She cried a lot, almost everyday. And throughout the day. It was a very quiet cry. It wasn't a cry like "I miss my mommy," it was a very quiet cry. . . . She was very sad. And I'm not sure, it was very difficult to get her to talk. She rarely said a thing. So it was a very hard adjustment, very hard. . . . She speaks a little bit more, but she's still very quiet when she speaks. But she seems to have friends now. So I don't know what her worries and concerns were, it was very difficult for her to express them and tell us."

Ms. Kemp then stated that academically, Tamera was "performing below grade level," was "extremely dependent" on the teacher and her assistant, and wanted a great deal of "one-on-one" instruction. And, she added later, "probably next year she will continue working at first-grade level." She noted that Tamera got very little done in the classroom, and when work was sent home, she did not return it. She commented several times that Tamera's earlier kindergarten experience had not prepared her for the difficulty of the work in this special program, and she described her supposition that that experience likely consisted primarily of "coloring," "just kind of learning colors," and "watch[ing] the TV programs" (this description definitely did not fit Ms. Hill's kindergarten class). She gave numerous examples of Tamera's inability to complete even the simplest work. She told how within this school's structure, children were expected to seek help from one another, and noted Tamera also seemed unwilling and unable to do this. And she talked some of interaction with Tasha at the parent-teacher conference in November—that she seemed "very nice, you know, was real cooperative, [and] listened to what we talked about." But as far as her reaction to the suggestion that Tamera repeat first grade, "she was very respectful, but said no, she would not think about it and reconsider. She wants her to start second grade."

She also described a Thanksgiving classroom activity that Mr. Mitchell had attended, and said Tamera's interaction with her father was "aloof," and "they didn't seem close . . . she just didn't seem to talk to him." Finally, the teacher noted Tamera's physical ailments, including the bout with pinkeye, and also persistent stomach problems. Once Tamera complained of a stomachache, and Ms. Kemp sent her to the office to have her temperature taken. She was returned to classroom when no fever was apparent, and she promptly threw up on the carpet.

For each particular problem Ms. Kemp described—the sadness, crying and extreme quietness; the illness; the inability to complete work; and the unwillingness to interact with peers—she stated that these problems seemed much worse early in the year, and all had improved considerably, although Tamera still had great difficulties. The timing of these problems suggested Tamera might have been overwhelmed by the two major changes in her life that had occurred at the beginning of the school year: first, coming to a new school and adjusting to an all-day schedule and different school environment; and second and likely more important, her father leaving the home. To my surprise, however, Ms. Kemp knew nothing of Tamera's parents' separation. Instead, she vaguely attributed the child's sadness and other difficulties to something else: "It makes sense that she could be very afraid of what might happen to her if she does something wrong. And it's very possible that fear could be, you know, stifling her here a little bit. And it might take a while to develop a good relationship because of the fear of, you know, what could happen to her if something was done wrong. Or whatever. It's—it's a possibility."

She never expressed her suspicions more clearly, nor did she reveal that she had made a report to authorities. In fact, she openly stated that she was "reluctant to go too far into depth with certain things," and it was clear the teacher was understandably (given the history of her relationship with Tasha) holding back in her comments to me during our interview.

At this point in the interview, I decided to tell Ms. Kemp of the Mitchells' separation at the beginning of the school year, and I suggested Tamera may have been extremely troubled over this when school began. This may have instigated her initial academic problems, which then became difficult to overcome. Much as in my interview with Zena's teacher, Ms. Majors, from this point forward Ms. Kemp seemed to reconsider some of her own perceptions of Tamera's difficulties. For example, she said, "That's probably why she was responding so strange" to her father at Thanksgiving, and "Oh, yes, that does make a difference." She then continued:

> For whatever reason she thinks why her father left, you know, was it something she did? Children begin to think like that. And they are—she's definitely not verbal, so she's not able to express herself real well. So she's keeping it all inside herself. This probably could have been part of her tears, the sadness that was inside her that she wasn't letting out. . . . See, we had no idea. And we're expecting a little—you know, our expectations—could I have been a little more understanding about what the situation was? Although we were trying to be really pretty patient with her. It would really have helped, you know, for her just to say some little word, some little clue, and she was so silent.

Although it did seem clear Ms. Kemp was reconsidering her own assessment of the situation in response to the information I provided, I felt quite certain this information came much too late (mid-April) to make a significant difference in Tamera's school experience that year. In fact, the strongest impression I brought away from this interview was that given both Tasha's and Ms. Kemp's remarks and attitudes, there was little possibility of future positive, helpful communication that might mend the rift between the parent and teacher and encourage cooperative action to alleviate Tamera's problems in school.[6]

Mary and I joined Tasha and her children for dinner during the summer of 1992, and I knew Tamera was to return to the neighborhood school for second grade. Tasha had refused to permit her retention in first grade, and IPS routinely honored parents' wishes in such matters. It was not until our fourth interview in December 1992, however, that we discussed the situation with Ms. Kemp again. During this interview, Tasha responded to my questions about Tamera's experiences and performance in second grade with her assessment of the true nature of the problem the year before. She first noted that Tamera continued to struggle with reading comprehension. Her second-grade teacher, however, believed she belonged in second grade, and Tasha reported that both she and the teacher felt Tamera was doing well overall. I was pleased and not surprised, I said, since I thought "that was really a fluke last year." Tasha responded: "Yeah, well, nobody had anything good to say about Ms. Kemp. . . . I think most of the teachers knew it, a lot of people thought she was prejudiced. And I thought she was, but then I thought, well, maybe that's just my opinion. But they said I wasn't the first parent who said it. . . . There was a classroom assistant, her son was in the classroom, and she couldn't wait to get him out of there."

A number of things should be kept in mind at this point. On the one hand, the problems that Tamera had in first grade were uncharacteristic of and contrasted with her experiences up to that point, and apparently in second grade she was gradually returning to her earlier pattern of achievement. The first-grade teacher's fears about the treatment and care she received at home also contrasted with my own perceptions of this family's home life. These factors lend support to Tasha's suspicions that something about this particular teacher contributed to Tamera's problems. In addition, I had heard reports from another mother (Evelyn, chapter 9) about racial problems in a second "special" IPS school organized in the same fashion. At that school—where a relative of Evelyn's taught—racial tensions among teachers were apparently mounting over white teachers' open statements concerning their preferring not to teach the neighborhood children (both schools were located in low-income black neighborhoods). As the "School Features" table in the appendix indicates, only 34 percent of students in Ms. Kemp's school received free lunch, suggesting that relatively few neighborhood children attended there.

On the other hand, however, it is also conceivable that Tamera's parents' separation could have contributed to temporary and unusual neglect of the children in this family at the time. Tasha always seemed to try to do too much; when she and Warren separated, the removal of his considerable contributions to the daily care of the children may also have led to a period when Tasha was unable to handle all her responsibilities alone, especially with her new job.[7] Clearly, it is possible that the mistrust and misunderstanding between the two women might have been allayed had Tasha disclosed to the teacher that the family was adjusting to a major disruption in their lives, but Tasha never told Ms. Kemp of their situation. And finally, of course, interviewing Ms. Kemp for two hours on one afternoon certainly did not place me in a position to pass judgment on her racial attitudes or to assess the accuracy of Tasha's later claims that the teacher's "prejudice" lay at the heart of Tamera's difficulties.

But although actual racial bias on the part of teachers can of course have serious negative effects on children's schooling, parents' perceptions of such biases may also contribute to difficulties, whether accurate or not. Tasha was clearly angry with Ms. Kemp—for calling Protective Services, for pressing to retain Tamera in first grade, and for what Tasha believed was her bias against black children. The action Tasha took in response to these things was essentially retreat—she removed both children from the alternative program and enrolled them back in the neighborhood school that had earlier displeased her, even though William had done well in this special program. She also kept all the children in the neighborhood school the following year, even when she had many other options under the Select Schools program.[8] Tasha's unpleasant experience with Ms. Kemp effectively convinced her that her earlier strategy of seeking out alternatives to traditional public school arrangements had been unwise, which may have been an unfortunate consequence. In addition, Tasha—who had previously demonstrated her willingness to seek help on child-rearing issues from Head Start and public school personnel—would likely now be more cautious and less willing to trust teachers, especially white teachers, in the future. This would be especially tragic for a parent like Tasha, who recognized her need to improve her parenting and made many purposeful steps in that direction.

I do not want to suggest that teachers not report suspected neglect or abuse in their students' families. Rather, I would argue that more effort could be extended to understand families' situations before such steps are taken. I also suspect that had Tamera's problems in first grade occurred at the neighborhood school, where Tasha was a well-known and respected parent, they would have been handled differently, but this is purely supposition on my part.

But the responsibility in this and other cases goes both ways.

Teachers should indeed consider and investigate (rather than making assumptions about) events outside of school that may be affecting their students' performance, but parents like Tasha whose families experience unusual stressful events would also be well advised to inform teachers that their children may be under additional strain. It is not possible to know whether such information would have made a difference in Ms. Kemp's handling and assessment of Tamera, or in her interpretation of where the problem lay. However, her reaction to this information when I provided it certainly suggested that possibility.

CONCLUSION: REPRODUCING PATTERNS

Tasha had a strong desire for self-improvement, and she actively worked to interrupt negative intergenerational reproductive processes that she identified. Like other mothers', Tasha's efforts to help her daughter overcome difficulties she encountered were commendable. However, the success of those efforts was questionable.

I spoke with Tasha in the spring of 1995, and we visited on the phone only briefly. She told me they were all doing well in their new neighborhood, and Tamera was doing well in her new neighborhood school. Tasha and Warren had not yet divorced, but she was saving money to cover lawyers' fees since she was convinced there was no chance for reconciliation. We talked of the possibility of getting together that summer (which did not occur). Finally, as we ended our conversation, Tasha told me: "You wouldn't recognize Tamera, she has put on so much weight. I don't know why, but maybe it upset her more than any of us knew when her father left."

This was a disheartening observation, especially in the light of Tasha's own struggle with her weight, and her enduring pain over childhood memories of her own parents' problems and the effects she believed these had had on her. Hopefully, Tasha's attempts to break the reproductive patterns she identified would more clearly pay off in the future. Encouraging her children's autonomy was one potentially effective strategy she employed to this end, but this tactic is risky in light of the poor choices children can and do make. This is, in fact, one of the lessons of the next narrative, devoted to Ramone and his mother, Samantha.

8

INDEPENDENCE, CONNECTION, AND ADAPTABILITY

Before meeting Samantha Winters, I had observed remarkable similarities between her son, Ramone Becker, and Rhonda Craft's daughter Cymira (see chapter 4). Although the children had attended different Head Start classes and displayed quite different interests, both shared sophisticated language skills and clear precociousness. Like Cymira, Ramone stood out among his classmates as a child with an unusually mature intellect and advanced reasoning and social skills. As was true of my initial meeting with Rhonda, then, I approached my first interview with Samantha looking for family qualities and circumstances that might have encouraged such characteristics.

There were clear differences in the two families' circumstances. Cymira was the oldest child of a never-married, AFDC-dependent young mother with virtually no experience in the labor force, while Ramone was the youngest child of a divorced older mother with extensive employment history and a decent income. Despite these differences, common themes did link the families, and I discovered many similarities between the views and strategies of the two mothers. Most striking was the mothers' shared emphasis on what some might consider contradictory socialization goals.

First, they were similar in their active encouragement of independence, self-reliance, and individuality in their children. Most mothers at minimum gave lip service to such values, and others besides Rhonda and Samantha also practiced them to some extent. But it was within these two families that valuation of children's autonomy was most routinely and consistently translated into everyday practice. In turn, both Cymira and Ramone exhibited a great deal of self-confidence in their interactions with others, and this generally served them well in classroom settings.

Rhonda managed to integrate emphases on both independence on the one hand, and family obligation and commitment on the other, and this paradoxical melding was true of Samantha as well. Samantha placed high value on family members' pulling together to advance the interests of all, and like Rhonda she expected her children to understand and share this traditional emphasis. At the same time, she held individuality and uniqueness in the highest regard, and her respect for her children's expressions of autonomy was clear. And finally, also like Rhonda, Samantha had an expressed desire to let her children "be children" as long as possible; this, however, seemed overridden by more pressing concerns. She too felt it unwise to continually shelter her children from real-world issues and problems, and Ramone had access to a great deal of information about adult issues.

Samantha's tactics seemed to contribute to Ramone's achievement and precocity. But there are certainly risks entailed in the combination of such emphases, as the startling experiences of Ramone's teenaged sisters bring to light. Ramone's relationships with his sisters added greatly to his life, but their own adult experiences contributed to Samantha's growing lack of confidence in her ability to effectively marshal her children's construction of satisfying and productive futures. And here, Samantha presents another dramatic example of the emergence of fatalism that I observed in so many of these mothers.

SAMANTHA'S NARRATIVE: HOUSEHOLD ADAPTABILITY AND FLUIDITY

Samantha's family lived in a small and somewhat dilapidated duplex in a neighborhood that had clearly seen better days. This was not, however, an area of the city that was particularly threatening or depressing. Like many others I visited, Samantha's street contained both well-maintained and inviting homes and homes fallen into disrepair. There was little off-street parking, and this contributed both to my persistent difficulties finding a spot in front of Samantha's house, and an impression of busyness in the neighborhood and much activity on the street.

Samantha—who was thirty-nine at the time of our first interview—had four children, of whom Ramone was the youngest. More so than those of other mothers, Samantha's circumstances had varied widely throughout her life: She had lived in several cities, had considerable postsecondary education, had worked in several different fields, and married several times. Samantha's economic situation had fluctuated from her lower-middle-class origins, to a lifestyle approaching affluence, through low-income status that included AFDC receipt at two points in her life. One stint on welfare occurred shortly before this study began. When we met, Samantha's full-time job as a hospital clerical worker provided a steady but modest income. Although she continually struggled to make ends meet, her family's financial well-being was surpassed by only one other mother in this study (Evelyn, chapter 9).

After attending several different high schools, including one in a nearby state where she lived with relatives, Samantha graduated from Crispus Attucks High School and began working in an entry-level position for a large company. Shortly thereafter, at age nineteen, Samantha had her first child. When she returned to work, the company offered her a transfer to the West Coast, and she and the baby's father (later her first husband) decided to relocate. The couple left their son, Timothy, in the care of Samantha's parents, the Randals, where he remained until adulthood.

While living in Seattle, Samantha held many different jobs. She left her original position to work for the postal service. Later, while doing secretarial work in a university department, she took classes in a variety of fields, including criminal justice, fine arts, and education. She attended for three semesters, then "took a break" before enrolling in another institution, where she became certified as a medical assistant and hematologist.

Samantha and her first husband had two more children, Simone and Jessica, who were sixteen and thirteen at the time of our first interview. The couple eventually separated and divorced on good terms. Soon afterward, Samantha married Ramone's father, who was a successful advertising executive. Five years later and just before Ramone's second birthday, Samantha dissolved this marriage as well, and returned with her three children to Indianapolis after nearly seventeen years on the West Coast.

Prior to relocation, Samantha's family had become accustomed to a nice home and many material possessions. With their return to Indianapolis, their comfortable lifestyle changed dramatically. Samantha rented an apartment in a low-income neighborhood, and there was little money for extras. Although Ramone was too young to recall his life in Seattle, Simone and Jessica were not, and the girls often complained of missing the lifestyle they had enjoyed there.

With her considerable work experience, Samantha had no trouble finding employment. She first worked part-time in a day-care center that Ramone also attended, and later obtained a full-time clerical position in a hospital, working second shift. After she quit the day-care center position, she could no longer afford to send Ramone there. When Samantha's uncle, who had a supervisory position in the transportation department of Head Start, urged her to enroll Ramone in the program, she was surprised to learn her family met the income-eligibility criteria. In fact, with Samantha's three dependents, her income was less than the federal poverty level ($12,675 for a family of four in 1989). Over the next few years, Samantha received periodic promotions and raises, but money problems persisted, and the family's difficulties were exacerbated when Samantha took other people into her home. This included a cousin's daughter, who stayed for several months during Ramone's kindergarten year, and Samantha's son Timothy and his family, who stayed in the family home for nearly a year beginning in the winter of 1990–91.

A Different Kind of Extended Family Network

There are further examples of the fluid household boundaries that existed among members of Samantha's extended family. Samantha lived with an aunt while attending high school, her oldest child was raised by her parents and then moved in with her as an adult after he married, and a cousin's child also lived briefly with Samantha. Samantha's parents also took over raising Samantha's sister's son, who had serious difficulties both in school and getting along with his mother. Samantha's daughter Jessica also lived with the Randals for most of her freshman and sophomore years in high school. She did so in part because this arrangement eliminated a lengthy bus commute, but also because her mother's three-bedroom home was overcrowded with the addition of Timothy and his wife and stepdaughter. Finally, Ramone also spent considerable time at his grandparents' home during much of his kindergarten year, and often met the bus or was dropped off at their home in later years.

Samantha also had close relationships with many of her male relatives. The uncle who worked for Head Start often assisted with transportation to the children's various activities, and was also routinely available to fill in child-care gaps during Ramone's Head Start year. Samantha also reported frequent contact with a male cousin to whom she turned for help, advice, and emotional support. Finally, she stayed in close contact with another male cousin who lived out of state, whose home she had shared during high school. Samantha valued the support and involvement of these male relatives, and was pleased with their involvement in her children's lives.

On the surface, the network of extended family members that Samantha drew upon was similar to that of other mothers involved in this research (especially Amy, Rhonda, and Evelyn). But relations among Samantha's family of origin were so remarkably strained they were more comparable to the very problematic relationships described by Marissa than to other mothers' close-knit networks. Samantha spoke bitterly of her relationship with her sister, who was unwilling to mend long-standing hard feelings between them. Samantha also felt her mother favored her sister, and she was frank about her jealousy over their relationship.[1] In addition, Samantha's father had suffered a painful and debilitating injury over thirty years earlier, and he tended to be morose and was addicted to painkillers. Although Mr. Randal was often remarkably helpful to Samantha's family, he just as frequently threatened to withdraw his support and break off contact with his daughter and grandchildren. While Samantha was accustomed to her father's threats and appeared to rarely take him seriously, the unpredictability of this relationship added considerable stress to the family's daily life.

Samantha identified herself as the "black sheep" of the family, and often said other family members were "judgmental" of her lifestyle choices. Samantha felt she'd alienated her family by leaving the city for those many years, and she never felt accepted after her return. Although there was always much routine contact, Samantha's relationships with her parents and sister were problematic. Despite the continual friction that existed, however, Samantha and Ramone also lived with the Randals for several months beginning in the fall of 1992, before she married her third husband the following spring.

Nonkin Sources of Support

Samantha's parents were strictly Apostolic, and although Samantha rejoined the family's congregation when she returned to Indianapolis, she no longer wholeheartedly embraced the rigid prescriptions of the church. Much like her relationship with her family, Samantha's relationship with the church of her youth was strained and marked by periodic estrangements. She was often critical of church dogma, and was especially displeased by its exclusionary teachings. As she once remarked, "Apostolics do not own heaven. . . . God wouldn't have made all these races and religions just to have one chosen people." Despite her feelings of alienation, Samantha remained a member and sporadically attended throughout the study years.

In part, Samantha maintained these ties because she believed regular church attendance was important for Ramone's upbringing. However, prior to his kindergarten year, she gave up attending church on a weekly basis. She often worked Sundays and quickly grew tired of "running in the rest room to change and go to work." When Samantha began to frequently miss services, her mother occasionally brought Ramone to church, but this was not a regular arrangement. During his kindergarten year, however, Ramone developed a unique relationship with his teacher that, among other things, enabled him to attend church every Sunday.

Ms. Bancroft was a white woman of about fifty, who had taught lower elementary grades for seventeen years in the school where Ramone attended kindergarten. This school was located in one of the poorest areas of the city. Kindergarten classrooms were nearly 100 percent black, and free-lunch participation was higher (92.6 percent) than at any other school attended by the study children. Though at times frustrated with "some of the parents who don't give a hoot," Ms. Bancroft was very happy with her position and "couldn't picture teaching somewhere else." She proudly described the relationships she'd developed over time with families and children in the surrounding neighborhood, and she seemed to take extraordinary steps to enhance her students' lives. Although Head Start and Follow Through teachers appeared to most consistently demonstrate appreciation for the complexity of socialization tasks faced by low-income parents, Ms. Bancroft was one of several other teachers who were also sensitive to the challenges these families faced. In addition to benefiting from his membership in Ms. Bancroft's afternoon class, Ramone was the beneficiary of her unusual devotion to students in two additional and distinct ways.

Ramone spent considerable time at his grandparents' home during his kindergarten year. When the year began, Samantha worked a shift that began at 2:00 P.M., and she dropped Ramone off at school before her workday began. Samantha's father drove some distance to retrieve him when class was dismissed at 3:15, and Ramone typically remained with his grandparents until Samantha picked him up or someone brought him home to his sisters in the evening. This worked well initially, but soon Samantha's schedule changed, and she began to work from noon until 8:30. Though her parents initially agreed to care for Ramone before and after school, Mr. Randal suddenly refused to make the lengthy trip between their home and Ramone's school twice daily. Samantha then quickly arranged a transfer to a school very near the Randals' home.

When Samantha informed Ms. Bancroft that Ramone was leaving her class, the teacher expressed concern the transfer might upset the smooth adjustment and clear pattern of achievement Ramone had established. Ms. Bancroft later told us she hoped Ramone could stay because his advanced skills and high motivation set a good example for the other children, and she quickly offered the family an alternative plan. If Mr. Randal would agree to transport Ramone to school, she would return him to his grandparents' home herself at the end of each school day. This arrangement was agreeable to all parties, and the transfer was avoided.

During our interview that year, Samantha also revealed that Ramone had begun to attend church with Ms. Bancroft every Sunday. The teacher had learned of Samantha's conflicting work schedule, and she offered to take Ramone to services at her own church. Ramone enjoyed this additional attention from his teacher, and when Samantha asked him, "What are you gonna do the Sundays that I don't work and we go to church?" he reportedly replied, "I want to go with Ms. Bancroft." Samantha was disappointed but decided, "Hey, why not? That's something positive." For the remainder of the school year, then, Ms. Bancroft collected Ramone each Sunday morning, and they attended church together. When we interviewed Ms. Bancroft, she surprisingly reported that this was not an unusual arrangement. In fact, she routinely took "quite a few of the children in the neighborhood" to church with her. She laughingly told of Ramone's frustration over the fact that he could not be the first child picked up on Sunday mornings. As I explain more fully later, Ramone demonstrated great concern over his social standing among his peers, and both his privileged relationship with his teacher and the fact he could not be first on Sunday mornings were likely important to him because of the status implications involved.

During Ramone's first-grade year, I was surprised to learn he continued to attend church with Ms. Bancroft although he no longer attended the school where she taught. Samantha became quite thoughtful when she spoke of Ramone's continuing relationship with Ms. Bancroft, and she paused and said, "It's funny. Ramone has these, um, these *women* in his life [laugh]." Apparently referring to Ramone's ongoing relationships with both Ms. Bancroft and with me, she then went on to wonder, as other mothers occasionally did, whether she and her family were unique among the families involved in my research, and to contemplate the significance of her own involvement:

S: One day, I set here and thought about it. . . . And I wondered if people would say you're just comin' over here just takin' me apart, usin' me as a guinea pig. But see, I look at this different, //

K: //Good! [laugh]

S: I look at it as different. It's for a reason. And it's good for me. Because this is somethin' that's gonna benefit people in the long run. You know, and this is how I feel. Sometimes Ramone says, "Well, has Katy called?" and I say, "Oh, yeah! You'll have to be callin'." I think it's good, and I wish that it could happen from now on. With not just my child, but with other children, too.[2]

Bill Corsaro and I have argued that "the willingness of the mothers to accept assistance from others and to welcome their involvement in the children's lives is an important parenting strategy in its own right," and we noted that the strategy of involving others seemed an acknowledgment "that children benefit from association with a variety of caring people" (Rosier and Corsaro 1993, 188).[3] Samantha's remarks supported this interpretation, and also begin to suggest the complex mix of collective and individualistic concerns that were often apparent in her talk. In this excerpt, Samantha first pondered her uniqueness, then implied that research that captures this uniqueness can benefit the larger society. Likewise, although her primary concern was for Ramone, she also believed other children would benefit from connections with others like those Ramone enjoyed.

Connection and Independence

Samantha clearly placed great importance on strong connections with others, and she often found those connections insufficient in her life. The inadequacy she sensed in her own support system may have contributed to the pleasure she took in Ramone's unusual relationships. Somewhat ironically, Samantha also took much pleasure in her individuality and in defying categorization. Her ready identification as Apostolic was coupled with efforts to set herself apart from other Apostolics, and two other characteristics also seemed to provoke this mix of both pride and motivation to differentiate herself: being black, and being a single parent.

For example, Samantha occasionally pointed out instances when she did not act in ways that fit with her coworkers' apparent expectations. During conversation over dinner before our third interview, Samantha told of a recent incident at work. After siding with a white coworker she felt was wrongly accused of a racist comment, she was chided by the other party for being "just not black enough." Though people had told her this before, she scoffed at such concerns, and in each interview made offhand remarks that downplayed the importance of race in her life and her thinking.[4]

Samantha also noted that people at the hospital occasionally commented on her easygoing manner, and she told of a co-worker who said, "I had no idea you were a single parent; you do not act like a single parent." When Samantha asked her, "What does a single parent act like?" the woman replied that Samantha was "just fun; I never hear you complain or anything." Although we laughed together about "What does a single parent act like?" Samantha took such matters quite seriously. She thought a great deal about her status as a single parent, and she was reflective about how this affected her child-rearing practices. While she noted several times that "I never thought I'd be a single parent," she was determined that this status not define her life, and she was proud she did not "act like a single parent." However, she often noted problems like "spoiling" her children in an effort to "make up" for the absence of their fathers.

Samantha thus portrayed herself as both dependent and independent, longing for closer connections with others yet thankful for her own "space" and protective of her individuality. She saw herself as someone whose life had turned out much differently from what she'd been prepared for, but she prided herself on her ability to adapt to the unexpected. These characteristics—independence, connection, and adaptability—were all highly valued and actively nurtured in her children, as these excerpts from our second interview illustrate:

> I tell [the girls] it's good to find a man and fall in love, and for the man to take care of you, but you need to be an individual too. Because you never know, you have to have a backup. You can have

the most perfect life and somethin' can happen. . . . Life's not promised to you.

I wanna be happy with family, I wanna be able to go over to my mother's, sit in the living room, tell jokes, like we do over here.

Some people get real bitter and hard inside, and I don't want to be a bitter person. Whatever, it's just life. But I want my children to be able to make major adjustments, you know?

Like Annette, Samantha believed everyone has a God-given talent they are obligated to respect and develop. Although Samantha at times mentioned Simone's very loving, giving nature and Jessica's maturity and good sense, she most clearly identified Ramone's intelligence as his special talent. She expected him to make the most of his gift and take his education very seriously. For example, when Ramone balked at moving to a "gifted" classroom in first grade, Samantha reportedly told him: "Everyone has somethin' special. God has somethin' special in you, you have this talent, so you need to use it." And when difficulties associated with being in gifted classes continued the following year, Samantha again called on Ramone to respect the talents he'd been given. "Everywhere you go, someone's gonna call you a name," she recounted telling him. "But everyone has a purpose in life. . . . Just ignore 'em, and keep goin'."

While Samantha was clear about Ramone's obligations in school, she was more flexible in other areas. For example, Ramone negotiated a later bedtime, more varied television viewing, and more lenient rules concerning permissible morning activities while other household members slept. Samantha acquiesced to Ramone's persuasive arguments and bargaining, but made her agreement conditional on his fulfillment of other—especially school-related— obligations. On numerous occasions, I watched Ramone convince his mother to eat at a certain restaurant, leave at a certain time, or permit a certain activity. In the context of such negotiations, Ramone's verbal and reasoning skills both advanced his interests and were undoubtedly developed and refined.

In addition to allowing him to challenge and negotiate rules and other directives, Samantha permitted other displays of Ramone's developing autonomy and independent thinking. During our second interview, Samantha reported an incident (before Ms. Bancroft began transporting him after school) in which Ramone's uncle had agreed to collect Ramone from school one afternoon, but had arrived quite late. Ramone did not panic, but remained waiting outside the school until his uncle arrived. But his displeasure was clear, and Samantha reported the following exchange between herself and the uncle: "He goes, 'Girl, I'm gonna have to knock the hell out of that boy.' I go, 'What's wrong?' He goes, 'Do you know he had the nerve to get in my car and not say a word to me?' I said, 'Well, you should have picked 'im up on time.' "

When I asked, "So he was just late?" Samantha replied, "He was super late, like twenty-five minutes. And Ramone just didn't feel like talkin' to 'im."

The uncle was angry with Ramone's lack of respect, and he apparently expected Samantha to punish Ramone for this transgression.[5] But consistent with her belief that Ramone should be allowed to express his feelings, Samantha not only supported her son; she also suggested he was justified in his behavior.

In these and other ways—including permitting Ramone assertions of independence that bordered on defiance in his interaction with her—Samantha demonstrated her encouragement of Ramone's individuality and autonomy. Yet she did not expect or hope he would become an independent individual, unconnected and unobliged to others. Instead, her child-rearing strategies and emphases suggested a view that might be summarized as an acknowledgment that both group and individual interests are best served by self-confident, autonomous individuals.

Family obligation and loyalty were high among values Samantha hoped to instill in her children. And Ramone's early displays of commitment to family pleased his mother greatly. She recounted, for example, that Ramone had said, "I'm the only man in your life you need, I'm gonna get a good job, and I'm gonna take care of you." And when she discussed his occupational goals (Ramone insisted he would be a dog trainer and a brain surgeon), she added, "He's very positive about what he wants to be and, when he gets grown, what he's gonna do for the family."

This expectation—that as adults, her children would work for their family's betterment as well as their own—is strikingly similar to Rhonda's expression of traditional values that emphasize the individual's obligation to and responsibility for the group. For both these mothers, however, these beliefs and expectations were coupled with high valuation of their children's individuality. Such a mix of individualistic and communal values is familiar in the literature on black family values and practices, and while the dual emphases may appear contradictory, they reflect the complexity of socialization tasks that confront these families.[6]

Jessica and Simone: Enrichment and Complication

Samantha held expectations of family commitment and support for her daughters as well as Ramone. Although Ramone was the primary focus of our discussions, Samantha often spoke at some length about Simone, Jessica, and happenings in their lives. Samantha's reflection on her status as a single mother included, during our second interview, her expressions of guilt about trying to overcompensate for the absence of the children's fathers by "givin' them everything." This did not last long, however, because financial concerns overrode Samantha's desire to indulge her daughters. In fact, she began to expect the girls to make sacrifices in order to provide Ramone with some of the opportunities and luxuries they had enjoyed when they were younger. For example, during Ramone's kindergarten year, Samantha showered him with gifts for Christmas while expecting her daughters to do without. She explained to them that "this Christmas is for him, because he has to know in the beginning what it's about, so that as he gets older, he can see that it takes on a different meaning." In the same interview, she talked somewhat vaguely about expectations that her daughters help support Ramone's future education: "If I can get my girls on a system where I get one into college and doin' something, then I can get 'em together so when Ramone gets there, we won't have any problems. I mean, we can work together and have him taken care of."

Finally, she expected both daughters, but especially Simone, to care for Ramone in the evenings, and Simone also took days off school to attend special performances or field-trips with her brother. Although Samantha worried that her expectations might be excessive, she felt her tactics were consistent with her belief that "families work together" for the benefit of all members.

Simone struggled and fell a year behind her peers in high school, but Jessica was a strong and responsible student who gave her mother little worry about educational matters. But Samantha hinted at other concerns, about Jessica's exaggerated maturity and her relationships with boys, during our second interview. At one point, she speculated about her reaction to a hypothetical pregnancy of one of her daughters: "My fourteen-year-old, she got a rubber for a birthday present. She said, 'If you're mature at fourteen, I don't think there's anything wrong with having sex at that age. . . .' I try, I say, 'Look, we've got Ramone. I'm not takin' care of a baby, because I want to get him straight first. I want to go back to school. . . .' I'm tellin' you, you say now that I don't let you have freedom to go places? You won't be goin' places with a baby. So you look at it that way.' And I can't say that if one of my children were pregnant, how I would feel."

Samantha's musings about such unwelcome future events were focused primarily on Jessica, but when we spoke by phone early in Ramone's first-grade year, Samantha reported Simone was expecting a baby in December. Samantha offered little further information, but did say she expected Simone would be a "great mother," especially given her apparent knack for caring for Ramone. She also noted Simone had quit school, thus eliminating the need for Ramone to routinely spend time at his grandparents' home before or after school.

When we met in December for our third interview shortly before her grandchild was born, all members of the family seemed in good spirits, despite Samantha's at times heartbreaking talk about Simone's situation. "It was really hard on me at first," Samantha understandably admitted, and she described the anger and denial she initially felt. This was gradually replaced, however, by a thoughtful acceptance of the changes that would now come, and she told her daughter that "whatever you want to do, I'm there for you." Samantha then talked of her concerns about how this would affect the entire family:

> I think it has brought us closer together. It has been a change for Ramone, but . . . he's been right there. He touches the baby, he talks to the baby. . . . I told Simone, the main thing is that Ramone doesn't feel threatened, and I don't want him to feel that he's not loved with this new thing that's happening. . . . And I think it was hard for Jessica at the beginning, but I think she's made adjustments to it, you know? Because she felt like Simone's having all the fun. I go, 'Well, it's not a fun thing. She needs the attention now, and we're to give it to her. You never know what's goin' to happen in your life, and it's only a natural thing that you're gonna have a time where you're gonna need the attention, so as a family we just have to roll with the punches, and be there for each other."

Samantha found ways to convince herself and help Simone view the situation positively. Not only Samantha's words, but also my observations of the family, suggested all were coping quite well with Simone's pregnancy and the imminent addition to the family. It was also clear Simone's pregnancy was viewed not as merely an individual matter but rather was a family event that affected and was shared by all members.

During this year (Ramone's first-grade year), Simone took on much greater responsibility for Ramone's care. As Samantha described Ramone's typical day, she said that even when she was present, Simone had the last word on Ramone's activities. Much like someone in a two-parent couple, she hoped to avoid sending Ramone inconsistent messages: "He does his homework and then he's outside to play. And when I'm off on Fridays and he asks me, I say, 'You ask Simone, because I don't know what she's told you during the week.' And I don't feel that I'm shiftin' the responsibility on her, I just don't want to give him more leeway than she gives him. . . . You know, try to be consistent with him."

When we next spoke by phone in March 1992, Simone's son had been born and was doing well. Other news included Samantha's family's move into a friend's large home in a mostly black, middle-class neighborhood twenty minutes from the duplex she'd rented for nearly five years. By August, however, Samantha's relationship with her friend had deteriorated, and the family again moved—this time, temporarily into Samantha's parents' home. Simone (who was nineteen and receiving AFDC) then chose to get her own apartment. Both moves that year necessitated school transfers for Ramone.

The family soon experienced other enormous changes. Samantha married in April 1993, and she and Ramone moved once again. When I phoned Samantha at her new home to arrange our fourth interview, I was once again startled by the news she immediately shared with me: "Jessica has a baby now too!" Samantha's second grandchild was born in March 1993, when Jessica was sixteen. Our later interview, then, was filled with talk of the many changes that had occurred in the family since we'd last met. Samantha and Ramone talked about their new neighborhood, where Samantha's husband owned a townhouse in a largely black, middle-class suburban community. Samantha also talked at length about her marriage and Jessica's pregnancy. Samantha and Bernard had dated only briefly before marrying, and Samantha's quick decision to remarry was likely influenced by both the several stressful months she spent living with her parents, and by the difficulties she'd had dealing with the pregnancies of both her daughters. The emotional upheaval in Samantha's life, and perhaps regret, were apparent when she reflected: "Being realistic as a mother, I never would have thought both my daughters would have been pregnant. But my mind's not closed to it, I'm not that shallow. I did everything I could, I was as tight as I could, but I realize I cannot watch them twenty-four hours, seven days a week. You know, I have to work. It's just one of those things. . . ."

Jessica stayed with her mother briefly after her daughter was born, then she and the baby moved in with Simone and her son. The girls' brother, Timothy, had also been living there since separating from his wife several months earlier. Whatever else Samantha may have felt about her children's situations, she was pleased with this living arrangement: "They're all together, the three kids. . . . They do have a sort of bond where at least they're together."

Perhaps in part because of her disappointment in the girls' pregnancies, Samantha's talk in our last interview suggested an increased sense of fatalism similar to that expressed by other mothers. While not formerly blindly optimistic, she now seemed considerably more tentative about Ramone's prospects for the future. She had done the best she could with her daughters, yet she'd been unable to prevent outcomes she feared would diminish their chances for satisfying lives. During our first interview, she'd expressed confidently: "There ain't gonna be no teen pregnancy in my house!" yet now she could only say, "I did everything I could . . . it's just one of those things." Although some measure of optimism remained ("I'm not sayin' they ruined their lives, because you learn from your mistakes"), Samantha's outlook concerning all her children's future prospects had definitely changed. Now when she spoke of her expectations for Ramone, she qualified these, belying a sense of impotence and lack of control: "I can't say because I've instilled this into you, that it's gonna stay in you. Because there's always someone that can come along and say 'Hey, man, I've got this' or 'Hey, girl, I could do this for you.' You just don't know how gullible your child is."

As with so many of the other mothers, while Samantha's hopes remained high, circumstances in her life contributed to a creeping sense of fatalism apparent in her views.

Ramone's Narrative: "He Meets No Strangers"

Ramone was an outgoing and outspoken child, socially adept, and very curious about and friendly toward others. Samantha mocked exasperation when she frequently said, "He meets no strangers." During our fourth interview, Samantha described two recent outings illustrating this quality. The first occurred at the grocery store: "Ramone went off in the store, talkin' to these people: 'Do you like your job?' The man that was watering the vegetables: 'Do you like your job?' You know, 'cause that's the way he is." Second, Ramone got into hot water with his teacher when his second-grade class took a field trip to the airport. After the teacher told the children, "You stay together," Ramone was left behind because "he's out there talkin' to the captain, about his job. And the sky-cap. So she said he was on punishment." Such incidents were common, and they underscored Ramone's friendly and curious nature.

As was true for Ramone's assertions of independence and autonomy, Samantha respected Ramone's intense curiosity about all manner of things by providing him with much advanced, adult-level information. For example, she was quite open about sex and sex-related issues (AIDS, pregnancy, "porno movies"); friendship and relationship issues (especially betrayals and disappointments); race and color (Ramone often questioned Samantha about people's racial identity, and once commented to me that he'd recently gotten much darker: "Look at these pictures. I used to be as light as a collie"); and current events (Ramone regularly watched the nightly news, and was especially well informed about the Gulf War, in which his older brother participated). Samantha believed it was better for children to learn sensitive "things about life" at home rather than "out on the street . . . because someone's gonna turn you around and tell you something that's not true. I love you; they may not love you."

Ramone also had an advanced and precocious intellect. While Samantha valued Ramone's "special talent," she at times found raising such an intelligent child difficult. She once commented that sometimes, "I don't even wanna have a conversation with [him]; I feel like I'm talkin' to somebody twice my age." She was also unnerved by Ramone's habit of listening in on her conversations, then offering solutions to her problems ("I can tell you how to work that out"). But this did not dissuade Samantha from continuing to discuss all sorts of adult issues in his presence. Although she claimed she did not want her son "to grow up too fast," I saw little evidence this desire was translated into practice. In fact, she seemed to deliberately teach him about the reality of "the world," offering both information and complex interpretation of many adult concerns.

Formal Recognition of Ramone's Gifts

Without exception, all the mothers involved in this study believed their children were smart, but Ramone was the only child formally identified as gifted. At the start of kindergarten, all IPS students were required to take a brief test that identified incoming students' weaknesses and in some cases determined placement in full-day kindergarten classes (some Chapter I schools had a full-day kindergarten class for children who were identified as needing additional instruction).[8] Both Samantha and Ms. Bancroft reported that Ramone scored highest of all kindergartners at the school that year.

In our interview with Ms. Bancroft in May 1991, she described Ramone's overall performance as "excellent." He had mastered all the kindergarten requirements quickly, and he was "very motivated" and "very well adjusted." Ramone's positive attitude toward school had influenced Ms. Bancroft's desire to personally resolve the transportation problems that could have caused Ramone's early transfer from the school. When Ms. Bancroft talked about their special arrangements, she noted: "He's so sharp, and he added a lot to the class."

While most of Ms. Bancroft's remarks were strongly positive, I asked about Ramone's possible weaknesses as well as his strengths. She first noted Ramone's leadership in the classroom, but then suggested some difficulties with competitiveness and also temper: "He can be a real leader, and he wants to do his best. . . . And he's kind of a leader of the boys, there's several boys who every once in a while have a little rivalry about who's who, you know. But he kind of controls the boys, you know, like what he says goes. And it's funny because he's kind of small to be the dictator in here. But anyway, he lets 'em know how it is. But one of his weaknesses is he can have a real temper and get real mad, and just stare like this [makes a glaring face] when he gets mad about something. . . . [And] he's not always as, um, congenial, as far as lettin' it slide. . . ."

Ms. Bancroft later talked of misgivings about the mandatory busing that sent many of her students to other schools. She noted Ramone would go elsewhere the following year, and then remarked: "I am going to recommend him for the academically talented program. And I'm sure he would have no problem with the program, no problem. And I think it might be more of a challenge for him, somethin' a little harder for him. Might strain his brain [laugh]. Everything seems like it comes very easy for him; that's why I was thinking of that class."

Upon her recommendation, Ramone entered a gifted class in first grade and remained in the school system's gifted program throughout the remainder of this study.

Consistent Patterns of Behavior and Achievement

Ms. Bancroft's comments supported our earlier observations of Ramone's experiences in the afternoon Head Start class. He was, indeed, a child for whom everything [academic] seemed to come very easy. Teacher-directed activities in the Head Start classroom presented no challenge for Ramone, and he nearly always produced correct answers when called upon. However, he often seemed impatient for instructional activities to end so he could move on to more important—that is, social—activities. A review of Bill Corsaro's field notes and of videotapes suggest certain patterns in Ramone's interaction with his peers. For example, he demonstrated greater concern about friendship issues than did the other children, including concern over his own and others' relative status within the peer culture, and he frequently displayed advanced language and reasoning skills, often demonstrated through inventive associations and topic shifts.

When the year began, Ramone was one of only two boys in the classroom, and Ramone and Darnell had something of a running feud as they engaged in many one-upmanship contests that at times ended in hard feelings. Since the boys had no other alternatives for same-sex playmates, they had extended interaction with one another despite their almost daily clashes. As the year progressed and other boys entered the classroom, however, Ramone and Darnell remained frequent companions. Eventually their competitiveness became routine, predictable, and—it seemed—enjoyable. Both boys became increasingly adept at one-upmanship routines, competing over such issues as whose sister snored louder, who got to sleep on the sofa, and whose dog ate the stranger foods. In the context of this competitive talk, their language skills were developed and displayed (see Corsaro 1993 1994; Goodwin 1990). Ramone's impressive skills in argumentative and other interaction also helped him secure a privileged position among his classroom peers.[9]

In his interaction with Darnell and other boys, Ramone's cleverness and maturity more than compensated for his small size, and in fact translated into popularity and high status. He had few problems getting along with—and often dominating—most of his class-mates. It was, however, his relationship with a girl that gave Ramone most of his trouble. Many of the boys in the Head Start classrooms talked of having girlfriends, and they at times bragged, competed, or teased one another about particular girls. Through-out the year, Ramone identified several girlfriends, but one in par-ticular was the primary object of his desire to have a special friendship with a girl. Daniella was an attractive and fashionably dressed child who was popular with both boys and girls, and she seemed to take great pleasure in denying Ramone's claims of their a special friendship. Here is one of Bill's numerous field note entries dedicated to these two children's relationship:

> [11/29/89] Ramone stayed very close by Daniella throughout the day. At one point he said he had been thinking about Daniella the night before and that she told him she had been thinking about him too. He also said they liked one another and were friends. Daniella did play with Ramone throughout the day, but I did not hear her say she was his friend. Later there was talk about Ramone going to Daniella's house after school. Darnell entered in this by saying: "Boy, you be getting into trouble going to her house. You not sup-posed to go there." Near the end of the day, Ramone said he told Daniella he liked her and then asked her if she liked him. She did not answer. Ramone was upset with this, and after telling me went back to ask Daniella again and she still did not respond. Finally, Ramone asked again if she liked him and Daniella said: "I sure don't!" This upset Ramone quite a bit, but he seemed determined to overcome her resistance as we walked to the buses.

Ramone was indeed determined, and throughout the remain-der of the year attempted to cement their relationship. Several times Bill noted Ramone's frustration and emotional upset as a result of interaction with Daniella that did not go as he would have liked. This occurred with other children as well, but Ramone was typically able to exert considerable control over his classmates. However, he also demonstrated greater concern with friendship and status issues than the other children, which contributed to his tendency to become frustrated when things did not go his way. (Ms. Bancroft's remarks about Ramone's "temper" and lack of "congeniality" indicate he continued to agonize somewhat over his relationships with peers the following year.)

Ramone never did resolve his difficulties with Daniella, who—despite the attention and even small gifts Ramone lavished on her—refused to confirm Ramone's claims of friendship. Although

Ramone talked of exchanging visits, and apparently convinced his classmates and Bill, I learned from his mother they never visited. Samantha did report, however, that she knew of this girl who Ramone was always giving his toys to: "He'd say I gotta have this for her, I gotta have it." It was also interesting to learn from Ms. Bancroft that the following year Ramone had again chosen one particular girl in his kindergarten class to be his girlfriend. This time Ramone was more successful, and the two children were close friends throughout the year.

Ramone's imagination was apparent not only in his talk about Daniella—Bill's notes indicated Ramone's play and talk were often quite fanciful, creative, and complex. For example, one afternoon while playing in the sandbox with another boy, Ramone announced he was going to the beach next summer, then initiated playful talk about fantasy events that could occur at the beach (drowning, being eaten by fish, and so on). He then pretended to bury treasure, and the boys play became quite elaborate as they built a road to the treasure, found the treasure, buried it again, destroyed the road, and built another. On another occasion, one child said he ate scrambled eggs for lunch at home, and—-when the children found this quite humorous—several others identified unusual foods they ate. Ramone's contribution was very creative and displayed complex thinking skills: "When my mother makes frozen fish, I have to knock the ice off it before I can eat it." This comment met with much laughter from the others, until teachers called for an end to the silliness.

These examples of Ramone's activities at the Head Start center only begin to convey the extent of his precociousness. This was a child who truly stood out among his peers as someone who—like Cymira—would likely experience great success in elementary school. Although Ramone was enrolled in the gifted program in first grade, his insistence on going alone on the first day contributed to a rather sour start to the year. When he arrived on the bus, he went with a former classmate to the wrong class, and no one realized the mistake for over two weeks. Finally, Simone commented on the "easy work" he was bringing home, and Ms. Bancroft called to say another of her former students, who was not in the gifted program, had mentioned Ramone was a classmate. Samantha then called the school, and found he was indeed enrolled in a "regular" classroom. Ramone then resisted changing classes, but Samantha urged him to take advantage of the "something special" God had given him, and he grudgingly complied.

Ramone's teacher reported problems with his behavior in the beginning, but these difficulties soon subsided. Samantha felt Ms. Frazier was quite understanding, and at the parent-teacher conference in October, she reportedly attributed Ramone's behavior to the fact that "he had to make that change, and those two weeks made a big difference, because the other children were under control, and the teacher had to start all over with him." Now however, Ms. Frazier "could see the change in him . . . and he's doin' good."

Samantha praised Ms. Frazier for her willingness to work with her family's situation. The teacher understood Samantha was not at home during the evenings, and she respected Simone's important role in Ramone's life. She reportedly felt his sister was "a good substitute" in Samantha's absence, "because she cares and wants him to do those things [homework] too."

Samantha was quite fond of Ms. Frazier, who was an "older woman . . . like teachers when I was a kid." And "any child," according to Samantha, "would want this classroom. It's big, it's spacious, they have their own aquarium—I mean, it's just what you would want your child to have."

Finally, Samantha suggested Ramone remained extremely interested in and aware of the place and personalities of other students in the class: "He does make a lot of comments [laugh] about his class. . . . This one little boy, he's a nerd, and he's a knows-it-all. And that girl, [S imitates someone talking through her nose] talks outta there. He's got somethin' down for everyone. And it's good, 'cause sometimes kids are in classes, those that are gifted, and they're just not tuned in to the other students, but he is. I think I could tell him, 'Here, draw the people in your classroom,' and he could do it. And I could see the expressions on their faces, by what he tells me."

It was no doubt stressful for Ramone, who exhibited such concern with friendship and status issues, to enter his first-grade classroom after his peers had already begun to establish a status hierarchy. This was likely especially trying because Ramone initially struggled with the more difficult work, and for the first time was not brighter than the others. I hoped to learn from Ms. Frazier how Ramone had dealt with these difficulties, but after Samantha's family moved late that winter and Ramone entered still another school, I chose to interview his second first-grade teacher instead. Of course, I suspected the midyear transfer would create even greater difficulties for Ramone than merely the slightly late entry he'd experienced when the school year began.

We interviewed Ms. Parson—a white woman about fifty years old—on April 30, when Ramone had been in her combined first- and second-grade gifted classroom for just under two months.[10] Although the student population at the school was over 80 percent black, Ramone's class was evenly divided between white and black children. Not surprisingly, Ms. Parson reported that Ramone experienced considerable difficulty fitting into the classroom. Ramone was accustomed to being at the top of the social ladder among his peers, and when he entered this class, he was "low on the totem pole." Not only was he "the new kid," but the majority of his classmates were older—only five of the twenty students were first-graders (four boys and one girl). In the beginning, Ramone "kinda got it—there were a few unkind things said to him—not only from the first-graders but the second-graders too." Ramone "weathered that well," however, and by the end of April, Ms. Parson felt he was fitting in and developing friendships with the other children.

Because of the difficult situation he faced establishing himself in the "pecking order," Ms. Parson reportedly ignored behavioral problems Ramone exhibited "too long" before attempting to rectify the situation. Early in the interview, she said she'd requested a conference with Samantha just days before, and I asked her, "What was the problem?" When she replied that "the problem is he's not getting his work done because he's being a very, very social," my somewhat humored sigh prompted her question: "Is this not new?" In fact, I explained, the sociability was indeed not new, but it had never before seemed to interfere with his work. Now, however, Ms. Parson reported that Ramone was distractable, almost continually talking, and rarely finished his work. Nearly all his free time was consumed completing neglected assignments, and although Ms. Parson had moved his desk to an isolated location in the classroom, he frequently left his seat without permission to talk with others. Not surprisingly, it was the lone first-grade girl who Ramone seemed most bent on socializing with.

Ms. Parson told of the "straw that broke the camel's back" and prompted her request to meet with Samantha. While she instructed the second-graders, Ramone characteristically began visiting with classmates, and Ms. Parson "bawled him out" in front of the others. Several students quickly reported that he had responded to her scolding "loudly enough for the children to hear but not me to hear—'Shut up.' " Ms. Parson felt Samantha was "very supportive yesterday, and not at all accusatory with me," but ineffective. The teacher was surprised Ramone did not appear impressed by his mother's visit. "His behavior did not straighten up very much after she was here. Twice I said, 'I can't believe you're doing this, and your mom was just in here.' "

Despite concerns about behavior, Ms. Parson expressed only praise for Ramone's academic work. After noting Ramone was "a good strong student . . . very aware of what's going on in the room, very observant . . . [and] will usually tell me what I've forgotten to do [laugh]," I asked whether Ms. Parson felt Ramone was "well placed in the academically talented program." Without hesitation, she replied: "From just what I've seen, yes, I'd say he was."

Throughout the remainder of the interview, she returned often to the topic of Ramone's behavior and continued to speculate on what lay at the heart of his difficulties—no doubt in part because she hoped to gain useful insight for the following year when she expected to again be his teacher. She remarked that Samantha had mentioned Ramone's teenaged sisters, and I questioned her about Simone's involvement in his schooling that year. To my surprise, Ramone never spoke of family members, and Ms. Parson saw no evidence that either sister took an interest in his education. Our discussion prompted Ms. Parson to remark: "I don't see him as very open in here . . . he's just not one to come up and really share something with me." In fact, although the children had a show-and-tell period each Friday, Ramone never contributed during this opportunity for sharing. These observations stood in marked contrast to the past; when Simone was highly involved in his education, Ramone frequently bragged about his family relationships, and he relished opportunities to occupy center stage.

Ms. Parson never got the chance to observe whether Ramone's behavior would improve or whether he would become more comfortable in her classroom the following year, because the family moved again, and Ramone began attending a school near his grandparents' home. Although another move in March 1993 could have meant still another transfer for Ramone, through Select Schools, Samantha was able to keep Ramone in that school near his grandparents' home not only for the rest of the school year but for the following year as well.

Samantha's reports of Ramone's experiences in second grade indicated that although he continued to get "in trouble" at times, he had an easier time, and his transgressions were minor. As was true during Head Start, kindergarten, and first grade prior to March 1992, Ramone apparently had many friends and was popular among his classmates (despite the fact that, as Samantha reported, he was repeatedly teased by children outside the program about his gifted status). After moving to his new stepfather's home, he was allowed greater freedom of movement than in the past, and for the first time he also developed several friendships with neighborhood boys that provided him new opportunities to socialize. When I visited with Ramone that summer he was cheerful, talkative, and impatient to return to his play with friends at the nearby tennis courts.

Although Ramone never attended the same school two consecutive years until second and third grade, he typically handled these challenges well, and found it relatively easy to negotiate satisfactory academic and social positions for himself in a variety of educational settings. The exception was, of course, his experience in Ms. Parson's first-grade classroom. Ramone's intense concerns with popularity and status issues impeded his ability to handle the midyear transfer. The several months he spent in this classroom marred an otherwise very successful transition into schooling that was likely to have laid the foundation for an exceptional educational career.

Ramone had contended with an especially daunting series of changes during his first- and second-grade years: his sisters' pregnancies and their eventual move to their own apartment; new babies in the family, who threatened his own position; three changes of residence; and his mother's marriage. Despite these disruptions, and despite behavioral problems he exhibited in Ms. Parson's classroom, he maintained his stellar academic performance throughout this period. At the end of his second-grade year, Samantha proudly reported he had scored above the 90th percentile in all but one subject (87th percentile in math) on the California Achievement Test.

CONCLUSION: INDEPENDENCE, ACHIEVEMENT, AND LINGERING DOUBTS

Samantha had seemingly contradictory socialization emphases on individuality and self-reliance on one hand, and a connection and obligation to others on the other. As was true for Rhonda and Cymira, it was often the case that Samantha's views and practices seemed to clearly manifest themselves in Ramone's both delightful and more problematic behavior as well. While it is impossible to predict the overall success of such parenting tactics at later ages, Ramone's and Cymira's open and supportive family environments certainly seemed to contribute to their outstanding performance in school. Despite the children's great success, however, both mothers expressed feelings of powerlessness to shape and control their children's future outcomes. Rhonda's memories of her own experiences as an adolescent contributed to these fatalistic leanings, while the pregnancies of Samantha's daughters inspired much uncertainty that Ramone would remain on the path she so wished he would follow.

Indeed, Ramone's sisters' early childbearing may warn against strategies like those employed by Rhonda and Samantha (though the dramatic decline in living standard experienced by the girls, and their mother's evening-shift work and resulting lack of supervision, should also be considered). In any case, while Cymira's and Ramone's family environments encouraged their confidence, self-reliance, and academic achievement, their mothers' decisions to inform them of adult concerns and issues at an early age may be associated with future costs as well as benefits. After presenting the final two narratives in chapters 9 and 10, I return to this issue of early access to adult information in the concluding chapter. Now I move on to consider the experiences of a mother and son whose circumstances were in many ways quite different from the others in this book. Despite their uniquely comfortable financial situation, however, many patterns apparent in the others' family lives can also be seen in Evelyn and Charles's narrative.

9

STRIVING FOR
RESPECTABILITY

Evelyn Widel earned a bachelor's degree from a state university, she held a supervisory position in a large downtown bank, and she never received welfare of any kind. In these ways, she and her family are certainly unique among the others in this study. Yet as this narrative demonstrates, Evelyn displayed many of the same concerns, and many of the same child-rearing strategies, that were common among the other families whose children shared the Head Start classrooms with her son, Charles. For example, familiar emphases on education, church, and a mutually supportive extended family are apparent. Evelyn also had great fears that negative neighborhood characteristics would influence her children, and, like Amy, she developed isolationist practices in response. Somewhat ambivalently, she attempted to reproduce the parenting successes of her own mother, and echoes of other mothers' claims of family difference are heard in this narrative as well (such claims certainly had valid basis in the relative material well-being of this family compared to others in their community).

Evelyn's claims of family difference were attached to the desire that her son have greater exposure to middle-class children and culture. Other mothers—especially Annette and Rhonda—also expressed this desire, but Evelyn clearly articulated the connection she saw between social class on the one hand, and "street" versus "decent" values and habits on the other. And in some of her most thoughtful and pessimistic moments, she noted that if nothing else, she hoped her kids would at least grow up to be "decent." Evelyn's actions in the service of these goals are clear throughout this chapter, but so too are her feelings of impotence as she encountered school and neighborhood processes that seemed to thwart her efforts. Unfortunately, Evelyn also encountered the final prejudiced teacher that mothers identified in this study.

EVELYN'S NARRATIVE: I DON'T WANT THAT FOR MY CHILDREN

Evelyn was thirty-eight and the mother of two children, Celia (age nine) and Charles (age five), when this study began. She was a very charming, friendly, and well-spoken woman, and was under five feet tall and very overweight. Despite this, she was quite attractive and appeared considerably younger than her age. Both her children resembled their mother, in both their appealing features and their stature.

Evelyn graduated from Shortridge High School, completed college in another state, then returned to Indianapolis and secured a good job working for a large bank. She married Joe Widel, Celia's father, when she was in her mid-twenties, but they divorced, quite amicably, not long after Celia's birth. Although Joe moved to another city, he often returned to Indianapolis, and the family maintained frequent contact with him.

During our acquaintance, Evelyn told me several times she did not want to marry again, especially not while her children were still in the home. "I just don't want to be bothered," she said, "I guess it's from bein' single for so long, that I don't know if I'd be a good marriage person now." Evelyn enjoyed her life as a single mother, and her job provided her with sufficient income to support her family relatively comfortably. Although Charles's father, Boyd Jones, thought her selfish and repeatedly pressured Evelyn to marry him, she was unwilling to give up her independence and her high level of involvement with her large extended family (this desire to maintain her independence was similar to the stance Marissa took concerning her relationship with her children"s father in chapter 5).

Despite Evelyn's rejection of marriage, it was clear from Charles's frequent talk at the Head Start center that Boyd was very active in his son's life. At Evelyn's insistence, Boyd kept his own apartment but often spent nights with the Widels, especially when he was experiencing health problems (Boyd was a large man with heart problems). Charles saw his father on an almost daily basis, and Boyd cared for Charles several afternoons a week during his Head Start year, and picked him up from school each day during his kindergarten year.

Evelyn, Celia, and Charles lived in a small single-family home that Evelyn owned, in a neighborhood several blocks from Tasha Mitchell's residence. They were also only a few blocks from the school Charles attended for kindergarten through second grade, and Celia attended throughout her elementary years. The street the Widels lived on was just two blocks long, and while some homes were certainly nicer than others, these were primarily single-family dwellings whose owners clearly took pride in their upkeep. Evelyn reported that most of her neighbors were elderly— "Besides the girl next door, I think we're probably the only ones under sixty"—and had lived in the neighborhood for many years. Although her interaction with most was limited to occasional greetings on the street, she felt certain she could turn to her neighbors if the need arose. In fact, after an ambulance visited Evelyn's house one night when Boyd became quite ill, most of her surrounding neighbors called or stopped by to make sure all was well.

Of all the neighborhoods I visited as this study began, this was the least run-down and threatening. I had ridden Charles's Head Start bus one day as children from the morning class were driven home, and I was impressed with the well-kept lawns and well-maintained houses I saw here. It was striking, however, how drastically the neighborhood changed in the matter of a block or two in any direction. Much like the Richys' block, the Widels' street seemed strangely out of place in the surrounding community, which was largely indistinguishable from the other low-income neighborhoods I visited.

Even with Evelyn's relatively comfortable financial situation, before Charles began school she had difficulties paying for full-time day care as well as after-school care for Celia. A private center for Charles proved too expensive, and she hired an elderly couple who lived across the street to care for both children. When one of her sisters suggested she check into Head Start, Evelyn felt certain she would not meet the income requirement, but she agreed to talk with an administrator of the program who was also a member of their church. Evelyn was correct in her assumption that her income would have made Charles ineligible for Head Start. But the Head Start administrator told her of program vacancies for handicapped children, and a slight and unnoticeable physical abnormality qualified Charles for a handicapped slot. Although she had reservations about Head Start (especially concerning the way the program seemed geared toward parents who don't work), Evelyn was pleased with Charles's opportunity to be in a preschool setting, and she was happy for the relief it provided from her high child-care bills.

Courting Decency in Church and Family

The Widel family's spare time was devoted to two general activities: spending time with Evelyn's large extended family, and participating in activities at their church. As was true for other families, the Widels' church was central to their lives, and they were involved in choir, Bible study classes, and Sunday school in addition to participating in regular services. I attended church services twice with Evelyn, Boyd, and the children, and services in their Methodist church were considerably shorter and decidedly less evangelical than elsewhere. Both times, my daughter and I were the only whites among the two hundred or so people there, and as was true of other black churches I visited, members of the congregation were friendly and welcoming toward us. I was impressed that this particular church had not relocated from its inner-city neighborhood, given the apparent relative affluence of the congregation. It was clear that few members lived in the immediately surrounding community, but rather that most must have traveled some distance from communities farther out from the central city. It was also clear that officials of the church understood challenges parents and children faced, and they hoped the church could be a source of strength for children dealing with difficult peer and community influences. During our first visit at Easter of 1991, Charles and Celia participated in a children's recitation program. Afterward, the pastor spoke briefly to the audience, stressing that "the presence and concern of family and community members is the most important factor in keeping children on the right track, off the streets and away from drugs and crime" (from field notes).

Evelyn is a middle child of six children whose parents divorced when she was in junior high school. Evelyn's mother and all her siblings attend the same church, and it was here that I first met her mother, three of her sisters and one brother (Evelyn's mother, and four of Evelyn's nieces and nephews, also accompanied Evelyn, Charles, Celia, and Boyd to one of the two picnics Bill Corsaro and I organized with the families involved in this study during the summers of 1991 and 1992). Members of Evelyn's family of origin all live in Indianapolis, and they maintain close ties to one another. For example, Evelyn speaks with each of her three sisters on the phone every evening, and she also delivers a wake-up call each morning to one sister who is a heavy sleeper. She also noted that if her mother did not hear from her each day, she would call at work, "just checkin' in." Evelyn and all her siblings and their families met at their mother's house each Sunday after church for a large Sunday dinner and socializing throughout the afternoon.[1] In addition, Evelyn is a member of a very large family reunion club, and each year she takes vacation time to travel with the children to that year's reunion, in cities across the country.

Evelyn's children do little socializing outside their extended family and school. Charles and Celia have many cousins, both close to them in age and considerably older. Throughout our acquaintance, it was not unusual for Evelyn or one of her sisters to have sleep-overs on the weekends, when the younger cousins would all spend the night together at one house or another. Even the older cousins at times came by and took Celia or Charles for an evening or overnight. During our third interview, midway through Charles's first-grade year, Evelyn expressed concern that perhaps she should encourage her children to develop more close friendships and activities outside their family. I had asked her to discuss how she went about encouraging Charles's social development, and how her strategies might have changed as he'd gotten older over the last few years. Toward the end of her lengthy reply, she commented: "I guess family has just always been the most important thing for me, and for us. And it seems like most of the things we do evolve around our family. And, I don't know, sometimes I wonder if we should be developing something outside of our family because we're so close knit. But then sometimes I think it's good, too, because [sigh], I'm just so scared about drugs and all the other things that are out there, maybe if they don't have to be exposed to so much of that, it won't be as tempting to them."

Other mothers in the study developed strategies aimed at shielding their children from the negative influences they all felt were so prevalent among children and adolescents growing up in their communities. Evelyn's discussion here and at other times indicated she took a tactic similar to Amy's—that is, isolating Charles and relying on extended family members (as well as church-related activities) to provide what she recognized was vital social interaction with children his own age. Evelyn was by no means the only mother to recognize this need, although her extended family provided her with more readily accessible alternatives to neighborhood playmates than most other families had available. Yet other mothers who did not have such resources sought out alternatives in organized recreation, church, and other activities. Most seemed quite aware that while protecting children from negative and dangerous community influences was a necessary precaution to insure their well-being and perhaps even their survival, taken too far such strategies could seriously hamper children's social development and their ability to construct positive relationships with others. For the time being, Evelyn settled on her tactic of restricting Charles's and Celia's social activities to situations involving relatives whom she trusted fully. But she knew this would not always be possible, and she continued:

> . . . Maybe if they don't have to be exposed to so much of that, it won't be as tempting to them. They're aware of it. Charles was tellin' somebody the other day about what crack looks like, he seen it on a movie. . . . They talk about it all the time, about how bad drugs are, and I reinforce that when they tell me that. "You see what drugs do to people, so you know, you don't want to." And they both agree, and I can only hope that they'll keep thinkin' like that. And that's the only thing I worry about, that even though they know better—because somethin' happens to all these other children out here that causes them to do it. And I don't know what it is, and I keep hopin' that whatever I'm doin', it's gonna keep them—we didn't. We didn't—and I keep thinkin' that if I'm doin' somethin' like whatever my mother did, she must have did somethin' right. And if I do anything that she did, hopefully it'll be carried through to them.

When Evelyn looked to the future, she worried a great deal about the extent to which her own efforts could really influence her children's outcomes. Perhaps attempting to account for what it is that "happens to all these other children out here that causes them to do it," she at times remarked on the apparent failings of other families. For example, in the first round of interviews I asked each mother if she thought preschool children from lower-income families had different educational needs than those from more affluent families. Evelyn answered affirmatively, and then explained:

> Don't ask me why, but for some reason, I don't know whether it's background, the parents, or the environment or what, in a lower-income situation the parents don't spend as much time with the children, givin' them basics. . . . Now that's the kind of things I do with my children in the evening. Charles has an ABC puzzle and we

work with that, and he's learned his telephone number and his address. And for some reason, the lower the income it seems like the less the time. Just like the people I was tellin' you about on our street? Now that little boy's mother . . . he's always outside, he's just kind of on his own, nobody watches him. . . . But she doesn't work, so tell me why she can't spend some time with him? And it bothers me because it seems like mostly in the black race it happens that way. . . . It bothers me that it happens so much in the black race where we're already deprived and we need that extra boost, need that extra push, because you're always gonna be behind.

Here Evelyn focused her criticisms of other families specifically on black, low-income families. Her income, of course, set her apart from that group, but she also made a point to explicitly contrast her family and her activities with Charles with the noninvolvement she supposed was common among other families—"now that's the kind of thing I do. . . ." Despite her own greater financial resources, these "other" families shared her neighborhood. Evelyn remarked several times that when you crossed the next street running perpendicular to their own, the neighborhood changed dramatically—"If you cross [Beaumont], it's an entirely different story"—and she feared the influence other community members might have on her children. In fact, during our fourth interview, Evelyn noted her plan to take advantage of the impending Select Schools program to move Charles out the neighborhood school and into a school in a more affluent, mixed-race community. She said: "I'm not happy with the environment at [PS#X] either. Because all the children there are neighborhood children, and this neighborhood is deteriorating."

These comments indicated that Evelyn, like other mothers, also relied on claims of family difference to make her children's futures seem less foreboding. Yet Evelyn's fear that there was really little she could do seemed often just under the surface, and she expressed these fears clearly at one point. As she and I discussed our similar experiences as single parents and both our tendencies to wait too long before disciplining or taking an unpopular stance with our children, she remarked: "When you think about it, all you really want is for them to just turn out to be decent. And you can go on and on and on and on, and make 'em do this or that, and they still may not, so what difference does it make? Seriously. You just teach 'em right from wrong and hope that they do the right thing, and that's all you can do."

Evelyn's comment indicates the same kind of fatalistic attitudes that were occasionally apparent in the talk of other much younger, and much lower-income mothers who were involved in this study and who feared their many efforts with their children would be to no avail (see Rhonda, chapter 4, and Marissa, chapter 5). Like Rhonda's admission that "sometimes I cry, because my mother saw all the same things in me," and Marissa's declaration that "you can bring a kid up the best you can, but that don't mean they'll be like that forever," Evelyn's rhetorical question—"What difference does it makes?"—could suggest a passive resignation to the power of fate. But this was clearly not the case for any of these mothers, who all strove mightily on their children's behalf despite their fears it might all be for naught.

Reproducing Proven Family Processes

Much as Rhonda often quoted her grandmother when discussing her parenting, Evelyn would at times quote her mother's advice. For example, during our third interview she said she tried "to set an example for [my children], 'cause I realize that children these days are not do as I say, but do as I do is more important than anything else." She then identified the origin of that belief: "My mother always said that you have to live the life before them that you want them to be." However, when she thought and talked about how she arrived at her own parenting strategies, Evelyn tended to express considerable ambivalence about her mother's parenting style. This was apparent during our first interview: "She was strict and I always said that I don't want to be like my mother. I don't know whether I'm tryin' to be the opposite of that or what, because she was strict, but she was a really good mother, and a lot of the things that she did, I see myself doin' and then I try not to."

She repeated this almost verbatim in our third interview as well, saying, "I always thought I didn't want to be the kind of mother that my mother was, 'cause I thought my mother was so strict."

In an excerpt from our third interview included earlier, when Evelyn expressed her worries about her children's potential future involvement in the drug culture, she stopped in midsentence to note that she and her siblings had avoided this and other temptations despite their exposure. She said: "I keep hopin' that whatever I'm doin', it's gonna keep them—we didn't." She then speculated somewhat vaguely on why she and her siblings had been so successful, both in avoiding drugs and other major problems, and in

attaining high levels of achievement (all six of the children in Evelyn's family had completed college—a remarkable record for any
family). Evelyn spoke about the kind of effect she hoped to produce on her children, by modeling her own mother's tactics:

> We didn't—and I don't know, I keep thinkin' that she must have did
> somethin' right. If I do anything that she did, hopefully it'll be carried
> through to them. Because that worries me a lot, and in those
> respects I do want to be like my mother. It wasn't that she was so
> strict that she put the fear of God into you, it was just that you
> didn't want to do it. Because you didn't want to disappoint her. And
> that's the way I want my children to be. And I don't know if I'm that
> strong, I think my mother was a lot stronger than me . . . because
> I know that I weaken sometimes, as far as disciplinin' them and car-
> ryin' through on things that I should do. She wasn't that way. She
> stood her ground. And in that sense, I would like to be more like
> her, because [pause] like, premarital sex? [laugh] You just didn't,
> because you knew that if she found out [laugh]—I'm serious. I'm
> serious. And that's just the way it was. And we didn't think about
> doin' drugs, or alcohol. . . . But that's just the kind of morality I want
> to instill in my children, that they know that it's wrong and they don't
> do it. . . . Not because Mommy says so, but because they want to.
> Not because somebody's else is makin' 'em do it. So I worry a lot
> about that, and I keep hopin' that I'm doin' something right, so that
> they do turn out to be at least decent.

Although Evelyn was unsure about just what it was in her
upbringing that helped her and her siblings avoid drugs, alcohol,
and irresponsible sexual behavior, she was quite certain the credit
lay in something her mother did. And it seemed to be those
unknown qualities that she hoped most to reproduce as she raised
her own children.

Unlike Tasha (chapter 7) and Marissa (chapter 5), who tried to
construct very different parental roles than those they were exposed
to in childhood, Evelyn found herself—like Amy (chapter 2)—purposefully attempting to model her own parenting after her
mother's, even qualities about her mother that she formerly disliked (Denise, chapter 10, also found herself reproducing her
mother's behaviors that she had disliked in the past). Aside from
asking all the mothers in our second interviews "how you remember your parents, grandparents, or others in your community talking about education when you were young," I never asked these
mothers to compare their own parenting styles with those of their
parents. It was clear, however, that general discussions of current

parenting concerns and strategies brought thoughts of reproductive processes to the forefront, and evoking childhood memories to
explain current practices and beliefs was one of the most common
patterns in interviews with the mothers.[2] In addition, the
metaphoric imagery used by mothers in discussions of these
processes was at times quite striking—for example, recall Tasha's
comment that her mother's "bad-mouthing" of men "had to plant
something" in her and her sisters, as well as Evelyn's wish that
"whatever my mother did . . . hopefully it'll be carried through to
[my children]." Both imply naturalistic processes at least partially
outside their purposeful control.

Evelyn's expressed desire that her children "turn out to be
decent" adults was a recurring theme in interviews with this
mother, and also a clear concern for many other mothers involved
in this study. While they did not necessarily speak in the same
terms, their distinctions between the decency or respectability of
their own families, and the street orientation of families they
believed were so prevalent in their communities mirror the distinctions Anderson makes among families he studied in Philadelphia.
Anderson's findings suggest that although "strong, loving, decent
famil[ies] committed to middle-class values . . . [constitute] the
majority of homes in the community," these families are compelled to encourage their children's familiarity with the street orientation "to enable them to negotiate the inner-city environment"
(1994, 82). Such arguments suggest that the isolationist strategies
favored by Amy, Evelyn, and other mothers may well become
unworkable as their children age. And Evelyn's remarks suggested
her awareness of this eventuality, and her emerging sentiment, in
common with Rhonda's, that exposure to "street" life is inevitable.
Encouraging high morals, a decency orientation, and a sense of
family difference may be these mothers' only chance for protecting
their children from the inevitable temptations of street life in their
communities.

CHARLES'S NARRATIVE: A CHARMER AND A PERFORMER

During our first interview, Evelyn described Charles in terms that
fit quite well with our Head Start observations. She noted he was a
"sweet" boy who had something of a stubborn streak at home, and
she was pleased and somewhat surprised to learn from Head Start
teachers that he was not "bad" in school. In addition, she worried
about his concentration, and said:

He don't want to stick with anything for a long period of time. His dad is teachin' him how to fish, tryin' to build up his patience. . . . He enjoys fishin', but . . . he wants to be doin' somethin' all the time, not the kind of fishin' [where] somebody's sittin' on the bank and just waitin' for the fish to bite. That's not the kind of fisher that he'll be. And I think that's gonna follow through to every thing that he does. He's not gonna . . . sit patient and wait for things to happen, he's gonna be the kind of person to make things happen for him. . . . He's a person that doesn't meet any strangers. We go places that we won't know anybody there but by the time we leave, Charles may know everybody there. And that's just the way he is. There's somethin' about him, somethin' in his personality that draws people . . . at church—that's a good example. He's just normal, he does all the things that the other little kids do, but there's several older ladies at church who always look for him . . . and I don't know what it is about him that's attracted those people, but everybody looks for him.

Like the "ladies at church," I was unable to resist Charles's outgoing friendliness, his fun-loving nature, easy expressive laugh, and unique and appealing looks. Evelyn said "he doesn't meet any strangers" (Samantha also used this phrase to describe Ramone), and I found this an apt description. I recall once commenting to Bill that it was very difficult not to have "favorites" among the children at the Head Start center, and Charles was the impetus for my remark. Like Jeremiah, Charles had lovely manners which, also like Jeremiah, were at times forgotten in his frequent excitement. The two boys were, in fact, frequent playmates in their morning class, although both also played well and often with most other class members. Unlike Jeremiah, who did not "like girls," Charles often played with girls and would at times make comments and sing songs about girlfriends. It appeared to me that Charles had the most extensive network of playmates, and was the most popular child, in the class. In addition, Charles developed a great and enduring liking for Bill, which continued long after the research was concluded.

Like other mothers in this study, in three of our four interviews, Evelyn expressed her surprise that Charles was not "bad" at school, and in our first interview she requested confirmation of the Head Start teachers' reports from me—"He really isn't?" "No, no he isn't," I replied. But in retrospect, Charles was one of the most frequent targets of the morning Head Start teachers' teasing admonitions and their directives to change the topic of conversation or stick to the task at hand. As Evelyn suggested, Charles had some difficulty staying still and remaining on task for long. Field notes indicate first, that Charles rarely voluntarily chose sedentary activities like painting, writing, cutting, or other creative arts projects; and second, that he often joined groups of children already involved in activities midway through the free-play period (suggesting he had quickly tired of the activity he initially chose). Evelyn's comments about Charles's fishing activities with his father were very interesting—both for the suggestion that this was purposefully aimed at increasing Charles's attention span, and because Charles frequently mentioned fishing and at times demonstrated how to fish while interacting with other children at the center (see chapter 4 for one example of this).

Charles's activities in Head Start demonstrated a real preference for active role play, and like many of the other boys at the center, he often participated in play that involved the imaginative use of weapons. In one case, he instigated activities with several other boys in the "family" area that included the transformation of bananas into guns and oranges into bombs. On many other occasions, the block area served as a site for Charles and other boys' "cops" and "bad guys" kind of play. Charles also participated in other types of fantasy play in which he demonstrated rather sophisticated knowledge and understanding of a variety of different roles, including much family role play, barbershop play, and other jobs-related kinds of activities (for example, worker in a fast food restaurant, truck driver, and construction worker). Finally, Charles was also clearly a performer, and he very often sang and danced—much to the delight of the children and adults present.

Delighting Teachers Despite Misbehavior

When Charles moved on to kindergarten, he attended the morning session at a school about four blocks from his home. He walked to school each morning with his sister, and this was a pattern that continued through the second grade. Charles's teacher was Ms. Hill, who also taught Zena and Tamera for kindergarten. Charles and Tamera—who were classmates in Head Start—both attended Ms. Hill's morning class, and the children thus were used to the routine of early rising for school and afternoons off. Ms. Hill was a young black woman with a no-nonsense teaching style, and she allowed little time for free play. She clearly had high expectations for her students, and after completing the required IPS kindergarten curriculum, she introduced advanced lessons in addition and subtraction, and vocabulary.

Given Charles's boisterousness, his showmanship, and his problems staying on task, it seemed likely he would have difficulty adjusting to Ms. Hill's highly structured classroom. This, however, did not prove true, and Charles did quite well his kindergarten year. When I interviewed Evelyn in February of that year, she reported she had attended two conferences with Ms. Hill at the school, and the teacher had said that academically, Charles was "progressing the way he should be." Evelyn did not elaborate more than this on the quality of his academic performance, but rather, she noted that Ms. Hill did not seem to be troubled by Charles's behavior. Although Evelyn reported Ms. Hill told her Charles "likes to talk" and is "sometimes slow getting finished because he's carrying on a conversation," the teacher reported that overall, Charles was doing "just fine." Evelyn also repeated to me Ms. Hill's comment that "sometimes she's gotta scold 'im, and he looks at her with those eyes, and then she forgets what she was scolding him for!" As was true in Head Start, this remark suggested that although Charles's behavior was not ideal, his charm and appeal made up for his minor transgressions.

That spring, Ms. Hill confirmed Charles's mother's remarks about his experiences in her class. The first thing she mentioned was that Charles was "one of my outspoken ones" and "I ask him if he's charged, sometimes, before he even comes in here." But she said these things laughingly, and in the end, she concluded that "he's very good, he really is, and always smiling, always happy." Just as Evelyn had reported, Ms. Hill described Charles's academic work as "doing fine," and she noted his satisfactory progress since fall. He had entered knowing only seven letters, and "in February he had mastered all of them." He knew "his colors" and his address and telephone number when school began, and could identify numbers to 10. Now, she reported, he could count to 100. Like Evelyn, Ms. Hill noted that "if he doesn't complete his work, it's because he's talking." But overall, he completed assigned work on time, and when he was too talkative, Ms. Hill said "just eye contact" with her, or the question "Do I need to speak to Dad as you walk out?" took care of any problems. Finally, she said both Evelyn and Boyd were "very supportive," and she could "call them anytime" if there was a problem, or speak with Boyd when he picked Charles up from school each day. Although she saved her highest praise for Tamera, Ms. Hill concluded: "So I'm very pleased with him. And I know he'll do well next year, too."

Charles's first-grade teacher was a white woman Evelyn described as "grandmotherly-like" (she was the oldest of any teacher I encountered in this study). After a brief career in social work followed by ten years off while her children were young, Ms. Holden had taught the same grade in the same school for twenty-four years (she retired the year after Charles was in her class). In our interview in April 1992, Ms. Holden noted that lately, she'd taught "children of children that I had in first grade," and she clearly enjoyed the many long-standing relationships she'd developed in the community. Like Ms. Hill, she had clear expectations for her students, and in addition to identifying what children should accomplish in first grade, she had definite ideas concerning the knowledge children should enter with in order to do well: "If they know their name, their address, their phone number, their alphabet, colors and numerals, then they're going to have a pretty good start." She stuck to a strict schedule but was not, however, strictly all business—her schedule included several free-time periods throughout the week, and she expected the children to "talk a little bit among themselves" as they completed seatwork that was waiting for them when they arrived each morning.

After spending the first twenty minutes of our interview discussing general issues like teaching philosophy and classroom organization, we moved on to discuss Charles specifically. I began to ask Ms. Holden how she would "evaluate Charles's overall performance over the past year, um, also any particular strengths or weaknesses that you feel. . . . " when she interrupted me to say: "Well, to start with, Charles is one delightful little boy." She went on to describe his sometimes naughty behavior in the classroom, but despite her criticisms, it was clear that she was, indeed, delighted to know him. For example, she noted, he was "pretty talkative and very social, and—and he can take it upon himself to do things that I haven't asked him to do." She told a humorous story exemplifying how Charles at times would go beyond what was appropriate behavior, but in a helpful and thoughtful way:

T: He'll ask to be excused to go to the rest room. Well, we always have to have a hall pass to leave the room. So he'll pick up our hall pass. Now over the days and weeks, our hall pass has become used and worn. But he'll take it upon himself to go into the office, and ask Ms. [secretary] if she'll make him a new hall pass.

K: [laugh]

Corsaro: That's—that's Charles.

T: That's Charles. Uh-huh. [laugh]

  While Charles was certainly out of line, it was obviously difficult to be angry or upset over this kind of confident, helpful behavior. At other points in the interview, Ms. Holden also described Charles as "just a good, sturdy, friendly little boy" who "can be a little bossy," but who "gets along very nicely with the other children." I asked her if the talkativeness she had identified was "at all a problem," and she replied: "No, not with Charles. Because he corrects easily, and he certainly is not one that will talk back to you."

  Ms. Holden noted some difficulty Charles was having academically. He was "reading nicely," but "finds math difficult." As I knew from my interview with Evelyn earlier in the year, he was receiving Chapter I assistance in both math and reading, but Ms. Holden repeated that "he is stronger in reading than he is in math." While his handwriting was "acceptable," he was "extremely slow doing his work." However, not surprisingly, Ms. Holden noted that "he certainly participates in class discussion." Finally, she said that although she had met them at parent-teacher conferences, contact with Charles's parents had been "very minimal." This, however, was normal for children who were not having any particular problems. Ms. Holden remarked that it was clear Charles "gets help at home," and he "gets his homework back every day."

  During our interview earlier in the year, Evelyn had described her contact with Ms. Holden, beginning with the parent-teacher conference in the fall: "She said, 'You should really be pleased to have a child like Charles.' I said, 'Uh oh.' [laugh] And she said 'he is just so helpful, and so cooperative.' And Charles is not the same child at home. She said, 'I just never have a minute's problem.' And the first six weeks on the report card she wrote how glad she was to have him in her class, and how he was so sweet and he was so this and so that. And this next six weeks she's wrote about how pleasant he was and how cooperative he was and [laugh], so she really likes him."

  Evelyn also reported that Ms. Holden said although "he likes to talk sometime . . . it's not a problem." In addition, while she mentioned Charles's involvement in the Chapter I program, she showed no particular concern that participation in Chapter I was reserved for children who were, as Ms. Holden said, among the "bottom quarter or the bottom half" of children in their class-

rooms. And given Charles's grades on his report cards—which Evelyn reported as "all As and Bs" except for a C in handwriting—
there seemed to be no cause for real concern.

Perhaps in part because adults reacted so favorably to Charles
despite his sometimes improper and unconstrained behavior, this
was a child who truly loved school. He seemed endlessly excited
about both what he was learning and his social interaction in the
classrooms. When I spoke with him on the phone and during my
visits for interviews and other occasions, he always told me in
some detail about his recent activities at school, and he often interrupted Evelyn and my discussions—sometimes first asking, "May I
speak?" or "Can I say something"—to add comments and details to
his mother's reports. When I visited them for our interview during
his first-grade year, he proudly told me Ms. Holden had chosen
him to read the school announcements one day recently over the
intercom. This was clearly an honor, and he was very pleased with
his accomplishment. Though more than a week had passed, he
repeated every word of the announcements he had made, much to
his mother's and my amusement.

During this interview, Evelyn captured her son's great enthusiasm and love for school, as well as his and his sister's commitment
to their education, with the following words: "I can sum that up in
about one sentence: The other morning when he couldn't go to
sleep, he laid there and he laid there and he laid there. I said,
'Charles, if you don't go back to sleep, you're gonna be tired and
you're gonna have to stay home.' And he said, 'Mommy, you know
I can't stay home, I want to learn.' And he has perfect attendance,
they both have perfect attendance again. Celia has perfect attendance for all the five years."

Second Grade: The "Prejudiced" Teacher

Charles remained at the same school for his second-grade year, and
in fact was one of only two of these nine children who did not
transfer at some point during their first three years of formal
schooling (Alysha Richy was the other). Evelyn reported during
our fourth interview that Charles continued to do well in second
grade, noting that "his grades are fine, and the papers that he
brings home are mostly one-hundreds." But this year Evelyn was
for the first time quite dissatisfied with Charles's teacher.

My daughter accompanied me to my fourth interview with
Evelyn in February 1993, as she, Charles, and Celia had become
friends over the course of this study. When we arrived, I set up the

tape recorder as Evelyn, Mary, and Charles made small talk, and then—as was typical for him—Charles wanted to be recorded as well as his mother.[3] He told me some about school, noting that "it is very good," and he and Mary were surprised to learn their teachers had the same last name. When Mary asked if Charles liked his teacher, he replied, "Well, she's kind of mean." Meanwhile, Evelyn said quietly to me, "*I* don't like his teacher."

When the children left the room and we began the formal interview, I did not immediately pursue Evelyn's remark about the teacher. Rather, I stuck to our established pattern of asking first about Charles's typical day, and then about changes in his life since we last spoke. When we had exhausted these topics, I returned to her earlier comment and prompted: "You started to say that you didn't care for the teacher so much." Evelyn replied, "I don't," then somewhat vaguely described a "teaching style" she found unusual and unsatisfactory, especially for math. She also complained that the teacher had failed to respond to several notes she'd sent to school with Charles, which she found perplexing and irritating given the school's insistence on the importance of parent involvement and parent-teacher communication. She noted that she had "thought two or three times about calling" this teacher, but had decided, "Oh, forget it! I just want 'im to hurry and get out of her class. I just don't like her attitude about anything." She then explained that she had initially been pleased when Charles had been assigned to a second-grade teacher who had a reputation as a strict disciplinarian, as she continued to believe he needed to learn more self-control despite earlier teachers' glowing reports. She then continued:

E: So I thought that maybe that would be a good class for Charles, and I really was glad that he had gotten her at first. But I am not impressed at all. Apparently he's not having any behavior problems, because she's not written anything about it on the report card, and she's never called me or anything. But, um, she's just not real good at communicating. . . .

K: So, you don't think—this teacher doesn't seem, like, to fit her reputation?

E: Actually, I think this teacher is just a little prejudiced.

K: Is that right?

E: I do. Yes, I do. . . . [Evelyn told how older children complained about her class, then talked about her sister's experiences with apparently prejudiced co-workers at the school where she taught. Finally, I returned the conversation to Charles's teacher and asked:]

K: How's it—been like—interacting with her?

E: Now, I think that I can talk to anybody?

K: Um-hmm.

E: And I was not uncomfortable talkin' to her? But it was not a pleasant meeting at all. I felt like she felt like she had to talk down to me to have a conversation with me.

Evelyn was the third mother to discuss her perceptions that her child's teacher seemed to harbor racial biases, and like Harriet, she seemed somewhat hesitant to share these impressions with me. I was glad she eventually decided to do so, because Evelyn's case is important in that it demonstrates that such accusations of teachers are not made only by mothers whose children are struggling. Unlike Sheila and Tamera, who experienced quite low levels of achievement while in the suspected teachers' classrooms, Charles had continued to earn honor roll status and Evelyn reported that, despite his earlier remark to Mary, he seemed to like his teacher.

I am obviously in no position to judge the accuracy of Evelyn's, Tasha's, and Harriet's perceptions that their children's teachers were racially biased. However, whether they are reactions to real prejudice or not, it is clear that such perceptions can and do complicate or even effectively shut off communication between parents and teachers. This is extremely important, given the emphasis that virtually every teacher I interviewed claimed to place on open and frequent communication with parents. When parents' perceptions of teachers' racial bias leads to their withdrawal from communication with teachers, this in turn may contribute to additional problems and to deepening animosity between them, and may further complicate the children's educational experiences.

While Harriet continued to speak regularly and cooperate with Sheila's teacher in an effort to help bring her daughter's behavior in line with the teacher's expectations, both Tasha and Evelyn withdrew from further communication with teachers they perceived to be racially biased. Tasha waited until the school year was over, removed her daughter from the voluntary program (which she also felt was unsuited to her child's needs and temperament), and reenrolled Tamera in a school she knew and trusted. Evelyn also opted for a similar, wait-it-out strategy. Her experience with Charles's second-grade teacher also contributed to her decision to remove Charles from the school. Although all three mothers actively thought about and decided on strategies intended to help themselves and their children cope with these trying situations, to some extent their responses were passive. The mothers all chose private, individual strategies rather than challenging or opposing the teachers in a more open or public manner.

Teacher Bias and Evelyn's Past and Select Schools

Evelyn's talk about Charles's second-grade teacher prompted me to ask that she elaborate on remarks made during an interview two years earlier. She'd reported then that when her family moved to a home about ten blocks north of where she currently lived while she was in the second grade, she and her siblings became the first black children to attend their elementary school. It was 1959, and during our fourth interview Evelyn recalled feeling at times "like I was on top of the world, because you were the center of attention," and she made many lasting friendships in the neighborhood and the school. But there were painful memories as well. For example, Evelyn recounted the first time a classmate called her "nigger," and she described an extremely upsetting incident involving a classmate's birthday party: "My mother took me to the party and we got to the door, and her mother saw who I was and she told my mother I wasn't invited to the party." Although Evelyn remembered her first teacher at the school as someone who "did everything she could to try to make me comfortable in that class," her third-grade teacher was quite different: "I know she was prejudiced. And she had a real hard time dealin' with black people. She spent most of her time sendin' 'em to the principal's office and puttin' 'em in the hallway. I think that she—and a lot of 'em—just never had any interaction, and I think that had a lot to do with it. But by the time I got to fourth grade, there were probably three black kids in my class, every year there were more and more, as the neighborhood started changing. And the more of us there were, the better time the teachers had dealing with us. But we never had a black teacher the whole time I was in [elementary] school."

Evelyn then described some of her experiences at Short Ridge High School, and she recalled that "they actually had what they called a race riot and the school was closed for a couple of days during that year" [when she graduated, 1969]. When I noted that I had looked into the desegregation history of IPS, and knew about the "different court orders in Indianapolis," Evelyn brought the conversation back to the present and to her concerns about Charles's education:

E: It seems funny, that now they're talking about Select Schools, and you know, you're gonna go to school in the neighborhood. And yet they closed half of these schools up so that you really can't go to school in your neighborhood unless there's still one there. The school we went to in our neighborhood when we were children, before we moved up here, is the Head Start school now.

K: I guess part of the reason I wanted to ask you about this is I was wondering where your experiences fit in with, now that there's a choice, how that affects your decision of where you want Charles to go to school?

E: It has a lot to do with it. I don't want him to grow up in an all-black environment. I don't//

K: //Isn't this what's gonna happen to [PS#X] now? Don't you think?

E: Uh-huh, I sure do, because what's gonna happen is people are not educated enough about Select Schools that they're gonna even make the choice. It says on that form: "Your child has been 'quick-picked' for school [PS#X]. You may choose this and eliminate any choices, you won't have to do anything else." All you have to do is send it back, or if you don't send it back, you're still gonna get PS#X. I guarantee you that seventy-five percent in this neighborhood are gonna do exactly that. [PS#X]'s gonna only have kids from this neighborhood because it's convenient. I don't want that. And that's what's gonna happen in every neighborhood. That's why I'm anxious to see what they give me, for my children. Because I sent my forms in way before the deadline. . . . I didn't pick [PS#X] at all for Charles, [and] if I get a first, second, and third choice, there's no reason why I shouldn't be able to get in one of those schools. But I'm anxious to see. I just may move to the township [laugh]. . . . But I would like him to go to [PS#XY] [where she attended grades two through six], simply because that neighborhood, when you get north of Forty-fourth Street, that neighborhood is still a racially mixed neighborhood. The white people are not movin' out, and the ones that are, are bein' replaced with more white people. That neighborhood is very similar to the way it was when we lived there, for some reason it's not changin'. . . .

Having earlier complained about the "environment" at PS#X, and the "deteriorating" neighborhood from which most of the children there came, Evelyn here complained about the poor white "Appalachian" children who were currently bused to PS#X: "The type of white people that they're busin' into this school would not be my choice either." She then concluded: "Culturally I want my children to have somethin' besides that. Charles makes me angry; I listen to him talk. He repeats things that he hears other people say? And he sounds streetish to me. And I don't want him to be that way. And I don't know if that's bad or not, but I don't want him to sound like that. I don't talk to him that way, because I don't want him to talk that way."

Once Evelyn was provided a choice, her desire that Charles be exposed to something other than the "streetish" culture she believed the majority of his classmates at the neighborhood school displayed was translated into another purposefully reproductive strategy: he should attend the same elementary school she did, located in the (eventually) racially mixed, middle-class neighborhood where she did much of her growing up. Since Evelyn was so rightfully pleased with the outcomes she and her siblings experienced, she hoped to be able to reproduce for Charles the educational context that had contributed to those outcomes.

An important part of that context was the "type" of children who attended a school, and Evelyn echoed many early historical arguments favoring desegregation when she expressed her preference for middle-class peers—both white and black—for her son. She wanted Charles to have greater exposure to cultural influences that seemed absent in his present schooling environment. In addition, Evelyn was attuned to her son's great social abilities (and sociability), his interaction skills, and his popularity with others. Perhaps these characteristics exacerbated her concerns regarding the potential negative influences of other children's "culture" and their language styles. Part of Charles's appeal came from his sensitivity to others, and his ability to shape his behavior and talk to fit the expectations and pleasure of others. This, his mother may have reasoned, was all the more cause for concern over negative neighborhood influences.

In conversations with Evelyn after formal data collection ceased, I learned Charles was not assigned to his mother's alma mater in the fall of 1993, and in fact, his assignment did not reflect any of Evelyn's three choices provided by the Select Schools program.[4] This frustrating development was worsened by the fact that as the school year began, Charles was one of many IPS students whose transportation never arrived at the appointed place and time throughout much of the first week of school.[5] Although Evelyn was disgusted that her choices were ignored, the school to which Charles was assigned did meet some of her objectives. In fact, this coincidentally was the school Sheila Heath attended in first grade, which, as indicated in the "School Features" table in the appendix, was located in a middle-class, mixed-race community. Evelyn decided to make the best of the situation, and she kept Charles here for the remainder of his elementary years.

CONCLUSION: SOCIAL CLASS AND FAMILY DIFFERENCE

Evelyn and her family clearly were different in some ways from the other mothers and families in this research, and from most families who shared their neighborhoods. For this reason, I have often thought of this family as a sort of control group of one. When discussion turns to family and socialization patterns among low-income black families living in inner-city neighborhoods, questions always arise as to whether evident patterns should be attributed to race or class. My feeling has always been that these are inextricably mixed, and currently impossible to disentangle given persistent discrimination and racism suffered by even relatively well-to-do blacks. But in Evelyn's family, the general themes that have emerged in this research are apparent in the family of a mother who shares the racial identity and neighborhood conditions of the other mothers, but not their social class. While this by no means answers the perennial class-or-race question, it does suggest the possible greater influence of cultural/racial traditions, and neighborhood conditions, on families' socialization practices.

In the next chapter, I return to a final low-income family to complete the family narratives. Denise Washington lived in a "bad" neighborhood, and she shared with Evelyn many concerns about neighborhood influences. To an even greater extent than Evelyn, Denise also emphasized church involvement as a defense strategy against those influences. But, even more, she feared the effects of internal family dynamics on her children's future outcomes, and like the stories of so many of the other mothers, hers depicts thoughtful reflection on, and determined and consistent effort to overcome, the heavy burdens she shouldered.

10

CULTURE SHOCK AND FAITHFUL EFFORT

This final family narrative is, happily, a celebration of sorts of the fruitful efforts of a determined mother to construct a positive and sane family life from the remnants of a devastating upheaval. It is a portrayal of a lengthy process that I observed with both great concern and great admiration. Its conclusion will surely alarm some readers, but Denise's story must be judged at least in part on her own terms, through the lens of her own values. It portrays the real achievement of long term goals, even if the "hero" will not take credit.

This chapter also reiterates and further elaborates most of the themes introduced earlier. We see, for example, another mother's artful negotiation of a support network comprised of both kin and nonkin members. Denise also provides another example of heavy parental involvement in children's schooling, and she worked consistently to secure educational experiences consistent with her own values and objectives. As with other families, religious participation and teachings were very important in the lives of Denise and her children, and Denise's religious faith helped her make sense of, and combat, the negatives of their environment. But Denise also experienced great self-doubts, and the narrative connects these not only to awareness and fear of social reproductive processes, but also to unique biographical influences that seemed to render her incapable of confidence and self-assurance.

Martin's narrative also happily depicts one of the all too few overwhelmingly successful transitions into school. Martin began his educational career as a terribly shy and apparently frightened child, but his confidence and competence in school settings grew at an impressive rate. Not surprisingly, his success was encouraged by devoted individual attention from teachers in three different but remarkably consistent settings. And this too is a hopeful note to end upon. Martin's teachers in Head Start, Follow Through, and a small black Catholic school all demonstrated the sensitivity, compassion, dedication, and effectiveness that I saw so often over the course of this study, but perhaps have highlighted too little as I've focused on families' and children's struggles.

DENISE'S NARRATIVE: A FAMILY STARTING OVER

At age forty in June 1990, Denise Washington was the oldest mother involved in this research. She lived with four of her five children (who ranged in age from one to thirteen) in a dilapidated duplex in an area of the city that had once been a thriving neighborhood near the center of the black community.[1] Now, however, houses were splattered with graffiti, many had boarded-up windows, unoccupied homes were interspersed with occupied homes, and unkept lawns and lots were common. One block from the Washingtons' home was a small liquor and party store, and whenever I visited, I would see a group of men who stood on the corner in front of the store, drinking from paper bags, leaning into the windows of stopped vehicles, and shouting to passers-by.

Denise had grown up in a house just three blocks from her current residence, and as I came to know her, I was fascinated by her stories of life in this neighborhood in years past. Nearly all Denise's extended family had once lived in the neighborhood, and although most had long ago relocated, they still returned each Sunday to attend the large Baptist church on the main street about four blocks from Denise's new home.

Denise graduated from Crispus Attucks High School in 1968. She depicted herself as a mediocre and uninterested student who never considered college. Instead, after high school graduation, she continued to work at the small restaurant just blocks from her home where she'd been employed since she was fifteen.

Denise's early family-life provided many models of women who worked hard throughout their lives to support their families. Denise was no exception; with no expectations other than hard work, she had an extensive employment history. After developing a distrust of day-care settings after her second child was born in 1983, however, she became a "housewife" who had "worked part-time off-and-on" only when her husband or mother-in-law could stay with the children. Her husband's trade provided a decent income for the family, and for nearly seven years their lives followed this relatively comfortable pattern. When Denise and I met, however, she was separated from her husband, unemployed, with no source of income other than AFDC.

Denise's circumstances had changed dramatically in the months just prior to our meeting. She had not always lived in Indianapolis, but rather, after nearly fifteen years of living in another state, had returned to the city of her youth just six months before our first interview. Denise had quite suddenly realized she and the children could no longer safely remain with her husband. With her four youngest in tow, she made a hasty return to Indianapolis midway through the 1989–90 school year.[2] In something of a daze, Denise rented an apartment and enrolled her seven-year-old daughter in public school and five-year-old Martin in Head Start. She also applied for AFDC, which would support the family for the next three years. Her oldest child, thirteen-year-old Mandy, stayed with friends to finish out the school year, then rejoined the family that summer.

Denise's Comforting and Haunting Past

Although conditions in the neighborhood had deteriorated quite dramatically in the years since she'd left the city, Denise's ties to the community were strong, and she looked no further for a place to begin anew. She felt lucky to have the opportunity to take over the lease on a three-bedroom, two-story duplex from a nephew who had married just weeks earlier. An aunt with whom she remained close lived very nearby, and the house where her mother had died several years earlier was right around the corner. Remnants of the old, vital neighborhood remained—for example, the church and public school Denise attended while growing up still served the community, and the small restaurant where Denise worked for years continued to cater to residents of the neighborhood. However, the majority of businesses (drugstores, florists, furniture and clothing stores) had long since closed their doors and boarded their windows. What was once a thriving community was now among the city's worst in terms of poverty, unemployment, and general decline (see the "Neighborhood Characteristics" table in the appendix). Despite present conditions, Denise was comforted by the familiarity of the neighborhood, and her return to old roots helped her cope with the uncertainties and emotional turmoil she faced at this difficult time in her life.

Denise often spoke of her mother and grandmother with great respect and gratitude. She and her mother and two older sisters had lived in her grandmother's small shotgun home until she was ten years old. Her mother worked long hours in food service, and the girls saw her only briefly during the week. Although time spent with her mother was precious and spare, her grandmother stayed home and was largely responsible for the daily care of the three girls. Denise often recalled her grandmother's constant presence, and in fact pointed to this model as an important source of her own decisions regarding the combination of work and child-rearing. In addition to her child-care contributions, Denise's grandmother was part of a community exchange network within which she traded laundry services for a variety of foodstuffs. As Denise recalled, "The lady across the street, [Grandma] did her laundry, and she gave us sugar. Another lady gave us milk and stuff. And another, my grandmother did her laundry and she gave us bread. That's how I grew up; the neighborhood was real close-knit."

Through her mother's formal employment and her grandmother's participation in the informal economy, the family maintained a modest but not deprived standard of living, and to her knowledge, Denise's mother had never sought assistance from government programs.

Denise rarely mentioned father figures in her life, but I eventually questioned her about both her biological father and stepfather. Her replies suggested distant and somewhat strained relationships with both men. Although Denise's parents had been married, her father left the family before she was born. He resided nearby and visited occasionally, but "never supported us financially." Despite his desertion of the family, Denise could not recall her mother "ever saying any harsh words about him." Her mother remarried when Denise was eight, but it was several years before the family moved from her grandmother's house to a house just one block away. By then, Denise and her sisters had communicated their rejection of their stepfather's benevolent overtures, including his desire to legally adopt the girls. Her description of his participation in her life thereafter was that of a shadow figure, who remained outside family activities.

Like Evelyn, Denise was considerably older (twenty-seven) than the other mothers when she had her first child. Although she never made this attribution, her sisters' early pregnancies (one during eighth grade) may have influenced her in this matter, as her lengthy relationship with an older man surely did. As a young teenager, Denise began a relationship with a man whose family owned the restaurant where she worked, and for nearly a decade, her life revolved around Billy. Their relationship was complex and its impact more than a little ironic.

Billy was extremely controlling and increasingly psychologically abusive over the years. He belittled her constantly, and convinced her she was incapable of making decisions about her own life. Before it was over, Denise described a relationship in which Billy completely controlled her life: "I didn't do nothin' without askin' him." Despite the abuse she suffered, Denise credited Billy's insistence that she practice birth control for her avoidance of unwed pregnancy. And because he gradually turned over the running of the business to Denise (while he attended to his activities in the illegal economy of the community), and insisted that she keep her own apartment, their relationship encouraged her self-sufficiency and self-reliance. Over time, Denise came to recognize that she was a competent, dependable employee who worked well with the public and with other staff. While Billy's constant put-downs battered her self-esteem and contributed to feelings of personal incompetence that plagued her throughout her adult life, there was no denying her abilities in the workplace, and within this arena she developed great self-confidence.

A bus tour with her mother to several Southern cities instigated a sudden and remarkable break from all Denise had ever known. One city in particular, Birmingham, Alabama, had captured her attention, and as she prepared to leave Indianapolis, Denise recalled her mother's reaction to her departure: "Thank you, Jesus! Anything to get [you] away from that man!" Billy's angry prediction that "You'll never make it; you'll be back," merely added to her determination. She was soon in a Birmingham YWCA, where she stayed briefly while looking for work, then found an apartment after taking a job as a bank teller.

When Denise thought back on her move to the unknown city, she marveled at her courage as well as her competence. She recalled how everything had fallen almost magically into place, and she attributed this to divine guidance: "I wasn't in the will of God at that time, but God was directin' and guidin' my steps." Although Denise came home occasionally to see her family, she never seemed to look back or regret the dramatic break she'd made. She was happy with her new life and quickly made a place for herself among new neighbors, coworkers, and friends.

Denise soon began to date a new bank employee and within several months found herself pregnant. She seriously considered an abortion, but felt compelled by growing religiosity to discard this plan. The baby's father cared deeply for Denise, but she was now quite distrustful of men and dependence, and she kept him always at arm's length. After Mandy was born, her father remained involved and supportive in her life, but Denise never seriously considered marriage to this man, whom she always remembered fondly and with great appreciation (and with whom she maintained a cooperative, amicable relationship).

Denise's religious convictions had become increasingly important to her. Throughout her youth, Denise had been active in the Baptist church where her family worshiped, but her participation was perfunctory and not particularly meaningful. With similar nonchalance, she had joined another Baptist congregation in Birmingham. Her decision not to abort her pregnancy, however, marked the beginning of a qualitative change in Denise's religiosity. Soon after Mandy's birth, Denise accepted an invitation to vist a new church, and was quite stunned to find a white pastor and a racially integrated congregation. A white couple at the church heard Denise was looking for a new place to live, and they offered her a room in their home. After much prayer and soul-searching, she accepted. This turn of events introduced her to both Evangelical Christianity and a racially integrated community and congregation. From this point forward, Christianity became both a guide for living and a lens through which Denise interpreted her life.[3]

Denise soon met her future (and considerably younger) husband, and they married in 1979. Daniel was a licensed plumber employed by a large company, and after moving several times, the couple bought a home in the suburban community where Daniel's parents lived. Denise continued to work at the bank until their first child was born in 1983, then quit her job and over the next six years had three more children. She supplement the family's income with occasional part-time work, but for the first time did not need to rely on herself for economic survival. She settled into a comfortable life centered around family and church.

Denise recalled this suburban Birmingham community as an "isolated" place where her family "lived a sheltered life" and socialized primarily with church members and neighbors who shared their values. "I guess you could say we lived in a Cinderella world," she said, "where everybody kind of agreed on things." Her fairy-tale world, however, hid the increasing pain of Denise's relationship with her husband. Daniel had always been somewhat remote, but Denise had looked beyond this to his better qualities. Gradually, however, he became more and more critical, and emotionally abusive. She felt he was ashamed of her, he became extremely conscious of their age difference, and he insisted that Denise not discuss their family "business" (for example, that they had a new baby). His coldness turned to more blatant disdain, and he routinely denied any feelings for her. He also became cold to and resentful of the children. In addition, while he had always provided for the family financially, in the months before their breakup this too began to change. Only later did Denise learn that many of Daniel's changes were surely worsened by a well-hidden drug problem.

When Denise spoke of how her relationship with Daniel evolved, the similarities to her earlier relationship with Billy were striking. Both men's attacks on her self-esteem took a heavy toll, and Denise again felt weak, incompetent, and incapable of effectively managing her life. She took solace in her religious beliefs and her hope that things would improve, but instead they only worsened. When Denise was forced to suddenly leave Daniel and her life in Birmingham, she returned to Indianapolis with little self-confidence and a great deal of fear about the future. Much like Samantha, who "never thought [she'd] be a single parent," Denise remarked that "I never even considered all this, I never thought I would be back here and things would be *so* different." Throughout our first interview, she seemed to be still reeling from the events of the prior winter.

Constructing a New Family Life

Although Denise was devastated by these events, when she arrived in Indianapolis she set about constructing a new life for herself and her children. Denise found an apartment, enrolled her children in school, and applied for AFDC. She had never before received assistance, and applying for welfare was quite difficult for her. During our first interview, Denise revealed a former dislike of AFDC recipients, and she made her "confession" of the stigma she'd attached to welfare receipt: "I used to be against, and talked about people that was on AFDC. . . . But I never knew that I would be in the situation I'm in today, and I had to say 'Lord forgive me for ever talkin' against those people,' 'cause in a thousand years, never did I think. . . . Whatever help I can get now so that my children have a place to stay and food to eat, I've just been so grateful."

After a lifetime of hard work, finding herself among people she'd formerly "been against" and "talked about" was certainly humbling. Later Denise spoke of God's benevolent hand in the unusual ease with which she was able to secure AFDC for her family. Though acquaintances told of nightmarish delays, hostile case-workers, and mountains of paperwork before they could establish an AFDC case, Denise had no problems. "I knew it was the Lord," she said. "He just had everything set up for me."

Once she knew her children's physical needs were met, Denise turned her attention to helping them make sense of the situation. In particular, she talked of her efforts to help them cope with their abruptly severed relationship with their father. She was concerned that her children would be irreparably harmed if they did not find ways to express their hurt and confusion. Denise sounded much like Rhonda (chapter 4) as she described the metaphoric advice she gave her children: "For a while they wouldn't cry, and I could see it wellin' up in them, and I said, 'It's OK to cry,' cause it'll hurt you if you shove it down in your throat and it goes into your heart. . . . As long as it's in your throat, you can cough it up, cry it out, but if it get down in your heart, then you get hard, and bitter, and you don't want that to be a part of your life.' "

Denise worked hard to keep her children's needs paramount. "They love their dad," she said during that first interview, and "however things work out, I never will change that." As I came to know her better, it was clear she had made monumental efforts to shield her children from her own problems. During our third interview, she described the apparent positive effects of hiding from her children details of the incident that precipitated their move and her own emotional pain.

> It amazes me that with all the changes we've been through in the two years, my children have remained happy . . . I tried to keep a positive attitude about their dad as much as it hurt me to do so at times. I'm glad I did. I think that helped them come through a tragedy as well as they did. . . . I could be down and depressed about all this happenin', but because I haven't allowed them to know fact upon fact, and don't allow other members of the family to remind them of all the ugly that happened, it hasn't been such a big change. . . . Now, it's almost like nothin' really happened, it's just

like we've been separated for a while, and all that ugly stuff that normally happens in a family with the children takin' sides, I can praise God and say that has not happened.

Denise had not left Daniel with certainty that their marriage was over. In fact, within a year I realized she was committed to making every effort to reconcile. She was extremely cautious, however, and moved only very slowly in that direction. In the meantime, Denise was concerned that Martin should enjoy contact with positive male role models. She had few appropriate male relatives, so she instead sought assistance from a couple at church with a son Martin's age. Martin participated in various activities with this family, including bowling, Little League baseball, and a basketball league.

In addition to her valuation of a male role model for her children, Denise's commitment to her marriage was influenced by her sincere love for Daniel despite his faults, her religious beliefs, and her determination to keep her children's best interests at heart. However, concern for her oldest child's well-being slowed this process. Mandy was dead set against returning to live with her stepfather, and despite Daniel's efforts to win her trust, Mandy remained unconvinced of his sincerity. Denise was deeply troubled by this, and she talked to Mandy of biblical teachings that counseled forgiveness. Like other mothers, she also drew on recollections of her own mother's practices to help her through this difficult time:

> I used to look at my mother and feel that I could just use her. But when I think about her [now], she had a forgiving heart and she was a warm person. . . . I used to want to say, "Mom, why you let 'em do this?" . . . Now I can see it. I can see a lot of my mother in me. Different things that I did not like about my mother, now I have those same qualities. . . . People don't understand why I even want to try and go back with my husband. . . . Especially Mandy. . . . She goes, "I can understand you forgive him, but still love him? I don't get that yet." But I try to say, "You're gonna do some things in life, and there will be things that you're gonna have to ask that I forgive you for. And you're gonna be prayin', 'Please, Lord, let 'em forgive me.'"

Denise told Mandy that in order to be forgiven for your own misdeeds, you must first forgive others. She hoped Mandy would come to understand her reconciliation efforts, and she felt the prospects of this were good, given her own change of heart about her mother. Despite the comfort Denise derived from her hind-sight understanding of her mother's practices and attitudes, how-ever, Daniel and Mandy's relationship presented a major stumbling block for the family's reunification, and Denise was torn by her children's conflicting desires. The delay of three and a half years before she and Daniel were reunited was influenced by Denise's insistence on protecting all her children from potential ill effects of her troubled marriage.

While Denise did all she could to protect her children from the ugliness of their parents' relationship, she found it impossible to shield them from the reality of the street life that now surrounded them. As with other mothers who worried about negative commu-nity influences, this was another major concern for Denise as she tried to help her children cope with their drastically changed cir-cumstances. During our first interview, Denise noted her children's reaction to life in their neighborhood: ". . . If we go in the back-yard, we see people in the alley and they're drinking and smokin'. . . . And they say, 'Mommy? Everybody here do that, don't they?' So it's almost like they're bein' shocked into reality of life. It's like, everybody is not like they were where we came from. . . . I grew up here in this type of environment so it's not strange to me. But to them, it's like we're in a different culture here! You know, what's goin' on?"

In later interviews Denise returned to her children's culture shock, but noted they had "adjusted to it pretty well." And when they questioned her about "the little men that hang in the alley," Denise reportedly told them "you just pray for those people." She explained that continual reinforcement of "biblical principles" was the best way to combat the negatives of their environment. Much as Rhonda did with her children, insisting, for example, that "drug addicts are people too," Denise wanted Martin and his siblings to "know your stance in life, know your morals, and stand with it" and reject the undesirable behaviors of individuals who populated their community. However, they needn't reject the humanity of the individuals themselves: "You can still get along with people like that, still treat them like human beings." Thus although Denise routinely suggested to her children that they were different from others who shared their community, she encouraged an atti-tude of nonjudgmental acceptance. The loss of her own judgmen-tal attitudes been a hard lesson, and she hoped her children would be better people for what she'd learned.

When Denise again brought up the men who met daily on the

corner to drink during our fourth interview, her comments suggested a new concern. The familiarity of the men's faces was
troubling, and for the first time Denise talked of the possibility her
children could end up in similar situations: "I'm seein' a lot of
people I went to school with down on the corner. And those boys
was smart in school! . . . And I'm so determined that my kids just
won't go that route. Especially my boys! I mean . . . there's gotta be
some good men out there, and my boys are gonna be! And I hope I
don't push 'em so hard till they turn from it."

Denise did indeed push her children to do well in school, and
among the mothers her routine involvement in their educations
was rivaled only by Amy. She accompanied Martin's Head Start
class on field trips and occasionally helped out in the classroom.
She attended all special programs at the various schools her children attended, and she enrolled Martin in an alternative public
school program and later moved all her children to Catholic
schools in hopes of finding the optimum environment for their
educational needs. She visited all her children's schools regularly
and never missed a parent-teacher conference, and she routinely
took her family to the public library as well. She also involved
Mandy, Martin, and Monique in a church-sponsored tutoring program. Finally, she insisted the children spend at least an hour each
evening completing their assigned homework, reading, or working
math problems.

Although she did not want to push too hard, Denise was convinced they needed to see her stressing education. She noted that
her own mother had "worked so much, she didn't have that time
to reinforce education." Denise felt this had contributed to her
own indifferent attitude, and she certainly did not want her children to follow in her footsteps. "I have this fear about my children
bein' like me," she said. Like other mothers who expressed regret
over their own lack of education, Denise looked to her own childhood for answers and attempted to improve on the upbringing
she'd received.

Fostering Self-Confidence

By all appearances, Denise was a resourceful woman who succeeded in constructing a stable and nurturing family life for her
children despite great obstacles. She also appeared quite successful
in instilling a high valuation of schooling in her children.
Monique and Martin were both very strong students, and later
their younger brother's and sister's early performances suggested

they would do equally well. Although Mandy struggled at times with poor grades (Denise considered Cs poor grades), she graduated from high school in June 1995, and began to make plans for college. The Washington children's accomplishments were even more impressive when considered in the light of the upheavals in their family life. Denise had good reason to be proud of all she had done to encourage their success. But remarkably, she was not. Instead, she remained full of self-doubt and continually questioned the quality of her efforts, the wisdom of her decisions, and her overall adequacy as a mother and a person.

Often, Denise's self-criticisms focused on her past failure to be a better student and how this lessened her effectiveness with her children. For example, she lamented that "I'm not a study person . . . I hate that I never got that in me." She also noted her shame when her children asked for assistance and she had to reply, "I don't understand." Even when noting successes, she managed to convey more fundamental failings. This was apparent in our first interview, as Denise noted skills Martin possessed when he entered Head Start: "The church that I attended [in Birmingham] pushed home school a lot, but I just never felt confident enough in myself to do it. But surprisingly enough, I taught Martin everything he knew before he went to Head Start. . . ."

I noted earlier Denise's decision to enroll her children in Catholic schools. Late in the summer between Martin's kindergarten and first-grade years, Denise saw a commercial on television announcing the Golden Rule Insurance Company's Choice Charitable Trust program. The company offered to pay a portion of low-income students' tuition at private schools, and Denise quickly called for information, filled out applications, convinced her husband in Alabama to pay the tuition Golden Rule did not cover, selected a school for Monique and Martin to attend, and was accepted by the program—all before school began that fall. She also enrolled the children at Our Redeemer knowing she would have to provide her own transportation. Despite her remarkable effort, the following year when she began to doubt the quality of the school's instruction, she berated herself for failing to choose a school more carefully.

It also seemed that whenever she noted her children's failings, she'd comment that "I guess he gets that from me." On the other hand, remarks about their finer qualities were often followed by "I don't know where she gets that," or suggestions that God provided her children with talents she could not model ("Where I'm lackin', she picks it up. I'm not proud of that, but I'm proud to see that God got to my little girl"). And when she talked of how she'd like her children to be, she contrasted these desirable qualities with perceived self-failings.

While I doubt Denise was aware of the extent of her self-criticisms, she certainly knew she lacked self-esteem and confidence. This was, in fact, probably her most frequent criticism. "I lack a lot of self confidence," she said during our second interview, "and I don't want my kids to pick that up." She did, however, see evidence that her children already shared this quality—for example, as she described Martin during our first interview, she noted: "He doesn't have a lot of self-confidence, and he probably got that from me. He doesn't know how to initiate things on his own."

Denise often noted her pride in Martin, but she was also concerned that she saw much of herself in him. Martin's school experiences were to some extent a reflection of his mother's concerns and his family's circumstances. Martin's transition into schooling coincided with many other transitions as well: transitions into poverty, into a single-parent family situation, and into inner-city living. Like his mother, Martin initially appeared quite dazed, and Denise's suggestion of "culture shock" seemed an apt description of his experiences in his early days in Indianapolis and in the Head Start classroom.

MARTIN'S TRANSITION: INCREASING
CONFIDENCE IN SUPPORTIVE SETTINGS

Denise's relatives saw the pressure Denise was under, and they encouraged her to enroll Martin in Head Start for both their sakes. Although enrolling Martin was "a hard pill to swallow," she took their advice and began looking into the program. She again encountered helpful people, and was lucky to find that her area's center had one opening in an afternoon class.

By the time Martin entered this classroom, personnel there had stabilized. Although other children dealt with several teacher changes throughout the first half of the year, by late January both the head- and assistant-teacher positions were filled by teachers who remained for the duration of the year. This class contained several assertive, articulate, and boisterous children who dominated most of their peers. These children presented new challenges for Martin, whose contact with peers had previously been limited to family members and children who attended their church in Birmingham.

Initially, Martin was painfully silent, at times appearing to be frightened of both peers and teachers. The teachers thought him extremely shy, and they tried to comfort him and encouraged him to talk. This was a difficult task, however, and early on he often responded to questions by casting his eyes downward and perhaps whispering a response. Occasionally, tears would flow. Ms. Wilcox in particular took pride in her ability to gradually bring such children out of their shyness, and she showed patience and determination as she worked with Martin one-on-one throughout the spring. She also kindly but directly questioned him during group activities, and as he gradually gained confidence in these situations it became apparent Martin was one of the most academically capable children in the class.

Martin's participation in peer interaction was minimal, and he was only a peripheral participant in nearly all mentions of him in Bill's field notes. Despite this, he did make progress toward greater social comfort. Early on, he involved himself only in quiet activities such as puzzles or crafts, or doing household tasks in the family area. He stuck to the task at hand and rarely contributed to other children's conversations. For example, in mid-March, Martin, Ramone, and Dustin were seated at a table making collages. The other boys' conversation was animated and wide-ranging as they discussed Dustin's bad behavior, Ramone's relationship with his "girlfriend," and other children's use of "cuss words." Despite the spirited talk, Martin said little or nothing, and this was typical of his early participation.

As time went on, however, he began to join other children in more physical play. In mid-April, Martin entered the block area where two boys were playing battling Ninja Turtles. He first stood off to one side and was ignored. But when a teacher called one boy away from the area, the other introduced an activity in which large blocks were spread out and the object was to jump from one to the other. Martin joined him enthusiastically, and both enjoyed placing the blocks farther and farther apart to increase the challenge of the game.

A third episode in mid-May was captured on videotape. Martin again joined other children in the block area, this time with no initial period of hesitancy. Jerald—who talked loudly and animatedly—directed LaKeesha and Martin in building a house, and soon introduced the threat of an alligator and a shark trying to enter.

Screaming frantically about the great danger, Jerald encouraged the others to work with him to fortify the house against the attackers, and Martin was soon feverishly helping the others keep out the threatening agents. A problem arose, however, because Martin (perhaps not understanding Jerald's excited instructions) kept demolishing the walls of the house. Jerald soon called to a teacher that "Martin keeps messin' up the house," and Martin then began to cry. Jerald appeared very sympathetic and concerned, but Ms. Wilcox then called Martin out of the area, and he left without hesitation.

Martin had made no verbal contributions to the activity, while Jerald produced nonstop commentary and LaKeesha laughed and screamed throughout. At one point, however, Jerald turned to Martin and asked, "Do you live in a house?" "Yes," Martin replied, and they returned to their construction. Jerald's interaction with Martin, and his sympathetic response to his tears, was typical of the children's reactions. They included Martin in their play when they easily could, and occasionally asked direct questions but otherwise did not push for greater involvement. They also did not tease or insult him, as was common among these children. Rather, his classmates seemed sensitive to his painful shyness, and they altered their normal style with this apparently in mind. For his part, it was clear from Martin's frequently wide-eyed expression or his cocked head that he watched and listened to his peers very carefully, though he rarely spoke.

Martin never became outgoing during his time in Head Start, and he never participated in the playful banter of the children. But he did make clear improvements and by the end of the year responded readily to direct questions from teachers and peers. His tears were less frequent, and he appeared to enjoy his time at the center.

Denise was well aware of Martin's painful shyness. Although he had always been reserved, the problem had worsened with their move. Denise felt Martin's increased shyness stemmed from their family difficulties and from her own uneasiness. However, she also saw improvement by the time the school year was over: "I really can see where he did open up, and I think it helped take his mind off a lot of what happened." She was thankful for Ms. Wilcox's work with Martin, which she felt was responsible for differences she saw in two church performances—one at Easter, the other in early June. In the first, "he got up there and would not say a word." In the second, "he had two parts, and he was the loudest, clearest thing you ever heard."

Although it was never apparent in the classroom, in each of our four interviews Denise expressed concern about Martin's temper and the anger she feared he harbored. For example, in our first interview she noted that "I get frightened when I think of the anger that he has built inside. If one of the children approached him in a fightin' manner, how he would react?" Denise hoped he would find ways to release bottled-up anger that might otherwise have serious consequences. She also characteristically added, "I guess he gets a lot of anger from me, 'cause I stay angry a lot."

Like some of the other mothers, Denise was amazed by Martin's teachers' reports of good behavior. In addition to being concerned about his occasional displays of temper, Denise complained of Martin's lack of obedience and his overboisterous play around the house. Martin's very different behavior at home and school came up in each of our interviews. In our second interview, for example, she said simply that "it's like I don't know the child that they're talkin' about."

I spent considerable time with the Washington family, and Martin did indeed behave differently at home. However, by my standards I never saw especially bad behavior. Martin and his siblings liked to climb and jump on the furniture, and they seemed to take advantage of their mother's distraction during my visits and would push the limits. I also observed Martin's tendency to pout and whine when he felt ignored, left out, or picked on. But I never saw the anger Denise so worried about, never saw him defy her requests, nor did I hear him speak to her disrespectfully. Denise once summed up her hopes for Martin by insisting, "I just want him to be a good young man, a *gentle*man. Like we used to have, a good, honest, young gentleman." Although he was certainly less reserved at home, what I saw of his school behavior was consistent with her wishes.

Following Through on Head Start Gains

When Martin began kindergarten the following fall, Denise was pleased and proud that he could attend her own "alma mater." The school was conveniently near to both their own home and Denise's aunt. Martin went to the aunt's house after school, and she helped with his homework. Denise appreciated her aunt's involvement in Martin's care and schooling, and she later recalled that the same woman had "helped us with our homework" when she and her sisters were young.[4]

Along with Cymira, Martin attended the full-day Follow Through kindergarten classroom. Like Rhonda, Denise was pleased with both the teacher and the program. She felt "blessed to get him in this" program, and similarly "blessed" to have Ms. Roth for Martin's teacher. She praised the teacher's patience, then continued: "Even if her students are real bad . . . she has a way of saying something nice even about that bad thing they are doing. And it's hard for me to do that. Sometimes I think, well, what would Ms. Roth say? What would she do? 'Cause she has a way of turnin' them around."

Denise's comment about Ms. Roth's way of "saying something nice even about bad" behavior and somehow "turning [their behavior] around" was consistent with the Head Start teachers' styles. Ms. Roth's talents dealing with the challenges presented by her students were clear, and our limited observations in her class suggested both devotion to her students and her ability to bring out their strengths while gradually extinguishing their problematic behavior.

Extinguishing bad behavior was not, however, an issue with Martin. Like the Head Start teachers, Ms. Roth worked throughout the year to increase Martin's self-confidence, hoping he would become comfortable displaying and developing his considerable academic talents. When I asked her to "evaluate Martin's overall performance" and describe his "strengths and weaknesses," Ms. Roth immediately responded, "Martin's real quiet." She described efforts to encourage his participation that were reminiscent of Ms. Wilcox's strategies the year before. "You kind of have to pull things out of him," she said. "He knows, but you gotta give a little extra. . . . When I do point-blank ask him, he responds always in the correct way."

Ms. Roth's patience and determination to "pull" and "give a little extra" were facilitated by the small class size and full-day schedule made possible through the Follow Through program. It was easy to imagine Martin's needs being neglected in a more typical kindergarten classroom, especially since he displayed no behavior problems that would have demanded attention.

We then briefly discussed Martin's academic performance and his mother's involvement. Ms. Roth's comments demonstrated Martin's growing competence in academic matters, and were highly consistent with Denise's reports and with our observations.[5]

K: How about his academic performance?

T: Excellent. Just excellent. His handwriting, his papers, are just neat, almost to perfection. He's not really perfectionist, I would not classify him there, but it leans towards that. You know, he's very precise, and a excellent listener. He has good listening skills.

K: OK, and again, how would you characterize your relationship with Martin's mother?

T: Oh, we have a good relationship, she comes in, and we visit and talk and we really have a good relationship, um-hmm.

K: And how do you feel she is about encouraging him to do well and//

T: //Oh, I think she does, yes. From all indications, homework-wise or whatever. But she was a little amazed when I said I didn't have any problems with him. When we had our conference in the fall, she just couldn't believe that Martin didn't misbehave. But he's very patient, and just doesn't get involved in negative situations.

The tendency toward perfectionism that Ms. Roth noted is something we observed in other children as well (particularly Jeremiah and Zena; see Corsaro 1995 and Corsaro and Rosier 1992). Denise worried that "I hope I don't push them so hard they turn from it," and we shared the concern that at some point overzealous encouragement of academic excellence could become counterproductive (as did Jeremiah's kindergarten teacher in chapter 2). However, though she found it worthy of comment, Ms. Roth did not believe this was a serious problem.[6]

I came away from the interview with Ms. Roth feeling Martin had steadily progressed toward the self-confidence that his talents warranted. While his experiences in educational settings were helping him progress toward social competence, he was also gaining and refining his literacy skills in contexts other than school. This certainly was true of his family environment, where Denise worked diligently (though she felt less than adequately) to encourage development of academic skills. In addition, church activities also contributed to Martin's growing educational competence.

One Sunday in August 1991, my daughter and I attended services at two different churches with the Washington family. Denise was agonizing over her pending decision to leave the Baptist church where her extended family had worshiped for decades to join an Evangelical Biblical congregation. A week earlier, Denise had described the all-black Baptist church as "stuffy" and unable to meet her spiritual needs, while the church she was considering was more open, informal, and expressive, and Denise was pleased that the congregation was also racially integrated.[7] She much preferred the latter church, but leaving the former was complicated by relatives' resentment of her desertion of the institution that had long served the family. Denise invited me to attend services and observe the differences myself, and I gladly accepted her offer.

Contrasts between the two services and congregations were striking, and although the Baptist service was livelier than mainstream white churches I attended in my youth, it was much more sedate and formal than other black churches I visited over the course of this study. The Evangelical service, on the other hand, was lively and informal, the music was modern and engaging, and the congregation was much more involved and excited.

More relevant to the current discussion, however, were the many ways both churches encouraged literacy and connected church activities with reading. Martin showed me around outside the Baptist sanctuary, and he proudly read the inspirational posters that papered the walls. During the Bible-reading portion of the service, he asked his mother to follow along the text with her finger as he listened and tried to read it. This was the same church where the children attended Bible school that summer, and also where they went for tutoring during the school year. Though such emphases were less apparent at the Evangelical church, literacy development here was encouraged through lessons in Sunday school, and also the prominent display by overhead projector of scriptures sung before the service began.

The Washington children's academic efforts were therefore reinforced by their participation in formal religious activities. I also knew Denise read to her children from the Bible on a regular basis, and this too served to reinforce the practical value of education. Finally, on more than one visit to the Washingtons' home, I observed the children engaged in role-playing activity that Denise called "playing church." Much like the more common "playing school," this involved preaching, taking up collections, spirited singing of gospel music, chanting, and reading from religious materials.

Choosing Religious Education

Denise was very pleased with Martin's first year in public school, but she knew his experience had been enhanced by the Follow Through program. After its demise, Denise sought an alternative arrangement to traditional public school classrooms. I knew Denise felt strongly about the absence of religion in public schools, for she often made comments like "We lost out somewhere, and I am a firm believer it was when they took prayer out of school."

Since their move north, Mandy's father had been paying the "Catholic rate" tuition for her to attend a Catholic junior high and high school, while Denise worked off the difference by cleaning at the school each week. It was, therefore, no surprise that Denise would choose Catholic school for her younger children when she was presented with that opportunity.

What was somewhat surprising was Denise's choice of an all-black Catholic school, given her discomfort with the extensive segregation of Indianapolis. During our fourth interview, Denise thought back on why she had chosen the school. Her decision had been rushed by time constraints, and she had acted on the recommendation of a cousin who was pleased with the education her daughter received there. More important, "the main reason I put 'em in there is spirit," she said, noting that public schools did not reinforce the religious values she tried to stress at home. Finally, she added that "they need to learn about prejudice," and Our Redeemer personnel taught children to deal with such difficult situations through prayer: "They teach them to pray for this, pray for that. And that's what I try to teach 'em at home." The continuity of values and emphases between home and school helped ease her concerns about academic shortcomings, as did evidence that her children took these teachings to heart.

Denise was unhappy with the segregation of everyday life in Indianapolis, but she may have felt the all-black school would provide her children with tools for interpreting and coping with this unfortunate situation. Our Redeemer placed great emphasis on teaching its students the history and culture of African Americans, and this was a required curriculum component at even the earliest grade levels. The hallways were lined with pictures of influential blacks, and a large portrait of a black bishop was the first thing visitors saw upon entering the school. One evening my family joined Denise's at a program celebrating Black History Month and Martin Luther King Jr.'s birthday. While I expected a typical children's performance (that is, simplicity, many errors, and at least a somewhat tedious and dull program), the sets and costumes were elaborate, and the children performed complex skits almost flawlessly. One fifth-grader stole the show with a powerful rendition of King's "I have a dream" speech that brought tears to my eyes as well as to those of many others in the packed auditorium.

Martin did well at Our Redeemer, and both he and his sister consistently earned honor roll status. Denise felt Martin had also become more comfortable with social aspects of school. Several times she described comments he made about other children, and she laughed and told me that "there's a little girl in the class, and they're supposed to be close friends." There were problems as well, however, because Martin's teacher had left the school with little notice in late November. Before she left, Denise said, the teacher "was always really praisin' him a lot about his work and behavior." When we met for our third interview in December, the school principal was sharing responsibilities for Martin's first-grade class with a man who taught computer classes to all grade levels, while the search for a new teacher was in progress.

Denise believed the original teacher had had little ability to deal with unruly students. She had visited the class for an afternoon and "noticed there wasn't control in the class like it should have been." Denise felt the teacher's inability to control the students had been "holdin' Martin back." Thus although she was concerned that "it's like we're startin' all over at the beginning," she hoped a new teacher would better manage the children and therefore be better able to meet Martin's needs for more challenging work.

Late in April I interviewed Ms. Garfield, who took over Martin's class when students returned from their Christmas break. She was a very expressive and articulate black woman around fifty, who had considerable teaching experience in a variety of school settings. She told of her dreams of opening an academy for African-American boys, and she talked at length about the "mission" of Our Redeemer, and about many issues specific to educating black students. This fascinating interview lasted nearly two hours and was the longest teacher interview I conducted.

Ms. Garfield knew of Denise's concerns about Martin's behavior, but felt these were unwarranted. In fact, Ms. Garfield believed Martin "was almost too good." I was pleased to hear, however, that Martin was "beginning to talk a little more," and she occasionally had to tell him "to stop talking or go back to your seat." Ms. Garfield offered further evidence that Martin was developing greater social ease and confidence, and perhaps his shyness was subsiding.

Like all his teachers before her, Ms. Garfield was impressed with Martin's academic abilities. "He's a very good student," she said, who "understands more than the basics." His skills, she noted, were apparent "across the board"—in math, reading, social studies, and so on. Like his mother, Ms. Garfield was concerned Martin was not being adequately challenged. She believed Martin might be better placed in an accelerated class, but since Our

Redeemer had no such offerings, she tried to meet his needs in her classroom. She planned to give Martin and two others "extra work . . . to challenge him. Because if you don't challenge them, they start slipping back. . . . And I don't wanna lose him."

Ms. Garfield qualified her high praise by noting some additional concerns reminiscent of Ms. Roth's remarks a year earlier. She noted Martin's apparent expectation that he make the very best grades, win every contest, and receive every award, and she then elaborated: "I think he's gonna be his own worst enemy, because I think he's going to put a lot of pressure on himself. And I think his mother will have to be careful that his push for excellence is at a normal rate, and not where it becomes a pressure, something more destructive than good. . . . We know it's gonna get difficult, and he needs to know that when you've done your very best, that's all that's expected. . . . He becomes easily frustrated if he finds something he has to struggle with. . . . And I don't want him beginnin' to think I have to live up to this image that I always have to be right and I always have to be the top."

She added that "I don't think [his mother is] doin' it to him so much as it's Martin's opinion of himself. I think her expectation is you do your very best, and you behave." While I tended to agree that Denise did not expect perfection, I felt that— like Amy with Jeremiah—Martin's increasing perfectionism surely reflected to some extent his mother's push for excellence. For her part, Denise recognized she might be walking a fine line between encouragement and paralyzing pressure. But she felt so strongly about her own rejection of educational pursuits that she dared not risk withdrawing the pressure.

Ms. Garfield knew Denise was worried her husband might not be able to afford the half-tuition at Our Redeemer the following year, and she talked of the reception Martin might receive if he had to enter a typical public school classroom at this point:

T: . . . I would like to see him stay in a setting like this, because in all honesty, unless it's a very understanding teacher, and especially a white teacher, he would have the ability to turn teachers off. Because the way he approaches things, he approaches them with confidence. And I have seen this happen with some of [the] black girls, where they have had this from a early age, and I have seen it destroyed.

K: They think it's like cockiness or something?

T: Right. I still have a person that's not speakin' to me today, because . . . she described a kid as smart-alecky, I says, no, he's defending his honor. I says, isn't that what teachin' is all about? You teach them how to think, but now you don't want him to think? She said he was bein' smart-alecky, bein' disrespectful. . . . He wasn't gonna back down. I think Martin would back down, because his mother has taught him that kind of respect. And so he needs an environment that encourages him to think, to reason, and to bring out his ideas. If he's not in that kind of environment, I think he will not be assertive enough to challenge.

Two years earlier, Martin had been so immobilized by fear and shyness that he could barely speak in a classroom setting, and it was striking to hear he had progressed to a point where a teacher could express concern that he might display too much confidence as he approached his schoolwork. At the same time, Ms. Garfield worried he still lacked the personal confidence to stand up to a hypothetical teacher who might attempt to break him of a (misinterpreted) assertive stance. In addition, Ms. Garfield's insight into what she believed was many teachers' reactions to black children's "defense" of their "honor" provided much food for thought. Could such processes help explain conflicts between Zena and Ms. Majors, Sheila and Ms. Jackson, or Ramone and Ms. Parsons? Ms. Garfield also suggested that many black children respond to a teacher or classroom situation by rolling their eyes and affecting impatience, and teachers interpret this as "talking back." In fact, Ms. Garfield said, "A lot of times when I'm upset with myself, that's how I respond because I don't want anyone to see I'm embarrassed. Because, in this community, you never show embarrassment, you show a toughness, like I don't care. But I really do care."

Back to Alabama

Denise did keep both Martin and Monique at Our Redeemer the following year, and their younger sister, Melanie, joined them there as well. Although she continued to worry that Martin was not adequately challenged, Denise was comforted by knowing this school reinforced her own values. As she had said long ago in our first interview, "I believe in education, but if a person doesn't have the right type of character to go with it, what are you even goin' for?" To compensate for Martin's unchallenging classwork, Denise began to introduce new material at home, including using her daughter's fourth-grade math book as a source for problems. And Martin continued to do exceedingly well in all areas, receiving As and occasional Bs on report cards.

Daniel and Denise continued to work through issues in their marriage, and he began to visit quite often. As early as December of

Martin's second-grade year, Denise considered returning to Alabama. Despite Daniel's impatience, however, she decided that "I wouldn't do that to the kids, just rip them off of school like that." But the following summer, Denise and the five children rejoined Daniel in Birmingham, three and a half years after their hasty departure. Within a year they had moved again, this time to a large city in Ohio. Denise was pleased with the transfer because it allowed her to maintain the ties she had (re)built in Indianapolis. She reports quite regularly that all is well: the children—especially Martin—are doing very well in the public schools they attend, and they are happy to be living with their father and enjoying a more economically comfortable existence. And she assures me her relationship with Daniel is solid and good, and she is happy to be with him.

CONCLUSION: DENISE'S COMPETENCE

Martin's narrative is surely a success story, and his movement through the early years of schooling was a pleasure to observe. Despite the traumatic events that brought him to the Head Start center, thereafter his family and school settings meshed remarkably well and together encouraged dramatic personal development. Within three quite different settings, Martin transformed himself from the most painfully shy child I had ever seen into a confident student and increasingly social young man.

When children involved in this study changed schools, the discontinuity often created difficult challenges that at times undermined their previous achievement and positive adjustments to schooling. For Martin, however, school changes appeared to provide a continuity of emphases on parental involvement, social skills, and individualized attention that served his needs exceedingly well. For this, Denise deserves much credit for recognizing and acting to secure available opportunities. Only a small number of Head Start graduates were enrolled in the Follow Through program (that is, eighteen), and Denise acted quickly to take advantage of this program she hoped would continue to encourage the progress he'd made during his half year in Head Start. That year, Ms. Roth's Follow Through classroom fit Martin's needs quite well, and her special attention encouraged great social and academic gains. The following year, when Follow Through was eliminated, Denise again took advantage of a special program to act on her misgivings about typical public school arrangements. Although she was not entirely pleased with Our Redeemer, the steady progress

Martin made in this setting was clear, and he appeared well on his way to exceptional achievement.

Throughout these years, Denise worked diligently to ensure that Martin's school and home contexts supplemented, accommodated, and reinforced one another. Denise, of course, would argue that God guided her decisions on Martin's behalf and He deserved the credit for Martin's success. I, however, see things differently. In fact, since our earliest acquaintance I have been puzzled and fascinated by what I perceived as the contradictory role of religion in Denise's life. On one hand, her faith provided her both strength and comfort in the face of great turmoil and challenge in her life. As was true for many families involved in this research, Denise's church participation also provided her children with alternatives to neighborhood playmates, and church sponsored programs enriched their lives.

On the other hand, I saw a darker side to Denise's religiosity. Garbarino, Kostelny, and Dubrow have referred to religious ideology as a "paradoxical resource," providing critical support but also serving to "truncate moral development" if held to with "fanatic intensity" (1991, 383). As was true for Annette, however, Denise seemed to offer her children many opportunities to develop and express their own opinions, and she was adamant that they not judge others. But in Denise I see a different religion "paradox," of which I find no mention in the literature. That is, as I observed all her self-sacrifice, innovative strategies, and thoughtful planning for the future, I was continually startled by her routine negation of her own efforts. Instead of taking pride in her accomplishments, she attributed all good fortune to "the grace of God," crediting herself only for negative events or shortcomings.

Denise, however, was determined that her children not suffer the same lack of confidence and self-esteem that she recognized in herself. The growing confidence Martin displayed is yet another testimony to both Denise's monumental efforts in the face of great obstacles, and her clear parental competence.

11

COMPLEXITY AND CONTRADICTIONS: CONSTRUCTING HOPE IN DISCOURAGING ENVIRONMENTS

M any patterns are apparent in the lives and experiences of these nine families; the families share common environments, common concerns, and common socialization tasks and strategies. However, the complexity and diversity of the family lives within which these patterns are constituted is great. The task for this chapter, then, is to synthesize the various themes and patterns developed in the individual narratives into a composite picture, summarizing patterns apparent in the families' home lives, linking these with patterns in the children's school lives, and tying these discussions, finally, to the extant literature. I begin with perhaps the most obvious characteristic the mothers share, and that is their common orientation toward their children's schooling.

HIGH VALUATION OF EDUCATIONAL ACHIEVEMENT

All the mothers display very strong valuation of education and intense desires for their children's high achievement in school. They believed it was through such achievement that their children might realize more prosperous and satisfying lives.

The high hopes these mothers had for their children's educations are not surprising, given consistent findings from other studies. Black parents have traditionally placed great value on their children's education. Since the Civil War era, black parents who themselves have most often been poor and undereducated have viewed education as their children's most likely route out of poverty, and have gone to great lengths at considerable personal sacrifice to secure it (Anderson, 1988; Slaughter and Epps 1987). Several recent studies (Alexander and Entwisle 1988; Stevenson, Chen, and Uttal 1990; also see MacLeod 1987) indicate that black parents tend to be more encouraging of and have higher expectations for their children's educational careers, to value education more highly, and to be more likely to teach their children basic skills prior to school entry than their white counterparts.

The mothers in this study consistently displayed high aspirations for their children's educational careers, and they employed an impressive array of strategies in support of those aspirations. Direct strategies aimed at promoting their children's academic achievement included in-home teaching of academic skills, purchasing or constructing educational materials, involving children in library or tutorial programs, and seeking out alternatives to traditional classrooms. Other strategies focused more on instilling values and encouraging attitudes the mothers believed would help keep their children motivated and interested in schooling.

RELIANCE ON NETWORKS OF SUPPORT

The mothers were involved in complex and interdependent networks, and the critical importance of these supportive networks for mothers' ability to consistently provide for their children's well-being is clear. This family feature is also among those most often noted in the literature on black families. These extensive, cooperative "domestic networks," which often include both kin and nonkin, have typically been viewed as a functional adaptation to the limited economic opportunities and discrimination they have historically faced (see Stack 1974; see also Martin and Martin 1978, 1986). Dodson (1988) argues that kinship ties are strengthened by minority status in a hostile society, and the "importance and pervasiveness" of extended-family support networks among blacks is well documented (Taylor et al. 1992, 16).

In addition to their importance for black families' economic viability, domestic support networks positively contribute to children's development of academic, language, and social skills (Slaughter and Epps 1987; see also Heath 1989), and to adults' psychological well-being and personal happiness (Taylor et al. 1992; see also Ellison 1990). McAdoo's research (1978, 1986) examining black families' use of extended-family networks is especially important because it demonstrates the prevalence of this pattern at all socioeconomic levels, thus implicating the importance of cultural norms. Numerous scholars have argued that the roots of these norms are traceable to West African traditions (see, for example, Nobles 1988; Sudarkasa 1988; Taylor et al. 1992).

The families in this study made extensive use of support networks in meeting the challenges of their daily lives. Even the most financially secure mother (Evelyn) relied on and was a primary member of a close-knit extended family network that was critical for her ability to act on her child-rearing values. This study included three-generational households, families who utilized both permanent and temporary informal adoption arrangements (see Collins 1991b; Minkler and Roe 1993; Stack 1974), and households that contained unrelated adults. More generally, these families continually participated in and benefited from the exchange of material, practical, and emotional support with nonhousehold relatives and friends. Managing these complexes of relationships can also be stressful, however, and in addition to the critical support they provided, it was also clear that participation in such networks at times complicated everyday life in these families.

Strong support networks facilitated most mothers' ability to cope with the challenges they faced. But for several mothers (Marissa, Harriet, and Tasha), networks were unstable, underdeveloped, or overextended. Marissa and Tasha were both somewhat estranged from their families of origin, and both harbored ill will toward their mothers. Both also took considerable pride in their ability to do without the support of extended-family members, but, especially for Marissa, it seemed clear they were at times distressed by this state of affairs.[1] The experiences of these two mothers were in line with a quite recent trend evident in the literature. That is, there is growing evidence that in the most disadvantaged, dangerous, and alienating neighborhoods, support networks are breaking down and low-income black families are becoming more isolated (Collins 1991b; Cook and Fine 1995; Heath 1990), compared to the kin networks found by Stack (1974) and others in the past.

Harriet's situation was different—she received a great deal of support from both kin and nonkin, but her circumstances were often so dire, and her parents and others had already provided so much, that she had exhausted many of her network resources. In addition, Harriet was rarely in a position to reciprocate, and thus could not legitimately seek assistance while also maintaining her own sense of dignity and worth. Instead, Harriet's family at times went without basic necessities—that is, food and shelter—when she either could not bring herself to ask, or network members could not provide for the needs of this very troubled family.

In addition to having the least viable networks, Marissa, Harriet, and Tasha were the mothers of children who experienced the greatest difficulties in school. Coincidentally and somewhat tragically, these three children—Zena, Sheila, and Tamera—were all bused during their first-grade years. The busing of these children further isolated their mothers from actual or potential sources of support they might have found within neighborhood schools. In fact, Tasha and Marissa both demonstrated their willingness and ability to seek assistance from neighborhood school personnel during their children's kindergarten year, while Sheila's sitter had acted as an advocate for Harriet and Sheila at the school Sheila attended for kindergarten. When these children moved to more distant schools, both they and their parents became more isolated from support sources.[2]

CONCERN OVER NEIGHBORHOOD INFLUENCES

A third characteristic the mothers in this study shared was grave concern over the potential negative influences of their neighborhoods on their children. Except for Annette (who—at the start of this research—felt her children were too young to be influenced by the drugs, crime, and despair evident in their neighborhood), all the mothers expressed tremendous fears that they would be unable to protect their children from the undesirable and threatening aspects of their low-income urban communities. Parental strategies for protecting children from negative community influences and dangers have also recently received much attention in the literature (Anderson 1994; Cook and Fine 1995; Furstenburg 1993; Garbarino, Kostelny, and Dubrow 1991; Jarrett 1997), and this study is exceptional in finding intense concerns among parents of such very young children (but also see Anderson 1994). In the literature, the most commonly noted tactics of parents are monitoring and isolating children, often severely restricting or prohibiting entirely their interaction with neighborhood peers. Several families in this study exemplified this strategy, but typically in something less than its most extreme form. While all the mothers expressed concern about both negative peer influences and life-threatening violence in their communities, these families varied in the extent to which they restricted their children's neighborhood activities. Some mothers prohibited or closely monitored all or nearly all neighborhood interaction, but others were considerably less restrictive. Mothers' biographies appeared more important in shaping these strategies than objective neighborhood conditions or parental concerns and values.

Another protective strategy families used was seeking out alternative—especially church-related—activities where children could interact with peers in organized, adult monitored setting (see Rosier and Corsaro 1993; also see Furstenburg 1993; Jarrett 1997). By pursuing such activities, the mothers demonstrated awareness that peer interaction is an important element of their children's socialization. As Garbarino, Kostelny, and Dubrow (1991) and Furstenburg (1993) argue, denying children opportunities for such interaction with peers can have serious developmental consequences.

EMERGING FATALISTIC ATTITUDES

The mothers' perceptions of threatening neighborhood conditions surely contributed to the emerging fatalism apparent in their discussions about their children. Collins notes that "the pain of knowing what lies ahead for black children while feeling powerless to protect them" is a fact of life for black mothers (1991a, 135). She thus suggests that feelings of "powerlessness" or fatalism are rooted in knowledge, not in character flaws. This fact commonly goes unacknowledged by researchers who have examined "externality" among blacks and other social groups. Although "fatalistic attitudes" or an "external locus of control" is a prevalent theme in the literature on blacks, most studies fail to consider the appropriateness of such orientations, or to examine individuals' active resistance of processes they nonetheless feel may be outside their control.

A great many studies have portrayed low-income blacks as "fatalistic" and "externally" oriented, especially low-income black students (for reviews, see Banks et al. 1991; Lefcourt 1972; also see Gecas 1979 for an assessment of the evidence that social class is negatively related to locus of control).[3] Externality has been described as a "self-perception as an inactive pawn of fate" (Lefcourt 1972, 22), and it is argued that such perceptions "should result in a minimum of effort to achieve and a lack of interest in achievement-related pursuits" (Lefcourt and Ladwig 1965, 380).

Findings from quantitative studies strongly suggest the mothers in this study have a triple status that puts them "at risk" for such perceptions and attitudes. That is, they are low-income, black, and female (female subjects have also repeatedly been found to be more external than males). And like quantitative researchers, I have also seen in the mothers what we have called a "creeping sense of fatalism" (see Corsaro and Rosier 1992).

In initial interviews during the summer prior to their children's entry into public school, all mothers expressed great expectations for their children's academic achievement. They saw their children as well prepared and enthusiastic about learning. Yet over time, a variety of factors—including time and financial constraints that prevented them from securing basic as well as enriching opportunities for their children; insecurity over their own abilities to adequately assist their children and frustration over children's resistance to their help; structural features of the schools such as half-day kindergarten programs and mandatory busing; and mothers' perceptions of teacher characteristics, especially perceptions of racial bias—all contributed to a tempering of initial high expectations, and to emerging fatalistic attitudes among some mothers concerning the likelihood their own efforts could foster their children's success and mobility.

In addition, while the mothers involved in this study demonstrated clear motivation to provide their children with environments that encouraged commitment to education, they felt extremely challenged and frustrated by neighborhood characteristics that seemed to oppose their efforts. As their children aged and made more, and more insistent, bids for independence and freedom of movement, mothers feared their children's greater vulnerability to drugs, crime, and other negative influences. They often felt powerless in the face of powerful neighborhood forces, and the contribution of neighborhood dynamics to mothers' development of fatalistic attitudes cannot be overstressed.

RECOGNITION OF SOCIAL REPRODUCTIVE PROCESSES

But perhaps the most powerful impetus for mothers' emerging fatalistic views was their recognition and consideration of social reproductive processes. It was striking how many of these mothers sadly acknowledged fears their children would follow in their footsteps and repeat their own regrettable missteps. Marissa recognized parallels between her own experiences with homelessness and unstable family relationships and her mother's similar situation when she was young. This was coupled with Marissa's matter-of-fact anticipation that her own children would experience similar hardships. Rhonda reported fears and tears as she contemplated the great promise she saw in her daughter while understanding that her mother "saw all the same things in me." Tasha had the insight that parents' negative words and behaviors "plant something" in their children, which is all too easily reproduced in the next generation. In addition, several mothers lamented the difficulty of maintaining control over children once they reached the teen years, and they drew on memories of their own youths to construct these expectations for the coming rebelliousness of their children. All these instances speak to the burdensome sadness—and sense of futility—that insight into reproductive processes can apparently generate.

Despite their fears that they would be unable to effectively interrupt such processes, the mothers did not give up under this tremendous weight. The mothers' active resistance of fatalism was a directive force in their lives. Rather than succumb to the reproductive processes they feared might seal their children's fates, they instead enacted creative strategies aimed at breaking the cycles they identified. These included, first and foremost, all the various actions the mothers took to encourage their children's academic skills and motivation (for example, direct instruction in basic skills; frequent expressions of educational values and the use of cautionary tales to underscore benefits of education; involving children in extracurricular activities; identification of role models). Other strategies were focused on shaping children's interpretations of life in their own communities and the possibilities available elsewhere.

I want to repeat that while other studies employing different methods also uncover fatalistic leanings among such parents, it is rare for researchers to consider the origins or reasonableness of such attitudes. It is also typically assumed these attitudes are translated into inactivity and "a lack of interest in achievement-related pursuits" (Lefcourt and Ladwig 1965, 380). However, this study indicates the translation of attitudes into practice is considerably less straightforward: although such attitudes were in evidence, they were actively resisted through strategies intended to interrupt reproductive processes and defy fate.

CONTRADICTORY SOCIALIZATION GOALS

Furstenburg (1993) argues that in anomic inner-city neighborhoods, parents must be "super motivated" and "exceptionally competent" at seeking out opportunities and monitoring their children in order to protect them from undesirable outcomes like delinquency and violence, school dropout, or teen pregnancy. He and others (for example, Clark 1983; Jarrett 1997) note that parents in such neighborhoods must be vigilant about restricting their children's interaction in tempting, exciting, and dangerous environments. But, as Garbarino, Kostelny, and Dubrow (1991; also see Franklin and Boyd-Franklin 1985) stress, isolation tactics carried to extreme can have serious detrimental effects on children's development of social competence. For example, they note that "prohibiting children from playing outside for fear of shooting incidents" denies opportunities for social interaction and athletic play, and "a very restrictive and punitive style of discipline in an effort to protect children from falling under the influence of negative forces, such as gangs," may actually encourage them to become more oriented toward violence and aggression as the way to control situations (1991, 379). The authors stress that parents must balance their desire to protect children with recognition of the importance of providing children with opportunities for social, intellectual, and moral development. Such a balance, however, is not easily achieved.

I noted in several chapters that mothers at times appeared to have contradictory socialization goals (see chapters 2, 4, 7, and 8). As was so often the case, Rhonda expressed this most clearly and succinctly. She said, "I don't want 'em to be rough, but I don't want 'em to be wimpy either. I don't want 'em to be takers, and I don't want 'em giving everything, you know what I mean? . . . Try to work yourself in the middle so you have room to tilt over."

Rhonda seemed most consciously aware that simultaneously keeping children safe from harm while also encouraging their independence, autonomy, and personal growth required complex socialization strategies. Her uneasy resolution of the dilemma was to accept her children's exposure to the "street" ways of her neighbors, and encourage them to be knowledgeable, competent and savvy participants in interaction with all variety of individuals they encountered (also see Anderson 1994). At the same time, she encouraged Cymira and her brothers to believe in both their potential to achieve better lives, and their ability and right to "use their own heads" rather than blindly following others' direction.

Collins has argued that apparent contradictions in the socialization practices of black parents may represent attempts to teach and instill a "delicate balance between conformity and resistance," in hopes of ensuring the "physical survival" of their children on the one hand, while also encouraging them to challenge and transcend various obstacles they will undoubtedly face (1991b, 54; also see Cook and Fine 1995). Although the dilemma of balancing concerns for children's safety with concerns for their healthy, normal growth and development was brought out most starkly in Rhonda and Cymira's narrative, similar concerns were expressed by most other mothers. Features of individual mothers' biographies, as well as mothers' variable access to support resources, influenced the parenting tactics they employed in coping with this dilemma. Mothers whose networks provided them with easy access to alternative peer groups, and those who recalled their own mothers' successful use of isolation strategies, were more restrictive of their children's neighborhood activities.

Despite their differences in actual practice, however, the mothers unanimously agreed in principle on the importance of encouraging autonomy and independence. This was true for even the most restrictive and controlling mothers, Amy and Evelyn, who appeared to hope their sons would learn to make good, independent decisions, but were unwilling or unable to grant them the freedom necessary to practice those decision-making skills.[4] Also regardless of their differential practice, when mothers noted their valuation of self-reliance and independent thinking, they typically also stressed that children must learn to be respectful and considerate of others when asserting opposing opinions, challenging rules or directives, or making other bids for independence.

Studies of black families have presented a mixed picture regarding encouragement of autonomy and self-direction on one hand, or obedience and conformity on the other. Some researchers have argued that black families tend to emphasize obedience to authority and conformity to external rules (see Gibbs 1990; Silverstein and Krate 1975; also see Kohn 1969). Ogbu (1980), however, has noted that this emphasis was more common prior to the civil rights movement, and represented parents' attempts to prepare children to cope with the realities of overt racism and discrimination. In contrast to the emphasis on conformity reported by others, Lewis describes a "high valuation for personal uniqueness" and "non-conformance within bounds" as typical in black culture (1975, 222; also see Heath 1989; Young 1974). There is also evidence that children "hav[ing] their own heads" (Heath 1989, 368), and "expressive-individualism" (Boykin and Toms 1985) are highly valued. Other studies that have noted black parents' encouragement of early independence and self-reliance have stressed that children are expected to take on responsibility and adultlike roles at young ages (Ladner 1978).It was this early, adultlike responsibility that Tasha sadly remembered from her own childhood and hoped her children would be able to avoid, while Harriet was proud that Sheila seemed willing and able to take on many adult responsibilities.

The confusion apparent in the literature regarding black parents' strategies and objectives concerning autonomy versus conformity is indicative of the complexity of the socialization tasks that black families confront. Ogbu's well-known assertions that black parents must prepare their children for competency in two qualitatively different and often contradictory worlds are widely accepted by other scholars (for example, see Boykin and Toms 1985; Harrison et al. 1990, Holliday 1985; Spencer 1990). As a result of these dual-socialization tasks, Boykin and Toms argue, "there is no obvious straightforward resolution of what it means to be an 'adequate' adult . . . and the potential complexity attendant to black child socialization is simply overwhelming" (1985, 34). These researchers speak of merely preparing children for interaction and competency in both white and black worlds. When one adds to this the world of the "street"—which is clearly a third world, not synonymous with black culture—parents' socialization tasks become even more complex. Despite this complexity and the lack of consensus concerning what constitutes adult adequacy, the mothers involved in this study are in agreement about the importance of decency and respectability.

Although surely every mother had greater hopes and dreams for her children, Evelyn's declaration that "all you really want is for them to turn out decent" captured the most basic wish that underlay many of the mothers' efforts. This goal is achievable even if mobility goals prove not to be. If children turn out to be good, decent individuals (or, as Denise expressed her wish for Martin: that he be "a good honest young gentleman") who spend their lives struggling within familiar confines of poverty and hardship, so be it—mothers can still take comfort in having raised them right and respectable. The goal of decency and respectability provides mothers with additional motivation to continue striving even if forced to recognize the unlikelihood of attaining mobility goals. Yet even this most basic goal may be threatened by the seemingly contradictory goal of teaching children to safely negotiate their environments. As Anderson (1994) points out, even families with very strong decency orientations must school their children in how to act and how to survive on the perilous streets. The threat is, of course, that this tactic may backfire, as children thus schooled may adopt as their own the street values they've necessarily come to understand.

Thus it appears that both mobility and moral goals that mothers set for their children exist in constant tension with goals of safety and survival. And socialization strategies practiced in the service of these goals—that is, the encouragement of autonomy and independence on one hand, and restrictiveness and insistence on obedience on the other—exist in uneasy opposition to one another as well. One final socialization pattern I observed appears to help mothers—and in turn, children—make sense of and integrate the many great, and often contradictory, demands that weigh so heavily on their shoulders.

WHAT MOTHERS MUST DO: CLAIMS OF FAMILY DIFFERENCE

Ogbu has observed that despite parents' many admonitions concerning the advisability of hard work and perseverance in educational pursuits, children learn "through the actual texture of life in the home and community—that even if [they] succeed in school they may not make it as adults in the wider society" (1988, 177). It is, indeed, difficult for parents to combat the constant negative messages children no doubt decipher from the "texture of [everyday] life." But combating these messages is clearly what mothers must do if they hope to see their children excel in school and experience social mobility out of poverty. It is also difficult to combat the creeping fatalism that so many of these mothers displayed, especially when these notions of lack of control over the future are based on accurate assessments of their own experiences and the experiences of others around them (and, for some, the experiences of their adolescent children). But again, combating these fatalistic views is precisely what they must do in order to continue striving on their children's behalf.

Parents like these mothers who live in depressed and oppressive neighborhoods and who face restricted opportunities are compelled to find ways to set themselves apart from others, else resign themselves to the inevitability of outcomes that are so common among their neighbors. One of the most powerful tools at these mothers' disposal for combating both their own and their children's feelings of powerlessness is the routine evocation of claims of family difference. Such claims enable continuing belief in some modicum of control over destiny. The logic that underlies and compels belief that one's own family is different from and superior to others' is quite simple—if families are different from the majority of others, they can then hope and expect their children to avoid the human tragedies they observe with regularity in their communities. But if, on the other hand, mothers judge themselves and their families as essentially the same as other community members, then they can expect only similar outcomes. This latter possibility is clearly to be avoided, for it suggests the futility of hope for a better future. In the face of incessant negative information that mothers receive about typical outcomes for people in their communities, the only psychologically comfortable position to take is that other families are inferior and ill equipped to meet the challenges that raising children presents.

Several other researchers have reported findings similar to these mothers' claims of family difference. For example, Jarrett discusses families' creation and maintenance of a symbolic "ideology of distinctiveness, often based on families' [own] purported respectability" (unpublished). She argues this can be an important tactic for protecting children from negative community influences and encouraging what she calls "community-bridging outcomes." In a study of several low-income Philadelphia neighborhoods, Furstenburg (1993) reports that so-called "resourceful" and "super-motivated" parents often encourage their children to feel different from and superior to their neighbors. Anderson (1994) also describes how parents in the crime-ridden, low-income neighborhoods he studied stress their own "decency," and contrast their values and habits with the "street" values of other families. And finally, in an earlier work, Nobles (1976—described in Nobles 1988) argued that the "provision of a family code" was a common strength of black families that helps members to interpret, manage, and respond to problematic situations.

The strong and unanimous belief in one's own family's superiority I observed in this study is in part a manifestation of other strongly held convictions. Like most Americans, the mothers involved in this research believed they now—as opposed to when they were children—lived in a meritocratic society where the quality and quantity of one's efforts are rewarded accordingly, in a just world where people get what they deserve. Mothers continuously communicated this belief to children, encouraging them to work hard and behave well in school in order to realize rewards of high achievement, good grades, and praise and appreciation from parents and teachers. And further, mothers repeatedly stressed that these positive school outcomes would translate into children's eventual realization of goals of social mobility; rewards would reflect inputs. Likewise, the mothers applied the "just-world hypothesis" (Lerner 1980) to their own lives and practices: If they could strive mightily and well to keep their children safe and encourage their achievement, they would be rewarded with their children's eventual mobility out of poverty and into the relative affluence of mainstream America. The alternative belief—that life is not fair—would inspire the fatalism and resignation these mothers strive so to resist.

So claiming—and believing in—family difference and superiority becomes an important routine that permits the maintenance of hope in the face of great evidence of others' hopelessness. It allows individuals to make sense of negative information about their group (race, community, income group, and so on) that they continually receive both from their own casual observations and from mainstream media sources, in a way that does not implicate them. Routinely setting oneself and one's family apart from seemingly similar others thus allows maintenance of self-esteem in the face of persistent messages of group pathology, and also provides impetus for action rather than despair. But routine beliefs and claims of family differences may have potentially negative effects as well.

I earlier described my initial meeting with Rhonda Craft, but I have not yet acknowledged the fear I felt as I waited for her to arrive at Davis Park. In truth, I was startled to discover that despite preferred self-concepts to the contrary, I was more than a little afraid. And as much as I would have liked to think otherwise, what I was afraid of was poor black people in inner cities and public housing projects. A lifetime of encounters with public discourse, popular media, journalistic accounts, and sociological studies had ill prepared me for interaction with these mothers and members of their networks. These encounters had also ill prepared me for the decidedly middle-class values and concerns they would exhibit, and for the extent to which I would identify with both their biographies and their child-rearing dilemmas and practice.[5]

In *Slim's Table*, Duneier (1992) constructs a persuasive argument that both journalistic accounts and sociological studies have collectively produced a distorted portrait of "the black community in terms of crude distinctions between 'respectable' black middle and upper-working classes, now supposedly departed from the inner-city scene, and . . . that segment of black society popularly known as the 'underclass' " (134).

Duneier argues that while classic ethnographies have succeeded in challenging many inaccurate stereotypes of urban black males, the "collective enterprise" has failed to "capture" the more "respectable" type of ghetto dweller (1992, 148). This is true, he argues, primarily because such studies have focused on segments of the black population that are most visible, selecting samples "based on pre-existing, popular images" (1992, 147). According to Duneier, stable working-class and working-poor inner-city blacks have received little attention from sociologists and journalists—who move quickly in and out of neighborhoods—and the "respectable masses" have been essentially ignored.[6]

In addition to their purposefully limited contact with neighbors, stereotypical portrayals of low-income black families constitute the bulk of the images and accounts that families who live in these communities see and hear, and must digest and make sense of. It should come as no surprise when these families respond to this information by constructing similar stereotypes, or "moral stories" (Stacey 1990, 225), of their own about the mostly faceless neighbors who share their communities. It should also be no surprise, then, to find they in turn routinely make claims that set their own families apart from the majority of these others.

While not surprising, these processes should be observed with some alarm. Claims of family difference can produce potentially positive effects. Notions of family difference provide the mothers with psychological comfort, hope, and a sense of control over their children's futures. Notions of family difference also may encourage an achievement orientation in children, promote self-esteem in both mothers and children, and strengthen ties and commitments to extended families. Finally, mothers' repeated claims about their families' difference, and superiority, provide children with a resource they can draw on to help them resist the many pressures and temptations that they face. These benefits support the idea that such claims and sentiments constitute an important resource for individual families and children, and other studies reporting similar findings among low-income urban black families also stress the benefits such sentiments provide individuals (Anderson 1994; Furstenburg 1993; Jarrett 1997; Nobles 1988). But this paradoxical resource may have quite negative effects on the larger communities in which these individuals reside.

The mothers who have participated in this and in other studies feel isolated from others who share their environments, but who they feel do not share their values or concerns. They look upon others with suspicion, and routinely withhold trust from, and avoid interaction with, their neighbors. But something is amiss here. Given this study's findings that all nine of these mothers felt so similarly different, and given similar findings in other studies as well, it appears the mothers are not as different and uncommon as they believe. It also appears their notions of family difference may effectively prohibit the realization of potential support from and cooperation with one another. And finally, it also appears such notions may make the possibility of collective action to improve their neighborhoods decidedly less likely. While notions of family difference may indeed be a positive resource for individual children, these same notions may actually contribute to the negativity of the environment they protect against.

Duneier argues that "without a consciousness of their own significance, the 'respectable' black masses cannot be harnessed to serve as an active force in maintaining stability within their own communities" (1992, 161). This seems so very true. As I listened repeatedly to mothers reporting their valiant efforts on their children's behalf, their strong values and admirable goals, and their beliefs they were alone in these things, I was amazed by their lack of awareness of others who were so much like them, and their lack of appreciation of "their own significance." While I derive some satisfaction in presenting the stories of nine families who are among the "respectable masses" Duneier claims have been ignored, I am unsure whether my satisfaction is warranted. Bringing knowledge to such families that they are not so different as they think might serve only to dash the hope that seems so critical for their continued efforts to shape and encourage better lives for their children.

BRINGING THE KIDS BACK IN

So far, this final chapter has neglected the children and their transition into schooling in favor of examining the mothers' experiences, interpretations, and practices. However, I began this research by asking questions about what happens to children's enthusiasm and clear promise, and I now return to this issue before closing. In part because data collection ended before the middle elementary years, when Head Start achievement gains typically begin to disappear, the answers are not clearly evident in these data.[7] Despite the inconclusiveness that must be acknowledged, there are certainly patterns apparent from children's school experiences that demand mention, and many of these can be linked to the themes I have delineated above.

For example, I noted the mothers' high valuation of educational achievement, and interviews with teachers and limited observations in classrooms suggest these children took this value very much to heart. With occasional exception (Sheila and Tamera during at least some portions of their first-grade years), they took pride in their work and showed great pleasure in their accomplishments. They were also certainly aware of the pleasure their achievement brought their mothers. For example, when Sheila deftly completed her delinquent work in a flurry of activity during one of her mother's severe illnesses, she demonstrated keen awareness that Harriet would be greatly cheered by good school performance.

Of course, as suggested in chapter 10, the mothers' push for academic excellence may have also contributed to the perfectionism we observed in some of the children (see Corsaro 1995; Corsaro and Rosier 1994). Not only Martin, but also, Zena, Alysha, and Jeremiah showed signs of such high expectations for their work that they were easily frustrated and hesitant to take risks when they encountered difficult material. And both teachers and mothers (for example, Ms. Sampsel in chapter 2, and Denise in chapter 10) expressed concern that the mothers' push for high achievement might have the unintended effect of spurring a rejection of academic pursuits in the face of standards that were impossible to meet.

Another apparent pattern is that busing seemed to have clear negative effects on the children's performance and behavior. At the start of first grade, three children (Jeremiah, Zena, and Sheila) were subject to mandatory busing to schools quite distant from the neighborhood schools they attended for kindergarten, and a fourth (Tamera) was bused to a distant school when her mother enrolled her in a special program. In three of these four cases, the children exhibited quite dramatic declines in both their academic performance and in their ability to produce acceptable behavior.[8]

These children's mothers tended to believe in the long-term objectives of mandatory busing (that is, desegregation of schools to increase opportunities for black children's achievement), yet they were frustrated by the immediate effects it had on their own and their children's lives. Marissa, Harriet, and Tasha had the least viable support networks among the mothers in this study, and the removal of their children from neighborhood schools also removed an institutional support they had demonstrated some willingness to call upon. Likewise, their children shared the mothers' insufficient networks, and the loss of supportive and familiar school personnel they'd become accustomed to likely exacerbated their difficulties as well. It is, of course, more than a little ironic that policy that theoretically was intended to increase opportunity instead in practice tended to diminish support for Zena's, Sheila's, and Tamera's successful integration into school culture and thus contributed to declining achievement for these children.

In children's perfectionist leanings, and in the negative impact of busing, we see two of the numerous ironies or contradictions apparent in the children's school experiences. Perhaps not surprisingly, their teachers at times characterized these children in contradictory terms—sometimes with startling clarity. For example, Ms. Weston, Alysha's kindergarten teacher, spoke metaphorically of her "bright" but "compulsive" and very "challenging" personality when she noted that "Alysha's like a double-edged sword." Alysha's significant academic talents were clear and not disputed, but Ms. Weston interpreted her displays of initiative as lack of self-control and her often stubborn stance as a sign of deep-seated emotional problems. Ms. Majors described Zena in a very similar manner. When I first contacted Ms. Majors to arrange an interview, she offered the opinion that Zena was "like the poem, the little girl with the little curl. When she's good she's very very good, and when she's bad, she's horrid." She then told me she'd concluded it was best "not to push Zena into something she doesn't want to do, because she's not going to do it." This "little girl's" bossy and stubborn behavior had a clear impact on the teacher's interpretation of her competence as a student and in addition may have inspired Ms. Majors to withdraw efforts to push Zena to excel.

Other teachers less explicitly suggested contradictions apparent in the behaviors and personalities of the study children. I noted that teachers at times feared that children's perfectionist tendencies might eventually end their active striving to achieve. In addition, several teachers discussed how children's behavior—especially too much talking, or wasted time spent brooding or sulking—interfered with their ability to complete work in a timely manner, or in a way that truly reflected their capabilities.

I have noted repeatedly that the mothers encouraged autonomy and self-reliance, and many of the children's so-called misbehaviors can perhaps be interpreted in this light. Too much socializing, stubbornness, rambunctiousness and lack of self-control, displays of temper, and occasional defiance of authority were all problems identified by the teachers, and all suggest these children were indeed coming to "have their own heads." It stands to reason that this should serve them well in various contexts outside school, where their mothers foresaw great need for children to think for themselves and stand up to negative peer pressure. But did the children's displays of autonomous thinking and behavior serve them well in schools? Most often, apparently not. It is another contradiction apparent in these children's lives that the tough self-reliance their mothers believed so necessary for survival seemed so unwelcome in their elementary classrooms.[9] These findings certainly lend support to Ogbu's (1980, 1988) and others' arguments that the complex worlds black children must negotiate demand the development of competencies that will serve them in a variety of settings. Unfortunately, these settings often call for different and, at times, contradictory skills and competencies, and children have difficulties adjusting their behavior to fit the particular settings in which they find themselves.

Part of the problem may lie in teachers' inability to understand and interpret the behaviors of students who are culturally dissimilar to them. Ms. Garfield made comments (chapter 10) about black children's confidence, their defensive stance when their behavior or ideas were challenged (which she called "defending their honor"), and their unwillingness to display embarrassment. Her observations of black children's styles fit well with the interaction we observed in the Head Start center, both between peers, and between teachers and children. The confrontational style the children used with one another was also evident at times in interaction with teachers, who responded in a similar manner with unrestrained teasing and direct commands. When teachers less familiar and less comfortable with such behavioral styles encounter a child's rolled eyes in response to correction, or stubborn insistence they have done nothing wrong, misunderstanding and overreaction seems likely to occur (Ms. Weston, Alysha, and the candy incident in chapter 3 is a case in point). Again, Ms.

Garfield's remarks on the importance of teachers understanding both the historical and cultural background of their students were insightful and provocative: "One of our children's problems . . . is teachers who don't know black children. It would be like if I went to teach your child (well, no, your child I could teach because that is who teachers are trained to teach). But say a poor white child, in Appalachia, I would not be prepared to teach that child. . . . I would have to understand the language, I would have to understand the mannerisms, I would have to understand everything about these Appalachian children."

Ms. Garfield makes familiar arguments, that teachers should be—but typically are not—well-versed on the cultural differences their students exhibit. Instead, teachers tend to be ill prepared to deal with children's behavior that falls outside the norm for white, middle-class students (see, for example, Heath 1983; Tabachnick and Bloch 1995). Evidence from this research supports this position. A simple observation underscores the point: Those teachers who described the greatest difficulties coping with the behavior of particular black students or black students in general (Weston, Majors, Jackson, Kemp, and Parson) were white teachers whose students were mostly white as well.[10] It seemed clear that greater familiarity with black children's styles of interaction was associated with greater understanding and tolerance for behavior that did not conform to expectations, or to white, middle-class norms.[11]

My interview with Ms. Garfield also illustrates another pattern apparent from our interviews with teachers. I asked Ms. Garfield to identify any "specific problems or strengths that either low-income children or African-American children bring to the educational experience that teachers have to deal with." Once again, her response showed both awareness of current issues in education as well as insight into potential sources of black children's frequent difficulties in school: "I think they bring the same things any child brings. I thinks it's how we as teachers see them. A lot of times teachers stereotype a low-income child, be it black or white, or they'll stereotype a minority child. Because society says they're not supposed to be able to do certain things . . . then those expectations aren't there. . . . Their mannerism might be different, the way they respond to something might be different. . . . [People] say the black male is a discipline problem, whereas when white males are doin' the same thing, it is bein' assertive! . . . So I think it's more the expectations of the teachers that is the problem."

Ms. Garfield argued strongly for the importance of teachers' expectations in shaping their students' experiences and achievement, and again, her arguments are hardly novel. Studies demonstrating the power of such expectations in elementary classrooms have alarmed educational researchers for quite some time and have inspired considerable research. Early influential studies include Rist's examination of a self-fulfilling prophesy of poor academic achievement set in motion by a first-grade teacher's low expectations for poor black children (1970, 1973), and Rosenthal and Jacobson's famous "Pygmalion" study of randomly chosen academic "bloomers" (1968). Both studies demonstrated the truth of W. I. Thomas's simple tenet: "If men [sic] define situations as real, they are real in their consequences." In the last several decades, it has become accepted wisdom that teacher expectations—which are translated into differential patterns of interaction with students—can have powerful effects on the success or failure those students experience.

I believe there exists within these data some evidence that supports arguments that race and social class do influence teachers' expectations for their students. But as a group, the teachers involved in this research—especially those with considerable experience working with low-income black children—were sensitive to the dangers of such stereotypical thinking. Many consciously worked to avoid such bases for their expectations. But these data suggest an interesting and rarely considered twist (for an exception, see Lareau 1987) on the simple argument that teachers' low expectations for poor black children contribute to an interactive climate that encourages children's conformity to these expectations. And that twist is the importance teachers place on parental involvement.

In recent years, parental involvement in children's schooling has received tremendous attention in the education literature, and it is viewed by both educators and researchers as essential for children's academic success (for example, see Epstein and Becker 1982; Lareau 1987; Slaughter and Epps 1987; Van Galen 1987; Wahlberg 1984). In her review of ethnographic studies that shed light on processes contributing to low-income black children's movement out of poverty, Jarrett (1997, unpublished) characterizes parents of successful children as active advocates of their children's interests who closely monitor school performance and involve themselves in school activities (also see Clark 1983).

The current focus on parental involvement reflects basic beliefs regarding the importance of parental attitudes and values, and it is generally agreed that parental involvement is crucial because it communicates to children parental values concerning the importance of education (see, for example, Robinson and Choper 1979; Valentine and Stark 1979). These values are thought to affect children's motivation to achieve in school, which researchers have long believed to be an important predictor of actual achievement (for example, see Lipset and Bendix 1962). As a general rule, then, parental participation and involvement is encouraged primarily because of its perceived ability to positively influence children's motivation to achieve (Epstein and Becker 1982; Lareau 1987; Seeley 1984; Wahlberg 1984).

Consider some comments about parental involvement made by teachers in this study. When I asked them directly to "describe the role of parents in encouraging their children's success in education," typical responses began with such statements as:

> I would say it's very important, and probably the earlier you can get parents to start to working with their children [the better]. (Ms. Sampsel, K)

> It's the pivot point—parent involvement—and that's what this school was based upon. (Ms. Weston, K)

> Extremely important. I think that if the parents don't encourage their children, more than likely the child is not going to put forth a lot of effort. (Ms. Nelbert, 1st)

> Ahh! The most important thing in the world! Without the parents' participation, you almost lose the child. . . , because parents have to provide the environment, they have to provide the incentive, for them to learn. (Ms. Garfield, 1st)

Several teachers introduced this topic on their own earlier in the interviews, typically in response to my request that they discuss the "most pleasing" and "least pleasing" aspects of their jobs. For example, Ms. Bancroft (Ramone's kindergarten teacher) identified "some of the parents that don't give a hoot" as among the least pleasing aspects. She noted the difficulty of getting parents to cooperate, and concluded that "parents just don't take time with 'em like I feel they should." The next year, Ramone's first-grade teacher responded similarly to the same question. Ms. Parson said that "the downside is . . . I don't see parents being involved with their children and being positive about school. . . . It's like ship them out the door and it's the school's responsibility."

Parental participation may be important for a variety of reasons, but its effect on teachers' expectations for students seems to me especially critical. In these interview excerpts, it is clear that teachers expect children of obviously involved and concerned parents to do well, while children whose parents' concern is not apparent are expected to "not put forth a lot of effort." Such comments were repeated over and over again by the teachers I interviewed, and I was struck by the underlying irony of the remarks.

The main reason teachers' perceptions of a lack of parental participation and concern may contribute to lower teacher expectations for the child is that teachers believe and act upon the idea that parents' values are conveyed to children, and in turn affect the children's own attitudes. Yet teachers were quite oblivious to the fact that their own attitudes about these matters—again, for example, "This student won't put forth much effort"—are similarly communicated to children through daily interaction and can be expected to have similar impact. Teachers' beliefs on this subject might not be particularly problematic if their perceptions of parental concern were always accurate. But as Marissa and Zena's narrative highlighted (see chapter 5), teachers' perceptions can be grossly inaccurate for a variety of reasons, and these false definitions of the situation can provide the foundation for a quite tragic chain of events.

The teachers I interviewed did not appear to lower expectations for low-income black students in general. However, they did seem to lower their expectations for children whose parents' concern was not obvious to them.[12] It was apparently those children—whose parents were not obviously involved and concerned—who the teachers involved in this study viewed as most "at risk" for failure in public school classrooms.

Swadener and Lubeck recently edited a volume intended to challenge the popular "at-risk" label: *Children and Families "At Promise": Deconstructing the Discourse of Risk* (1995). Essentially, the contributors to this collection argue that "at-risk" discourse represents a thinly disguised continuation of "culture of poverty" and "cultural deprivation" arguments. As such, labeling (or thinking about) low-income and minority kids and their families as "at-risk" places the onus of responsibility for their likely difficulties on their own overburdened shoulders and effectively shields from scrutiny systemic causes of school failure (for example, schools that are unresponsive to children's needs and cultures, and oppressive poverty that saps the strength of parents).

The pattern I have observed of teachers' lowered expectations for children whose parents they perceive as unconcerned fits with these authors' arguments about the discourse of risk. Even though one teacher—Zena's first-grade teacher, Ms. Majors—acknowledged that "I know there are reasons sometimes" for apparent lack of involvement, those "reasons" (for example, lack of transportation to a distant and unfamiliar school, and painful memories of their own failures in school settings) were insufficient to explain parents' perceived irresponsible failings (in this case, the teacher had "never met the mother," which "sent a signal" that Marissa was unconcerned). To this teacher, Zena was clearly at risk—not because the economic system failed to provide an adequate living for her hardworking parents, and not because the school system failed to consider her needs. Rather, Zena was at risk because her mother didn't care.

The authors represented in Swadener and Lubeck (1995) challenge educators to alter their expectations and instead begin to see and to cultivate the "promise" that resides within low-income and minority children. At the same time, they push us all to critically examine the structural conditions within which risks to these children and families are inherent. Surely children could only benefit from such alterations of perspective and definitions.

A FINAL IRONY

The complexity of these children's and their families' situations is, indeed—as Boykin and Toms assert—"simply overwhelming" (1985, 34), and the apparent contradictions and ironies are many and mind-boggling. One final and potentially critical irony requires discussion, and that concerns the mothers' repeated warnings about "street" alternatives to mainstream strivings.

The children involved in this study have always seemed somewhat old beyond their years, and their experiences with poverty and close proximity to crime, violence and despair unavoidably exposed them to adultlike concerns. Several of the mothers also purposefully provided their children with a good deal of adult knowledge in hopes of protecting them from potentially dangerous misinformation learned on the street. In addition, all the mothers told cautionary tales that warned their children of the regrets, sorrows—or worse—that would eventually befall them if they succumbed to the temptation of "street" alternatives.[13] Boys were warned to avoid gangs and violence, girls were warned to avoid early pregnancies, and both were cautioned about the dangers of drugs and the foolishness of dropping out of school. The mothers drew on their own experiences and the experiences of others to construct these cautionary tales, and they offered them with great regularity. Remarkably, such warnings were already in evidence when these children were barely five years old.

Where, then, is the irony in this? Perhaps these repeated cautions have the potential to encourage the opposite effect. Perhaps continual acknowledgment of such undesirable options makes their eventual choice more likely. Were Ramone's sisters' pregnancies encouraged by just such a process? It is possible that explicit and early knowledge about undesirable alternatives may increase children's propensity to consider and perhaps choose these alternatives. But as Anderson (1994) and the mothers in this study argue, such knowledge seems necessary to safely and successfully negotiate inner-city environments. So here, too, the contradictions with which parents and children must grapple are myriad and complex.

It is unreasonable to point the finger of blame at these parents (rather than at the larger environment in which they reside) and condemn their practice of schooling their children in the ways of the street. These women and their children could not afford the luxuries of silence, and the pretense that the world is safe. Cook and Fine note that "few parents haven't told 'white lies' to [their] children to allow them to believe in the safety of their worlds," but they urge their readers to: "Imagine a context in which you can no longer lie to your child because she hears shots out the window; where public institutions, your only hope, evince a strong ambivalence . . . toward you and your kin; where the most enduring public institutions are the prison and the juvenile justice system, and the most reliable economic system involves underground drug trafficking. . . . What kind of child-rearing practices would you invent?" (1995, 137).

A FEW POLICY IMPLICATIONS

The family narratives included in this book invite consideration of the often elusive linkages between "private troubles" and "public issues." Revealing such connections is, according to C. Wright Mills's classic work (1959), the special mission and obligation of sociology. Ethnographers and other qualitative researchers are often haunted, however, by their lack of control over interpretations and applications of their reported findings. While readers will no doubt—and rightfully—draw their own conclusions concerning social policy implications, the following seem clear to me.

Educational Policy

The issue of busing is one that stands out in many of the narrative chapters. Despite the problems it seemed to create for the children and families involved in this study, I am unwilling to take a stand against busing to achieve racial desegregation. Research indicates that attending desegregated schools is associated with modest achievement gains for black children when it occurs at young ages, and although desegregation does not produce similar gains for whites, no study has found a decline in the achievement of whites who attend desegregated schools. While overall short-term gains are relatively modest, long-term effects for blacks who attend desegregated schools are significant: They are more likely to finish high school and are more likely to attend college; they have higher GPAs in college and are less likely to drop out; in the South they are more likely to attend traditionally white universities; they earn higher incomes, and are employed in more nontraditional fields than blacks who attended segregated schools. Both blacks and whites who attend desegregated schools are more likely to work in integrated workplaces and more likely to live in integrated neighborhoods (for a review of desegregation research, see Stephan 1991).

While I believe these clear benefits of desegregation are compelling, findings from this study suggest that school changes in the early elementary years should be avoided whenever possible. When children enter initial school settings, they work hard to make sense of the situation and integrate themselves into the school and peer cultures they meet there. School changes that require young children to begin anew in culturally unfamiliar settings can severely upset their newly gained confidence in their ability to do well and get along with others. When new settings require new interaction skills, old habits—formerly successful but now deemed inappropriate—can be hard to shake.

The situation in Indianapolis seemed to encourage such a scenario. Since kindergarten was not mandatory, IPS did not provide transportation for kindergartners, and parents logically chose neighborhood schools. This strategy was not only convenient; it also reduced chances that children's schooling would be disrupted due to problems with transportation that are common for low-income parents. In addition, I saw no evidence that school personnel attempted to inform parents prior to kindergarten enrollment if and where their child would be bused the following year. If they did so, more parents might have chosen to enroll kindergarten children in the schools they would attend in first grade, for the sake of continuity.

Although the Select Schools program eliminated most forced busing, this reform did little to lessen the problem of school changes between the kindergarten and first-grade years. Busing remained unavailable for kindergartners, so parents who chose a school outside their neighborhood for first grade in effect also chose to uproot their children from the familiar school environment to which they had become accustomed. Since there was no guarantee parents' selections would be honored, attempts to transport kindergartners to schools parents hoped they would attend the following year would entail considerable risk.[14]

We have found that children leave Head Start excited and primed for the start of their formal school careers. They are ready to tackle new challenges and in most cases the Head Start program has contributed to feelings of self-confidence and agency. If these promising children—considered by many to be "at risk" for school failure—are to enter classrooms peopled with culturally unfamiliar peers, this is surely the time for them to do it. This also seems to be the time when the full-day schedule should be introduced.[15] The short-sighted, cost-saving tactic of refusing to transport kindergartners may lead to more long-term costs than it saves, in terms of lost educational achievement, increased grade retention, and perhaps lower lifetime productivity. Local school officials in Indianapolis and other similar cities would do well to consider these issues carefully and do away with this practice which seems so clearly counterproductive.

My arguments are not a condemnation of busing itself, but rather I suggest policies that encourage continuity in children's elementary school experiences. It is also clear from these data that, where busing of children away from neighborhood schools occurs, additional measures should be taken to facilitate parental involvement in and connections to the distant schools. These could include, for example, conducting parent-teacher conferences in the neighborhood school, and perhaps also developing a system of extension offices in neighborhood schools for encouraging and maintaining relationships with bused children's families. And all teachers—but especially those who teach in schools where children are bused from distant neighborhoods—need to reexamine their assumptions about parental involvement in general. Although parental involvement is associated with benefits for children, teachers should be extremely cautious about the attributions they make and the expectations they form when evidence of such involvement is not forthcoming.

Finally, we must do more to educate teachers and other school personnel about the family, neighborhood, and cultural backgrounds of the children they teach. When teachers seem insensitive to their students' needs and intolerant of their behavior, it is more than likely that they are merely ignorant of their shortcomings. As Heath's (1983) ethnographic study of language socialization in black and white low-income communities in the Piedmont Carolinas so clearly demonstrated, when teachers are given useful information about students' communities and families, their new understandings of the child-rearing values and daily practices of parents are translated into more effective classroom strategies that enhance children's success in and attachment to schooling.

National Policy in Support of Families

This is not a study of welfare mothers, and I will not linger over these points (but see Edin and Lein 1997). A striking observation must be made, however: those mothers who attempted to combine welfare and work, or move between welfare and work (i.e., Marissa and Harriet) were decidedly less able to construct secure and stable family lives than were those mothers who relied exclusively on AFDC (Rhonda and Denise). Marissa and Harriet both worked in the low-wage, traditionally female "pink collar ghetto" (Sidel 1992); Marissa in housekeeping and later retail sales, and Harriet as a nursing assistant. Both earned little more than minimum wage and they enjoyed no job security. Both found themselves and their children homeless at times, in both cases their own and their children's health was jeopardized when they lacked medical insurance, and both encountered an unsympathetic welfare system that— instead of applauding their efforts—made them suffer dearly when their efforts fell flat. As members of the working poor, both found the social safety net insufficient and much too slow to adequately protect them from unpredictable job losses or their own or their children's illnesses.

Rhonda and Denise, on the other hand, lived on meager grant awards, but these at least were dependable and assured from month to month. Both had good medical benefits, and Rhonda's low rent in public housing helped stretch the AFDC award. Both also occasionally supplemented their incomes through unreported contributions from relatives or their children's fathers, or through cleaning homes or watching other people's children (that is, they "cheated").

It is now somewhat well known that mothers on welfare are often better off than mothers who elect to enter low-wage and unstable jobs (see, for example, Edin and Lein 1997). Many policy-makers and political pundits contend that this suggests we must make welfare less attractive, or—as most recent reforms have guaranteed—simply less available. But this seems nonsense. The maximum AFDC grant in Indiana for a family of three in 1991 was $288—how much less attractive could it get? Surely the other logical conclusion is preferable and more sensible—make work more attractive for low-income mothers.

Harris (1996) argues that work is not the solution to the welfare dilemma—it is the problem. Women who work full-time all year should not earn wages that fail to bring their families over the poverty level. Women should not have to choose low-quality child care (or no child care at all) because they earn barely more than high-quality child care costs. The choice to work should not be accompanied by the threat of losing access to health care and the threat of becoming homeless when work unexpectedly ceases. Instead of reforming welfare, we should be reforming work. Low-income mothers shouldn't be harshly punished for doing what everyone says they should do. This country needs a humane system of social supports for all low-income families with children—working or not—that includes access to quality child care, health care, and housing. That recommendation sounds hollow in the present punitive political climate, but such entitlements would justify these mothers' beliefs in meritocracy and a just world, and anything less is surely a national shame that belies our professed concern for both children and equality.

We are all bombarded with images of young black male super-studs and hoodlums, immoral and irresponsible black "welfare mamas," and their uncontrollable children (see Gresham 1989). These images help to foster punitive attitudes among mainstream Americans who are disgusted and frightened by what they see on the nightly news, read in the papers, and hear from the lips of political candidates who attempt to outdo one another in the toughness of their stance. But we are also all seriously misled by these sources of common "knowledge." *It is perhaps the most impor-*

tant policy recommendation in and of itself to urge that politicians, jour-
nalists, and others who are in the position to manipulate public senti-
ment routinely acknowledge that the majority of families who populate
our inner cities, whose children populate our inner-city schools, are
respectable and decent.

The potential benefits of this message are substantial. Residents of inner cities are urged to organize and work together to
improve their communities, yet they are simultaneously told that
their neighbors are primarily dishonest and untrustworthy, lazy,
violent, and unscrupulous. And indeed, some are, but this segment
is able to "dominate public spaces" (Anderson 1994) in part
because their numbers are exaggerated by others for self-serving
interests. Awareness of "their own significance" (Duneier 1992)
and the values and concerns they share with their neighbors could
go a long way toward encouraging the "respectable masses" in
inner cities to put aside their distrust of their neighbors and work
together to take back and revitalize their communities.

In addition, the mainstream American public is increasingly
unsympathetic toward the problems of inner-city occupants, and
increasingly supportive of get-tough stances on such various issues
as education, welfare, and crime. Routine recognition of and
emphasis on the common decency and hard work of most families
who populate inner-city neighborhoods would surely encourage
more supportive, compassionate, and helpful attitudes. Current
popular ideological beliefs about the failure of helpful policies
notwithstanding, surely these are still the kinds of attitudes most
people would prefer to see exemplified in American social policy.

THE METHOD OF RELATIONSHIPS

The women and children represented in these pages have touched
and inspired me in ways I cannot adequately describe. I have
struggled with conflicting feelings of responsibility to research, versus responsibility to relationships and individuals, while writing
each of the narrative chapters. And through every stage of this
research, I have felt tremendous obligation to the women who
made it possible, obligation that at times immobilized me, as is
apparent from the lengthy interval between the study's conclusion
and the completion of this book. It is not, as Rhonda once suggested, an obligation to present these families in a positive light, or
to show only "something good about us." It is rather an obligation
to help others "know what it's like," and to demonstrate the diver-

sity—as well as the commonality—that exists among these inner-city families. Most of all, I've felt obligated to fairly and accurately portray the reality of these families' lives, and not "go for no stereotype."

Ruth Sidel has told her numerous readers that "statistics are people with the tears washed off." When we rely primarily on statistical portrayals of the poor—to teach our classes and to construct our own definitions of the world—we protect ourselves and our charges from the realization that poor people are "real people, very much like ourselves" (Sidel 1992, xxiv). Sometimes—and I would argue, much more often!—we need to see people with their tears still on them. And their hopes, their dreams, and all their other finery.

Rhonda once said that when she tried to explain this research to others in her network, they believed no good could come of it. They knew the portrayals that have dominated public discourse on low-income black families. I hope these same people, who know Rhonda and Cymira, could read this and conclude that it's OK.

.

Appendix

The tables in this appendix depict the study participants' neighborhoods, and the children's schools. The "Neighborhhod Characteristics" table employs 1990 Census tract data. Tract names are changed to indicate alphabetically if the family resided here at the study onset (A) or later (B or C); numerical identifiers indicate particular families. All tracts but C.7 are heavily majority black, and six of the twelve are over 90 percent black. All but one family lived in one of these overwhelmingly black tracts when the study began.

Many families in these communities owned or were buying their homes. Despite this suggestion of well-being, other figures suggest a more dismal picture. Many adults did not complete high school—in most areas over 30 percent neither graduated nor earned a GED; in several, fewer than half have high school credentials. Most black families in these areas are headed by women. The percentage of black families with incomes below poverty level ($10,860 for a family of three, $13,924 for a family of four, in 1991) is striking, and this official measure underestimates the number of families who experience grave financial difficulties (see Sidel 1992).

Official figures on labor force participation also underestimate those unable to secure viable employment. While the percent "unemployed" is less than 13 in all cases, adults "not in the labor force" exceed 40 percent in most tracts, especially in the tracts where families lived at the study onset (A tracts). It is not surprising, of course, to see low labor force participation among individuals who lack educational credentials and who are often without private transportation and/or phone service. As many as 18.5 percent of homes had no telephone (tract A.2), and 58.8 percent did not have access to a vehicle in tract A.9. Clearly, within tracts where participants resided at the study onset, poverty tended to be most severe, although there are exceptions.

The "School Features" table describes the schools attended by the study children for kindergarten and first grade. Three children attended full-day kindergarten classes that were in some sense "special." The other six children—like the majority of IPS kindergartners—attended only half days. This and other features of the classrooms and schools are summarized in the table. The top half of the table contains information on schools attended for kindergarten; the bottom half presents information on the six new schools attended by children for first grade.

Column 1 identifies the child and grade, and whether the child was bused. The second column connects the children with particular teachers, and here teachers' race and approximate ages are identified. In the "Location and Features of School" column, schools are described in terms of racial makeup and apparent income level. Schools with full-day kindergarten classrooms are identified, as are other special programs or features. The percentage of kindergartners (in 1991) who were black is also indicated. Since kindergarten attendance is not mandatory, IPS does not provide transportation, and most kindergartners attend the schools nearest their homes. Racial composition of these classrooms therefore tends to reflect the surrounding community.

The overall racial composition of the school, and the percentage of students receiving free lunch, are also depicted. Four of the eleven (public) schools were out of compliance with IPS desegregation orders that required 35 to 65 percent black student population. All but one child, Alysha, attended majority black schools in kindergarten, and three of the four children bused in first grade attended majority white schools, while the fourth attended a school that was 50 percent white. Finally, the percentage of students receiving free lunch suggests the relative poverty of the schools' families: well over half (in one case over 90 percent) in all but two schools in 1994 (the only data available). Exceptions were two schools that housed attractive special programs.

Appendix Table 1   Neighborhood Characteristics: 1990 Census Tract Data[1]

TRACT NUMBER[2]	% BLACK	% BLACK HOMES OWNED	% PERSONS >25 WITH <HIGH SCHOOL *	% BLACK FAMILIES FEMALE HEADED (W/CHILD <18)	% BLACK FAMILIES BELOW POVERTY	% BLACK HOUSEHOLDS WITH NO PHONE	NO VEHICLE	PERSONS ≥16 UNEMPLOYED	PERSONS ≥16 NOT IN LABOR FORCE
A.1	96.8	66.4	919/2078 (44.2)	203/363 (55.9)	19.4	7.7	17.2	246 (9.6)	1030 (40.3)
A.2	96.6	44.4	1181/2144 (55.1)	206/341 (60.4)	45.2	18.5	44.5	293 (11.2)	1155 (44.4)
A.3	98.0	45.1	502/1075 (46.7)	198/246 (80.5)	43.3	16.0	44.7	144 (10.7)	593 (44.2)
A.4B5	98.8	43.2	729/1679 (43.4)	335/443 (75.6)	48.6	11.3	36.8	275 (12.9)	919 (43.2)
A.5	73.3	57.6	511/2009 (25.4)	136/276 (49.3)	12.7	4.1	7.4	138 (5.4)	762 (29.6)
A.68**	NA	63.5	105/259 (40.5)	NA	NA	NA	NA	21 (6.5)	175 (54.0)
A.7C5	98.4	58.2	693/1767 (39.2)	195/320 (60.9)	26.5	10.2	29.4	166 (7.9)	823 (39.2)
A.9	93.8	36.3	443/634 (69.9)	47/74 (63.4)	32.5	16.9	58.8	54 (7.3)	434 (58.4)

Appendix Table 1 (Continued)

TRACT NUMBER[2]	% BLACK	% BLACK HOMES OWNED	% PERSONS >25 WITH <HIGH SCHOOL*	% BLACK FAMILIES FEMALE HEADED (W/CHILD <18)	% BLACK FAMILIES BELOW POVERTY	% BLACK HOUSEHOLDS WITH		PERSONS ≥16 UNEMPLOYED	PERSONS ≥16 NOT IN LABOR FORCE
						NO PHONE	NO VEHICLE		
B.3	89.6	19.6	950/1686 (56.4)	173/261 (66.3)	46.9	13.5	48.5	149 (7.2)	1033 (49.6)
B.4	86.4	18.5	877/2224 (39.4)	207/305 (67.9)	25.2	12.2	53.1	193 (7.3)	956 (36.2)
B.7	73.3	46.9	660/3492 (18.9)	290/722 (40.2)	9.9	7.1	14.6	281 (6.3)	956 (21.6)
C.7	45.7	***	728/3426 (21.2)	313/560 (55.9)	12.7	5.0	8.7	218 (5.2)	729 (17.6)

*"< High School" does not include persons with high school equivalency diploma.

**Only 452 individuals resided in tract A.68, and certain data were consequently not made available by the Census Bureau. Of the 196 households located in the tract, 137 (just under 70%) were black households.

***Data not available.

1. U.S. Department of Commerce, Economics and Statistics Administration, Bureau of the Census. 1990 CPH-3-179. 1990 Census of Population and Housing. *Population and Housing Characteristics for Census Tracts and Block Numbering Areas, Indianapolis IN MSA.*

2. Numerical identifiers indicate (1)Amy; (2)Annette; (3)Rhonda; (4)Marissa; (5)Harriet; (6)Tasha; (7)Samantha; (8)Evelyn; (9)Denise.

Appendix Table 2 School Features: Description of Teachers, Schools, and School Locations

CHILD (GRADE)	TEACHER (GRADE) RACE, AGE	RACIAL COMP OF SCHOOL* WHITE	BLACK	LOCATION AND FEATURES OF SCHOOL	**%STUDENTS RECEIVING FREE LUNCH
JEREMIAH (K)	SAMPSEL (K) WH, about 50	160 35.8%	287 64.2%	Low-income and working-class black neighborhood. Kindergarten 99% black.	73.6%
ALYSHA (K, 1)	WESTON (K) WH, Mid-forties CORBIN (1) WH, about 50	45	43	Small, alternative IPS school, stress language arts, community and democracy. Parents provide transportation. Full-day kindergarten (41% black).	28.4%
CYMIRA (K, 1) MARTIN (K)	ROTH (K) WH, about 60 NELBERT(1) WH, mid-forties	298 43.3%	391 56.7%	Site of Follow Through program. Low-income, primarily black neighborhood. Full-day kindergarten (79.3% black).	91%
ZENA (K) TAMERA (K) CHARLES (K, 1)	HILL (K) BL, mid-thirties HOLDEN (1) WH, mid-sixties	124 38.5%	198 61.5%	Another nearly all-black, low-income neighborhood. Kindergarten 96% black.	77.5%
SHEILA (K)	FULTON (K) WH, mid-thirties	169 35.6%	306 64.4%	Working-class, primarily black neighborhood, one-half day, traditional kindergarten (79% black).	62.8%
RAMONE (K)	BANCROFT (K) WH, about 50	57 17.3%	273 82.7%	Low-income black neighborhood. Kindergarten 98% black.	92.6%
JEREMIAH (1) (bused)	NORTH (1) BL, early thirties	144 68.9%	65 31.1%	Working-class white neighborhood. Kindergarten 12% black. Small class size accommodates temporary students from crisis care center.	68.9%

Appendix Table 2   (Continued)

CHILD (GRADE)	TEACHER (GRADE) RACE, AGE	RACIAL COMP OF SCHOOL* WHITE	BLACK	LOCATION AND FEATURES OF SCHOOL	**%STUDENTS RECEIVING FREE LUNCH
ZENA (1) (bused)	MAJORS (1) WH, early forties	275 68.1%	129 31.9%	Low-income white neighborhood. Kindergarten only 8% black	85%
TAMERA (1) (bused)	KEMP (1) WH, mid-forties	214 54.9%	176 45.1%	IPS Specialized program. Low-income black neighborhood. Student population balanced race and sex. Full-day kindergarten and g1 combined.	34.4%
SHEILA (1) (bused)	JACKSON (1) WH, late forties	113 50%	113 50%	Mixed-race, working–middle-class neigborhood. Kindergarten 30% black.	66.1%
RAMONE (1)	PARSON (1) WH, about 50	147 19.7%	598 80.3%	Working–middle-class, largely black neighborhood. Kindergarten 83% black. Academic talent classes, grades 1 and 2 combined.	57.7%
MARTIN (1)	GARFIELD (1) BL, about 50	# students unknown 100% black		Our Redeemer Catholic School. Student population 100% black. Curriculum stresses African-American studies.	NA

*These data reflect enrollments September 1991. From IPS Administration Building files.
**Data from September 1994, after "Select Schools" program was in place (data unavailable for earlier years).

Notes

1. Names of mothers, children, teachers, and schools have been changed throughout the book.
2. There are many social welfare programs (for example, school lunch programs, unemployment insurance, and subsidized housing in college dormitories), but the term "welfare" is almost exclusively reserved for AFDC, or Aid to Families with Dependent Children. Prior to the 1996 Federal Welfare Reform Legislation, AFDC was the main federal-state income support for poor families with children. There has always been much state-by-state variation in the amount of AFDC grants; in 1990 when this research began, the median state's maximum benefit for a family of three was $367 per month, while in Indiana, where this study was conducted, the maximum grant for a family of three was $288. Most families who receive AFDC are also eligible for and receive food stamps (which are spent like cash for groceries) and Medicaid (which provides health coverage for low-income families with children).

    AFDC was distributed in the form of a monthly grant check, which recipients used to meet housing, clothing, and personal needs. Any transportation or child-care costs were also paid out of the grant, although modest allowances for these items were added if the recipient was completing training or working. AFDC recipients who worked were permitted to keep only $50 of their monthly earnings; amounts above $50 were subtracted from AFDC and food stamp awards.

    Recipients were required to submit a monthly report verifying all sources of income, and all qualified expenses (expenses were not necessarily met by grant awards). Throughout the early 1990s, increasing numbers of AFDC recipients were required to complete education or training programs, or look for work under provisions of the 1988 Family Support Act. Failure to comply with these requirements could result in termination of the case. Good sources for further information on AFDC are Sidel 1992, 1996, and Edin and Lein 1997.
3. In these classes, I rely heavily on the arguments of B. Berger and P. L. Berger, 1983, *The War Over the Family*.
4. See the edited collection *Who Can Speak? Authority and Critical Identity* (Roof and Wiegman 1995) for an excellent portrayal of the issues and the discourse that structure this debate. Although this collection is authored and aimed primarily at literary critics, it has much to say to social scientists as well.

5. In 1996, the maximum AFDC grant in Louisiana for a family of three was $190 per month.

6. In 1996, the Republican-controlled Congress passed, and President Clinton then signed, a historic Welfare Reform Bill that did indeed fulfill Clinton's 1992 campaign promise to "end welfare as we know it." AFDC ceased to exist, replaced by Temporary Assistance for Needy Families (TANF). Three features of the law were particularly notable. First, welfare as an entitlement for poor families meeting eligibility requirements was eliminated. Instead, the federal government distributes block grants to the states; once these funds and additional state matching funds are distributed, eligible families with unmet needs are no longer entitled to assistance. Second, the federal legislation turned over much greater control of program rules and requirements to the states, which can develop their own innovative programs within rather broad federal guidelines. Finally, and most relevant here, new time limits stipulate that assistance can be received for no more than five years over a lifetime, and for no more than two years in a single stretch. Even if most states did not already disallow attendance at four-year colleges or universities, the "two years and off" provision effectively removed completion of a four-year degree from the list of acceptable education and training possibilities. See Cherlin 1998; Edin and Lein 1997.

7. As its name implies, the Head Start program was established to provide low-income children with a "head start" on their schooling. Founded in 1965 as part of President Johnson's War on Poverty, Head Start was touted as a program that would compensate for the supposed "cultural deprivation" that existed in the families of low-income—and especially black—children.

Unlike other "Great Society" programs, Head Start survived even the deep cuts of the Reagan era, and now appears to be permanently etched upon the nation's social policy landscape. In addition to its focus on preschool education, Head Start provides nutritional meals and snacks for children; health-care screening and social services for children and their families; a limited amount of job training for parents and some job opportunities within the program itself; home visits by teachers; and a parent involvement component that includes a role in local decision-making.

Although quite popular with both participants and policy makers, Head Start is a limited program that serves less than one-third of the country's eligible children. At least 90 percent of participants must live in families with incomes below the federal poverty level, yet there are not enough openings for even these very poor children. Most Head Start programs provide only half-day classes that meet just four days per week, and time needed to serve the required daily meal and snack typically cuts class time to well under three hours per day. While many believe Head Start's objectives include providing child care and thus encouraging parents' employment, its limited hours work against this possibility. In addition, other program features—including the parent component—also make it less workable and effective for employed parents. Since Head Start produces most lasting gains for children whose parents take an active role, working parents are often short-changed (see Zigler and Muenchow 1992).

Despite these and other problems (including a high adult/child ratio, low salaries, and high teacher turnover), Head Start provides children and families considerable benefits. I discuss these benefits at various points throughout this book.

8. Oakley argues that not only is "the goal of finding out about people through interviewing best achieved when the relationship of interviewer and interviewee is non-hierarchical," but this goal is also more likely realized when the interviewer is "prepared to invest his or her own personal identity in the relationship" (1981, 41). Investment of "personal identity" is especially important in longitudinal studies like this, which depend on participants' willingness to welcome the researcher into their lives time and time again. She argues further that "interviewees would not be prepared to continue after the first interview" if they did not gain some personal satisfaction from the process, and such satisfaction is most likely when reciprocal, honest relationships prevail. Such reciprocal relationships are based in part upon the interviewees' right to take active rather than passive roles in research endeavors.

Both Oakley and Cassell (1980) also maintain that researchers' presentation of authentic selves in interaction with subjects is methodologically as well as ethically sound practice. In addition to encouraging continued participation, researchers' willingness to answer questions honestly and to give other feedback—that is, their willingness to be themselves—clearly affects their ability to remain attuned to the unfolding discourse rather than self-consciously attending to the management of their own "front." Cassell's argument is essentially that interviewing practices that reflect excessive concern with self-monitoring and the presentation of a neutral or false persona (most likely done in hopes of reducing potential "bias") can seriously hamper both interviewees' ability and inclination to produce reports that actually reflect their interpretations of their daily lives, and the researcher's ability to interpret and respond to the ongoing interaction.

9. My experiences with single parenthood, poverty, and Head Start participation are of course not the extent of my biography. In fact, I have decidedly middle-class origins, and I grew up in a remote, and very white, town in Michigan's Upper Peninsula. Despite our differences, the most obvious of which was race, our common experiences nonetheless seemed to encourage the establishment of comfortable and open relationships between me and the mothers.

10. Data from the Head Start portion of the research include Bill Corsaro's extensive field notes, some notes of my own, and videotaped episodes of peer interaction at the center. I am grateful to Bill for the generous way he made these data available for my use. Interested readers should see Corsaro 1994, 1995, and 1997 for recent publications that draw on these and other data on children's peer cultures in a variety of settings. Corsaro's Head Start research was formally titled "Cultural Values, Child Care Policy, and Children's Peer Culture in the United States," and was funded by a grant to Corsaro from The Spencer Foundation.

11. This is clearly not a random sample, but it is generally representative (in terms of race, income, and household composition) of the families served by this Head Start center. The vast majority of children attending the center were black, as were all but one of the children (a Hispanic boy) in the classrooms we studied. Local Head Start officials estimated that between 91 and 94 percent of the children enrolled live in families with incomes below the federal poverty line, and eight of the nine families represented here met this criterion for participation. The diverse family structure and household composition represented here are typical of the variety of living arrangements black communities have traditionally relied on to provide children with secure home environments despite economic hardship.

Some would argue that this is an unusual and biased sample because, prior to their involvement in the study, these mothers demonstrated their motivation and concern for their children by enrolling them in the Head Start program. But while Head Start is voluntary, we estimated that approximately 50 percent of eligible children in the inner-city communities where these families lived participate in the program during the year prior to enrollment in kindergarten, and Head Start officials concurred with that estimate (given high rates of poverty, school dropout, and unemployment in the central township where these families live, the local Head Start program had targeted this area of the city as its top service priority). The mothers involved in this study should not be viewed as unusual simply because they chose to enroll their children; they are like half of all similarly situated families in their communities who do so.

12. The families and I remain in occasional contact, but my move to Louisiana several years ago has meant that this contact is infrequent and for the most part limited to cards, letters, and rare phone calls.

13. For example, during telephone conversations, I told mothers I was taking notes; I accepted several offers to dine with families both with thanks and with explanations that I was always glad for opportunities that would help me better understand their family routines; I visited churches after explaining that I hoped to gain insight into the role the church played in the family's life; while I gave one mother a ride to work, she described her happiness to have a "friend" who listened to her. I responded that I was glad she considered me her friend, but that she needed to understand I was always a researcher as well; and finally, one mother's teenaged daughter remarked once while her family and I were discussing the research, "Don't write anything I've said!" This quote represents the only time I have violated that command.

14. Corsaro accompanied me for about half the teacher interviews, and we completed the observations of first-grade classrooms together.

15. The first black high school in Indianapolis, Crispus Attucks, opened in 1927 and quickly became a center of the black community. It remained an important institution until its desegregation beginning in 1971, designation as a magnet school in the late 1970s, and

conversion to a junior high in 1986. Shortridge High was located near many black neigh-borhoods, and after desegregation of Attucks, it became the school of choice for many black students. Later desegregation efforts effectively led to the closing of Shortridge as well, in 1981. The loss of the two black high schools in rapid succession produced much anger among members of the black community, and also surely contributed to the isola-tion and alienation of many black students.

16. Court-ordered desegregation of IPS actually began in 1968, when desegregation of teach-ers occurred. The first trial addressing student assignments did not begin until 1971. The presiding federal judge, Judge S. Hugh Dillin, ruled that by setting attendance zones based on racial composition of neighborhoods, IPS was guilty of de jure segregation. He ordered the system to begin desegregation of students through both busing and redraw-ing of attendance zones. Although the system repeatedly appealed Dillin's rulings, they grudgingly began busing white and black students to achieve desegregation in 1973.

17. The most hotly contested aspect of the Indianapolis desegregation case centered around Dillin's 1975 order that nine suburban townships participate in IPS's desegregation. Dillin's decision was based on his findings that both the state and the townships were complicit in IPS segregation because of their roles in the 1969 Uni-Gov Act, which had transformed Marion County into a consolidated metropolitan government, expanding corporate boundaries of Indianapolis to include surrounding townships. Common law dictated that when corporate limits expanded, the limits of the school city would expand as well. However, the state legislature responded to suburban residents' protests and exempted Indianapolis from this law. After Uni-Gov consolidation, IPS boundaries remained unchanged.

Because of the high percentage of IPS students who were black, Judge Dillin believed an IPS-only remedy was unworkable. Redistributing blacks throughout the city would merely place all schools at or near the 40 percent minority enrollment that was consid-ered the tipping point for white flight from urban schools. In light of these considera-tions and the Uni-Gov history, Dillin added the suburban townships as defendants in the case. After a series of appeals by IPS, in August 1975 Dillin ordered immediate trans-fer of black IPS students to township schools. Another lengthy round of appeals delayed transfers, but the opening of the 1981–82 school year finally saw the busing of 5,600 black IPS students to six suburban townships. Busing of IPS students to the township schools continues today, at state expense (no suburban students are bused to inner-city schools).

With township schools educating over 6,000 IPS students each year, the large drop in enrollments led to closure of numerous IPS schools. Among them was Shortridge High School, and this loss reinforced blacks' perceptions that it was they who would bear the burdens of desegregation of a system that had victimized them for decades.

In addition to the black students annually bused to the suburbs, over 20,000 white and black students are bused within IPS's own borders. During the years this research took place, debate continued over the impact on students and communities, and over who is financially responsible for the ongoing desegregation efforts. The state had repeatedly denied IPS funds similar to those provided township schools for remedial classes, counseling, additional staff, magnet programs, and busing (*Indianapolis Star* 17 May 1989, 5 August 1989), and the system was financially strapped. In addition, stu-dents' involvement in school activities, their parents' ability to participate in their edu-cation, and their identification with distant schools both suburban and within IPS, all continued to cause concern as the 1990s, and this study, began.

Interested readers should consult Aquila 1980; Blee 1991; IPS 1981; Metcalf 1983; Warren 1994; Warren and Vanderstel 1994 for further detail on IPS system developments.

CHAPTER 2

1. This is the first of many interview excerpts. Presentation of excerpts follows certain con-ventions. A dash, —, indicates a self-interrupt, or an abrupt break in the continuity of an utterance. Occasionally excerpts include words or phrases enclosed in parentheses, which are approximate translations, while empty parentheses indicate a portion of the speaker's turn was inaudible. Two forward slashes (//) indicate an interruption of a speaker's turn.

I use the ellipsis (. . .) to indicate that a portion of the speaker's turn has been deleted, and I want to stress here that such editing has not been taken lightly. When readers first encounter verbatim transcription, they are often startled by the numerous errors, starts and stops, self-interruptions, and so on, that occur in normal speech. I believe much is learned about the negotiated nature of everyday interaction, and the meaning of exchanges is often clearer, when presentations of speech remain unedited. But practical issues of brevity and readability take precedence here. Although I have made many deletions, I've never changed participants' words, and I have worked to remain true to their intentions, actual words, and communication styles. I have also at times decided to retain errors and interruptions, for example, that seemed particularly important for understanding what was said and meant.

2. As the 1992–93 school year ended, children brought home forms for parents to select schools for the coming year. Parents were asked to choose the Quick Pick option—which automatically enrolled students in schools within newly drawn, neighborhood-sensitive districts—or prioritize three other school choices. In line with the federal judge's orders, the school system reserved the right to disregard parents' choices if necessary, to safeguard against resegregation that would occur if most parents chose the most convenient neighborhood schools. IPS documents indicated that for the 1993–94 school year, over 95 percent of students who returned their selection forms were enrolled in their parents' first-, second-, or third-choice schools—including over half who chose the Quick Pick option (these and other IPS documents, which were graciously provided by system personnel in the Administration Building, were typically without titles of any kind, and can be cited only as "IPS unpublished documents").

Transportation mix-ups and some lack of foresight by the plan's administrators made for a rocky start of the Select Schools program in the fall of 1993. The following year things went more smoothly, and satisfaction with the school system generally increased among its constituents. Resegregation remained a concern, however, as parents followed expectations and enrolled their children in nearby schools, eliminating busing when possible. While Select Schools did not begin without problems, it clearly responded to concerns of Indianapolis parents, among them several mothers involved in this research. As coming chapters illustrate, mandatory busing during the first-grade year contributed to significant difficulties experienced by several of the children. After Select Schools, all these children's families chose to enroll them in schools in or much nearer to their own neighborhoods.

3. An article in the *Indianapolis Star* dated 15 February 1973 (published midway through Amy's sixth-grade year) described desegregation plans for the upcoming school year. At that time, enrollment at Amy's elementary school was reported to be 99.3 percent black. The "white school" Amy was bused to was truly white—its student population was less than 1 percent black the year prior to transfers.

4. Annette Lareau reported that attempts to "customize" children's schooling by influencing teachers' practice or standards were much more common among the middle-class than among the working-class white parents she examined in *Home Advantage*, 1989.

5. Ms. North's comments (e.g., "when I was teachin' all black kids, I was a lot harder on my class") were similar to statements made by the other two black teachers who participated in this study (Ms. Hill, chapters 5, 7 and 9; and Ms. Garfield, chapter 10). These teachers seemed more demanding of their students, and placed less emphasis on social skills and more stress on academic achievement, than most white teachers I interviewed.

6. In IPS, "honor roll" designation requires all Bs and/or As in academic subjects, with the exception that one C is permitted.

CHAPTER 3

1. Judith Stacey (1990) describes similar uneasiness in the early stages of her relationship with a fundamentalist Christian woman whose family was the focus of extensive ethnographic study.

2. Throughout this research, I was occasionally startled by examples of mothers who worked hard, sacrificed personal interests, and devised innovative strategies to advance their children's success, and who then downplayed or even negated their own efforts by crediting successes or good fortunes to "the grace of God." See chapter 10 for more on this observation.

3. While it was I and not Annette who introduced the theme of leadership here, this was

not as leading as it may seem. Rather, I was tying our conversation to Annette's remarks on the phone a few days earlier, and she quickly made this topic her own, as indicated by her rapid agreement (//interruption) and elaboration when I brought it up.

4. It is worth noting here Annette's apparent comfort in stating her own beliefs with emphasis—she said "ladies should not"—even though I was sitting there wearing pants! At other times, she made similar comments about smoking, another behavior condemned by her church that she knew I was guilty of. Such remarks certainly speak to validity issues, as do Alysha's activities during this interview, which I note below.

5. While the issue of religiosity in black families' lives is generally treated very positively in the literature (for example, Hill et al. 1989; Poole 1990; Taylor et al. 1992), Garbarino, Kostelny, and Dubrow note that religious ideology can be a "paradoxical resource" for low-income urban black families. Strong religious beliefs can provide critical support, yet these authors warn that when such beliefs are held to with "fanatic intensity," they can serve to "truncate moral development" (1991, 383). While religious affiliations can help children and their parents make sense of violence, racism, poverty and other sources of stress, they argue that ideology that discourages parents from providing their children with open interactive climates may be counter-productive in the long run.

6. I never directly asked mothers their incomes. Many, however, provided much information about this without prompting. Annette on occasion referred to her family as "low income," and I've noted her disclosure that her family could not afford social outings. Additional information came from the children. During one interview, when Michael reminded his mother that they needed money for choir uniforms the next day or they would have to drop out, Annette's despondent "Yes, I know, we'll talk about it later" made clear the money was not available. In December 1992, Alysha, Melinda, Mary, and I had lunch at a Wendy's during a break from church. When I asked the girls if they were getting excited about Christmas, Alysha made a bored face as she told us all she got last year was a coloring book. Finally, teachers also conveyed their perceptions of the Richys' financial situation. For example, Ms. Corbin noted that "I've got very affluent children, and then Alysha, who's very, very poor."

7. In an ethnographic study of desegregated first-grade classrooms, Grant (1984) observed that an emphasis on social skills at the expense of academic development was common in teachers' interactions with black girls. She believed black girls were socialized at both school and home to provide the social salve necessary for diverse groups to get along and work together.

8. Readers should ask themselves why these high-achieving children would not be expected to go to college, but rather, to "some kind of trade school." Surely college was the expectation of their parents, who had—as the teacher notes—found ways to translate their high expectations into concrete supportive actions to date, despite their meager financial resources.

9. The "somebody" Annette refers to is likely Langston Hughes and his poem, "I, Too (sing America)". In chapter 4, I note Rhonda's and other mothers' routine use of colorful metaphoric imagery. Like Annette's words, Rhonda's talk also at times bore striking resemblance to the words of this famous black poet.

CHAPTER 4

1. When Rhonda described her child-centered family, with its emphases on respect for elderly members and the importance of blood relations over conjugal ties, she identified a traditional pattern of family organization that is apparent far beyond her own family. This pattern is well known in the literature on both historical and contemporary black families. While most stress the "adaptive" nature of such family organization in response to oppressive conditions (see Harrison et al. 1990; Taylor et al. 1992), others trace its origins to African roots. Sudarkasa notes that "historically, among Black Americans the concept of 'family' meant first and foremost relationships created by blood rather than by marriage" (1988, 39), and argues that although this organization has been criticized for contributing to fragility of black marital relationships, researchers should consider as well the stability that such family networks provide.

2. I argued in chapter 3 that such cooperation between teachers can contribute to difficulties for particular parents and children. However, when students and their families are viewed positively, such continuity seems likely to benefit rather than handicap most children.

3. I phoned the director of Follow Through the day after the graduation. Like Ms. Roth, Ms. Chase was clearly distressed that the program was ending. However, she explained that it had been funded by the President's Discretionary Fund since its inception in 1967, and federal funds were no longer available. In fact, the program had been being phased out gradually over the previous ten years, since early in the Reagan administration. While it was not entirely eliminated in June 1991, only twenty-five Follow Through programs nationwide would be funded in 1991–92, down from forty-nine programs the year before. Ms. Chase said the federal government had intended Follow Through funds to support short-term experimental and development programs initially, hoping local school districts would eventually take them over. There was "no chance" of this happening in Indianapolis, she said, where the system was under "tremendous" budgetary pressure.

CHAPTER 5

1. Ms. Hill was the kindergarten teacher of two other children involved in this study, although they were not Zena's classmates. Tamera and Charles (see chapters 7 and 9) were in Ms. Hill's morning class.
2. Marissa received only $50 of what Duane paid; the rest went to offset the state's costs of the family's welfare benefits.
3. As noted in chapter 2, this was a routine practice of Amy's during our interviews, and something that other mothers occasionally did as well, although I never asked to see papers or suggested the mothers save their children's work to share with me.

CHAPTER 6

1. In 1991, the average AFDC grant in Indiana for a family of three was $288, ranking 38th in the nation (Children's Defense Fund, 1992).
2. Eligibility criteria for Medicaid have varied by state, but federal legislation passed in 1990 resulted in greater standardization. By 1992, states were to extend coverage to all children born after 30 September 1983 whose families had income below 133 percent of the poverty level. All the children involved in this study were born in 1984 or 1985, and this policy change benefited several of them.
3. Harriet's stepfather was disabled, and granting her parents legal guardianship made these girls eligible for Social Security benefits in his name.
4. Like Miz Jones, I also observed the sorry state of Sheila's wardrobe that year, and gave Harriet several outfits my daughter had outgrown. Despite our attempts to assist in this way, Sheila's kindergarten teacher reported that Sheila's appearance was somewhat problematic: "Sometimes she looks unkept in a way. . . . A lot of my little black girls are just baby dolls, and Sheila doesn't look that way. Her shirt's out, just kinda draggin', skirt's a little big."
5. There is a great deal of literature that examines support networks constructed and maintained by African American families, particularly among those with very low incomes (for example, Martin and Martin 1978; Stack 1974; Taylor et al. 1992), and informal adoption of children is a well-known coping strategy.
6. For example, the oldest child in Samantha and Ramone's family (chapter 8) was raised by his grandparents, and a younger sister also lived temporarily in the grandparents' home. And Denise's (chapter 10) oldest child lived for six months with close family friends after the breakup of Denise's marriage.
7. Harriet rarely had access to private transportation, and also often worked Sunday overtime shifts. When not working, she relied on other congregation members—primarily Constance—for rides to services on Sundays or on Thursday evenings. Harriet was therefore unable to attend with any regularity the small church located several miles from any of the various places she lived over the course of this study. When my daughter and I attended services with Harriet, Sheila, and Jermaine one Sunday in March 1992, however, it was clear she was a well-known and popular member of the congregation, many of whom I met and chatted with throughout the afternoon (as in Annette's church, services here lasted most of the day).
8. This interview excerpt also provides an example of the general theme of evoking claims of family difference to explain the mothers' own values or behaviors. Harriet did not discuss her concerns with friends, and in fact had no friends at all, because she perceived herself to be so different from other people her age.

9. This visit included my participation in a rather elaborate scheme designed to secure permission for Harriet to leave her floor so that we could sneak outside for a cigarette. Together we fabricated a story about my daughter's intense fear of hospitals, and her unwillingness to venture further into the hospital than the first-floor lobby. Harriet successfully argued that since Mary had made the trip from out of town to visit, she should be granted five minutes downstairs to see her. For my part, I made one trip downstairs and returned to say that despite my best efforts, my assurances could not overcome the fear that a "scary movie about hospitals" had apparently created in my daughter. There was, in fact, no truth to this, and Mary initially waited in the lobby because I was unsure whether such a young visitor was allowed. When we finally got downstairs and then outside to smoke, we laughed a good deal about our silliness, and our conversation then quickly turned to rather personal topics. It seemed our collaborative deception contributed to what I sensed was a greater intimacy between us than had existed prior to this visit.

10. Harriet was transported by ambulance back to the hospital—again with chest pains—within two weeks of her initial release. In the following six months, she was hospitalized twice more for continuing heart trouble. Each time, Harriet believed she had been released too soon, before her health had stabilized, and she attributed this to her lack of medical insurance.

11. It could also be true that, unlike the great majority of children, Sheila may have been uncomfortable with Bill's presence. Two of the four times he observed play in which Sheila was a participant, she left the area within a few minutes.

12. Although her assessment of Sheila's experiences in kindergarten was positive, Harriet expressed frustration over Sheila's changed attitude toward her mother's assistance. Harriet described Sheila's reaction when she discovered Ms. Fulton wanted certain letters printed differently from the way Harriet taught her at home. Sheila reportedly complained, "Well, Mommy, that's not the way you taught me how to do it," and declared that "I'll just do everything my teacher say. Don't you tell me how to do anything." This remark fit well with other mothers' reports that their children increasingly resisted their attempts to provide assistance.

13. Harriet's report of the teacher's comment about parents from "our part of town" suggests that, like Zena's teacher did, Ms. Jackson may have been interpreting low-income black parents' inability to attend these conferences at distant schools as lack of interest in and concern for their children. A glance at the "Neighborhood Characteristics" table in the appendix suggests a different explanation: Nearly 30 percent of households in the census tract where Harriet lived had no vehicle, and in other neighborhoods represented in this study, that percentage was much higher.

CHAPTER 7

1. When Tasha told of this in our first interview, she did not hesitate to add that she had found it necessary to lie about her address in order to qualify for AFDC (she and her two children lived with her mother, but Tasha needed either to report she lived with someone who was not kin, or to count her mother's income, which would have made her ineligible). This candid admission suggested she'd decided to trust me from the start, and may also speak to the effectiveness of the veiled admission of similar AFDC "cheating" I had made when I originally told mothers of my own AFDC history.

2. When Tasha registered Tamera for kindergarten early in the summer, she learned of a special summer program offered at the neighborhood school for incoming kindergarten students. Tamera did attend this six-week program, which was designed and run by Tamera's future kindergarten teacher, Ms. Hill.

3. In this, she was in agreement with Evelyn (chapter 9), who lived several blocks away.

4. While I waited for Tasha to arrive, Tamera received two telephone calls. First, Tasha called to see if I had arrived. Second, Tamera's father called, and Tamera's side of the conversation suggested he was checking in on the children.

5. Of course, an alternative explanation is also plausible—that is, Tamera's apparent declining shyness reflected not a change in her personality, but growing comfort with me as she came to know me better. Most likely, both explanations are accurate—Tamera likely became more comfortable with me in particular, and more outgoing generally, over time.

6. It seems necessary to add here that, as was true of my interview with Zena's teacher as well, Ms. Kemp's genuine concern for Tamera seemed clear. Although I am quite critical of both teachers' definition of the situation, I did not believe either was intentionally callous or indifferent to parents, and certainly not uncaring toward the children.

7. As I've noted, Tamera was left alone to care for her younger brother during this school year, and—while there is some room for debate whether this is actually too much responsibility for a child of seven—the law is clear that such parental behavior does indeed constitute neglect. However, I should also note that after one visit to the home (when Tasha was not present) and one telephone call to Tasha, the social welfare agency took no further action in this case. Apparently, they were satisfied the complaint was not warranted.

8. With the advent of Select Schools, percentage of blacks at this school rose from 61.5 percent to 80 percent that year.

CHAPTER 8

1. Two other mothers, Marissa and Harriet, also complained that siblings enjoyed favored status with their mothers, and in all three cases, the pain and bitterness they harbored was apparent.

2. In the opening chapter, I quoted from a conversation with Rhonda that also occurred in November 1991. During that visit, Rhonda displayed similar consideration of her role in this research and justifications for her continuing participation. Like Samantha, she suggested that others communicated disapproval of her involvement, but she too had resolved the issue in her own mind. She said, in part that "people are askin' me all the time, 'What do you mean, somebody doin' research on Cymira?' And I try to tell them . . . you're gonna show something good about us." It is also worth pointing out that both women viewed themselves as considerably different from others in similar circumstances, and their felt uniqueness apparently influenced their continuing participation in the study.

3. Samantha's remarks also bring to mind a comment by Harriet, who noted that as she urged her daughter to work hard to improve her grades, she told Sheila to "remember, Ms. Katy will be checking on you." Such remarks underscore mothers' perceptions that this research benefited them as well as me, in part because it provided children additional incentive for achievement.

4. Readers may suppose such remarks were made for the benefit of my comfort, and although I believe Samantha was sincere, it would also be naive to suggest my own color did not influence her comments. Race was a salient difference between me and the mothers, and it is no surprise Samantha and others made a variety of attempts to establish their views on race and race relations, and their feelings about being black, though I never asked for such information. Denise and Rhonda also offered their feelings about whites, and they noted that their views seemed different from those of many other blacks they knew. This is, of course, another example of the mothers' routine claims about differences that set them apart from others.

5. Although it is disturbing, too much should not be made of the uncle's suggestion of abusive physical discipline. Like many of the children involved in this research, Ramone was occasionally physically disciplined by his mother, and on one occasion I was present when this occurred. After repeated warnings, Samantha responded to Ramone's continued misbehavior by hitting him smartly on his palm with the back of a hairbrush he had reluctantly fetched for her. I saw similar incidents in other families, though I saw many more threats of physical punishment than actual administrations. While such punishment was a fact of life for many of these children, "knocking the hell out of" kids was far beyond anything I ever observed or even remotely suspected. It is likely the uncle's comment was meant merely to underscore his displeasure and to suggest that punishment was in order.

6. D. Lewis described a "high valuation for personal uniqueness . . . individualism . . . and non-conformance within bounds" as typical in black culture. Lewis argues that this individualism "is experienced in a context of great interpersonal involvement" and she quotes Young's work on poor black families' child-rearing practices to clarify this integration of individual and group: "Strong individuality is paired with strong interpersonal connectedness. Not absorption in a group or acceptance of group identity as

higher than individual identity, but merely relatedness as distinguished from the isolation that characterizes individualism in the Western tradition" (Young 1970, quoted in Lewis 1975, 225).

These patterns are apparent in my own data, and in other contemporary literature on black families as well (for example, see Boykin and Toms 1985; Collins 1991a, 1991b).

7. In our first interview, Samantha expressed her strong desire to return to college and obtain a four-year degree. In each subsequent interview, she reiterated that desire, as she did here.

8. Chapter I funds are distributed as federal grants to schools determined to be eligible because a large percentage of their students are from low-income families. The funds primarily support tutors for children identified as needing extra help in math and/or reading and English.

9. See chapter 3 for a partial transcript of a lunchtime episode (the cable TV episode) in which Ramone was a major participant, and chapter 5, where Zena and Ramone patiently explained to Corsaro that they were not frightened by horror movies because they are "not real."

10. Ms. Parson was among the most defensive teachers I interviewed, and among the most critical of parents generally. For example, when asked to describe the best and worst aspects of her job, she quickly identified parents' changing attitudes as the primary "downside." After noting that "I don't see parents involved with their children and positive about school like they used to be," she continued: "Teachers now are not held at the same level of recognition and esteem as they used to be. I think that it's kind of like they're ready to catch us doing something wrong." I felt her remarks may well have been colored by the unique historical moment. The day before this interview, the not guilty verdict was delivered in the criminal trial of Los Angeles police officers charged in the beating of Rodney King. Our interview was delayed twenty minutes while teachers and administrators met to discuss how they might deal with angry parents or students in the wake of the L.A. uprising. Although we did not pursue these issues in the interview, Ms. Parson told us of an angry confrontation she'd had with a black mother that morning, and she believed the woman was especially hostile because of the national climate. Meanwhile, there were peaceful rallies in schools around the city that day, as well as several assault incidents at one inner-city high school.

CHAPTER 9

1. Evelyn phoned late in 1994 to tell me her mother, who was a heavy smoker, had died of heart disease. She talked of how she and her brothers and sisters had all agreed to work together to keep the family close in their mother's absence. She also urged me, as she had many times before, to please quit smoking.

2. Findings from a study of middle-class parents of preschool children by Harkness, Super, and Keefer (1992) also suggested parents often recall negative aspects of their childhoods when describing their own parenting tactics. Interestingly, however, they point out that although they also observed many positive parallels between their subjects' reported childhoods and present parenting activities, the parents rarely recognized these positive influences. The authors speculated that for their sample, "positive elements of one's own past are less consciously directive than negative ones" (1992, 173). This was clearly not the case for Evelyn and Amy, or for Denise, who is the topic of chapter 10. For these mothers, and to a lesser extent for Rhonda and Harriet as well, thoughtful and purposeful reproduction of their parents' tried-and-true tactics was very evident.

3. Charles's contributions are included in each of the four taped interviews I did with his mother. In two cases, Charles performed musical numbers—once a popular love song, and once a religious song. During this particular visit, Charles displayed some jealousy over the attention I gave his mother during my visits. In fact, the interview tape includes his question to me: "Are you my guest or my mother's?" He was not satisfied with my diplomatic reply that "I'm both," and said somewhat angrily to his mother, "She's not your guest, she's my guest!" I attempted to pacify him by suggesting that "Mary's your guest, and I'm both your guests," but he complained that Mary had gone into the other room with Celia. Finally, he said directly to the recorder: "See how mean they are to me? But Mary and Celia are nice to me," and then left the room.

4. Evelyn and Charles's experience with Select Schools options was quite unusual. As noted

in chapter 2, 95 percent of all parents received one of their three designated choices (including those parents who used the Quick Pick option).

5. A local television station doing a news report on the many transportation mix-ups learned of Charles and televised him waiting for his bus, which did finally arrive that day, and then arriving at his new school. Charles was, of course, thrilled with this opportunity to perform, and this surely eased his own frustration with the situation, if not his mother's.

CHAPTER 10

1. Mandy, thirteen; Monique, seven; Martin, five; Melanie, three; and Daniel Jr., one.

2. In the three years I formally collected data, Denise was the only mother to ever ask that I not tape-record a particular discussion. Denise wanted me to know what happened between her and her husband, but she did not want this information shared with others. "Turn that off," she said, before telling me of the events that led to their separation. As was often the case during my initial round of interviews, I was stunned by Denise's candor and the trust in me she displayed so early in our relationship, and I have no desire to defy that trust now. Although she later talked of the split with her husband more openly—suggesting perhaps that she had become less protective of the details—I will respect her wishes here and leave it to readers to imagine the particular incident that precipitated her sudden return to Indianapolis.

3. Denise told of these events during July 1991. She also announced she would give me her "testimony" concerning her feelings about whites. She began by describing herself as formerly quite prejudiced. Her joyous experiences within the integrated Evangelical church, however, prompted her to reevaluate her beliefs, and thereafter she had numerous interracial friendships while living in Birmingham.

Denise's interracial contact in Birmingham was markedly different from her experiences in Indianapolis. Although she had taken segregation for granted in her youth, upon her return to Indiana she was discomfited by this state of affairs. She'd come to view friendships with whites as unremarkable, and was distressed by reminders that others did not share this view. Denise's dilemma came into sharp relief during one particular visit. Denise's car was being repaired, and I arrived early to drive the children to school and help Denise run errands before our fourth interview. She asked me to pick up her aunt so she too could go to the bank and drugstore, and I naturally agreed. When we pulled up to her aunt's house, Denise looked surprised, then somewhat embarrassed as she worried: "Oh, no! I forgot to tell her you were white!" Although her aunt handled the situation unflappably and with grace, Denise's concern suggested this was indeed an unusual occurrence. She later remarked that "at one time, it would've bothered me to go get my aunt, for you to go pick her up. You know? 'Cause I wouldn't want anybody to say [disapproving and surprised facial expression, raised eyebrows], you know? They just don't understand."

4. During this and later interviews, I noticed that while Denise remained concerned about the neighborhood, she began to take advantage of some of the benefits of their location that had enriched her childhood. Her aunt's involvement in her children's life is just one example. During this year the children also participated in a tutoring program at the Baptist church. This and other churches had provided similar programs that Denise had attended with girl friends years ago. She also slowly began to participate in the informal economy of the neighborhood. For example, she ran errands for the elderly woman who lived next door, and in exchange the woman occasionally looked after the children. She also sought out the services of a man who had worked on neighbors' cars in his backyard since Denise was young. He was understanding of her financial constraints, would extend short-term credit, and could be trusted to provide high-quality repairs.

5. This excerpt also suggests the rushed nature of our interview by this point. As was true for the interview with Ms. Hill, it was difficult to discuss in detail more than one child in the time we'd allowed for the interview, and we had already spent much time talking about Cymira. The questions were also repetitive, which explains the opening, " . . . and again," to my request for information about Ms. Roth's relationship with Denise.

6. There was other evidence that Martin's performance in kindergarten did, in fact, approach perfection. During the graduation ceremony Ms. Roth held for her students, Martin received nearly every individual award presented. Denise beamed with pride as

Martin's outstanding performance was acknowledged in such diverse areas as reading, math, homework, attendance, and citizenship.

7. When I visited, the approximately 120 people who made up the congregation of the Evangelical church appeared to be about 30 percent black. In contrast, Mary and I were the only whites among the 250 or so people who worshiped at the Baptist church that day. Remarkably, I felt much more comfortable in the latter setting where I was clearly an outsider and observer, than in the former, where I felt others viewed my daughter and me as potential new members.

CHAPTER 11

1. To some extent, these statements hold true for Samantha as well. However, Samantha's situation was different in that she typically maintained daily contact with her parents, and received considerable routine assistance from them, despite her feeling ill at ease with their relationships.

2. It is also possible that lack of trust in these distant institutions may have contributed to Tasha's and Harriet's charges that teachers there were racially biased.

3. There is considerable controversy regarding the validity of the locus-of-control variable, perhaps especially when applied to black populations. It is generally agreed that personal control over one's own life must be differentiated from a more general orientation, which recognizes that discrimination, racism, and poverty interfere with the achievement of black Americans as a group (Banks et al. 1991; Gurin, Gurin, and Morrison 1978; Hendrix 1980). In addition, the misleading language that investigators have often used when narratively describing their results has come under fire (for example, see Banks et al. 1991; Ward 1986). Although these controversies are important, such issues are outside the scope of this discussion. Despite very real validity concerns, Banks et al argue that locus-of-control studies have been remarkably successful in "establishing a relatively stable belief system within the research community in externality for blacks" (1991, 188).

4. There are suggestions in the literature that black mothers encourage autonomy and independence in their daughters more than in their sons (for example, see Collins 1991a and 1991b), and it is easy to posit why this might be the case. Given the economic marginality of black men, black girls must be prepared to independently support themselves and their families without the assistance of a male partner. In addition, boys and girls tend to face different kinds of threats emanating from the street culture of their communities. While mothers fear their daughters' early school-leaving, teen pregnancies, and facing a life of poverty, gangs and life-threatening violence are more of concern for boys. Perhaps erring on the side of caution makes more sense, then, for mothers of boys whose concerns are focused on possible loss of life. In this sample, the mothers of boys did tend to be more restrictive, although Samantha is a clear exception. In addition, two mothers (Rhonda and Tasha) whose practices clearly encouraged autonomy and independence in their daughters also had sons they appeared to treat similarly. I am unwilling to draw any conclusions on this matter based on findings from this small sample, however, other than to note that this is an interesting question that begs further study.

5. Despite reviewers' and other readers' urgings, I find myself unwilling—without the cloak of anonymity that shields the mothers' privacy—to reveal many of the more personal similarities in our experiences. I am a strong believer both in reciprocal exchange between researchers and study participants, and searching self-reflection on the part of investigators. In fact, I would argue (along with many others) that reciprocal exchange and self-reflection may indeed be requisite for good and ethical qualitative research, and my research practice has reflected these beliefs. However, I do not believe that the content of such exchanges and reflections must necessarily be revealed to readers.

In this book, I have drawn some, but only a few, of the parallels I saw between these mothers' lives and my own. Beyond this, I've drawn a line, and my unwillingness to cross it represents a decision to protect my and my family's right to privacy. I acknowledge here that some readers may be bothered by nagging questions about my own experiences and child-rearing practices. Similarly, they may find my explanation for the lack of answers less than satisfying. Be that as it may, I am confident that most readers will both respect this position, and find adequate evidence of thoughtful, ethical research practice.

6. While I believe Duneier's arguments about the absence of "respectable" poor blacks from most ethnographies are compelling, his research in fact does little to rectify this omission. His study of patrons of a popular eatery on the edge of a large black ghetto in Chicago includes no *young* black males, and thus is ineffective in challenging or combating the stereotypes he decries.

7. Findings from this study underscore the need for qualitative research that follows children's entire educational careers, beginning with the earliest (that is, preschool) settings. The practical constraints on such research, however, are great, and obvious.

8. In the fourth case, Jeremiah's schoolwork remained essentially unchanged, and while his behavior also seemed little altered, his kindergarten and first-grade teachers differed in their responses to this behavior—with the first-grade teacher viewing it as somewhat more problematic.

9. Anyon's (1980) ethnographic research in classrooms serving children from lower-income, middle-income, and more affluent families suggests that autonomy and independent thinking is, in fact, encouraged by teachers of more affluent children, while conformity and following procedure is emphasized in schools that serve primarily lower-income and working-class students.

10. This does not mean that white teachers cannot be sensitive and talented teachers of black students. For example, Ms. Bancroft, Ms. Sampsel, and Ms. Holden were all white teachers who displayed great understanding of the needs of the students in their majority-black classrooms.

11. An alternative interpretation, of course, is that black children in majority white classrooms behave in more problematic ways. I suspect there is some truth to this explanation as well.

12. Many teachers seemed to feel attendance at parent-teacher conferences was an important—if not the most important—indicator of this concern.

13. This included Annette, who initially claimed her children were too young for concerns about gangs and drugs but later changed her mind after a her oldest son was briefly kidnaped by a car thief.

14. In the 1993–94 school year, about 87 percent of first-choice picks were honored—this included the 50 percent of all parents who selected the Quick Pick option, which enrolled children in their neighborhood school (IPS unpublished document). In effect, this means that just under three-quarters of parents who chose a school outside their neighborhood had that choice honored.

15. I do not intend to argue here that the Head Start program is without flaws. This is not the case. For example, curricular aspects of Head Start may contribute to the perfectionism we observed among many of the children. Language drills and cognitive and perceptual tasks that were presented as having only one correct answer, which the children were expected to produce in full sentences, seemed particularly problematic in this respect. Despite the program's failings, however, children's excitement about their coming entry into formal schooling was clear.

References

Alexander, K., and D. Entwisle. 1988. *Achievement in the First Two Years of School: Patterns and Processes*. Monographs of the Society for Research in Child Development 53 (2). Chicago: University of Chicago Press.

Anderson, E. 1994. "The Code of the Streets" *Atlantic Monthly* 273 (5): 80–94.

Anderson, J. 1988. *The Education of Blacks in the South: 1860–1935*. Chapel Hill: University of North Carolina Press.

Anyon, Jean. 1980. "Social Class and the Hidden Curriculum of Work." *Journal of Education* 162 (1): 67–92.

Aquila, Frank D. 1980. *Race Equity in Education: The History of School Desegregation, 1849–1979*. Monographs in Urban and Multi-Cultural Education, Center for Urban and Multi-Cultural Education, School of Education, Indiana University, Bloomington, Ind.

Banks, W. C., W. E. Ward, G. V. McQuater, and A. M. Debritto. 1991. "Are Blacks External: On the Status of Locus of Control in Black Populations." In *Black Psychology*, ed. R. L. Jones, 181–192. Berkeley, Calif.: Cobb & Henry.

Berger, B., and P. L. Berger. 1983. *The War Over the Family: Capturing the Middle Ground*. Garden City, N.Y.: Anchor Press/Doubleday.

Blee, K. M. 1991. *Women of the Klan: Racism and Gender in the 1920's*. Berkeley: University of California Press.

Boykin, A. W., and F. D. Toms. 1985. "Black Child Socialization: A Conceptual Framework." In *Black Children: Social, Educational, and Parental Environments, ed. H. P. McAdoo and J. L. McAdoo, 33–51. Newbury Park, Calif.: Sage.

Calabrese, R. L. 1990. "The Public School: A Source of Alienation for Minority Parents." *Journal of Negro Education* 59 (2): 148–154.

Cassell, J. 1980. "Ethical Principles for Conducting Fieldwork." *American Anthropologist* 82: 28–41.

Cherlin, A. J. 1998. "How Will the 1996 Welfare Reform Law Affect Poor Families." In *Public and Private Families: A Reader*, ed. A. Cherlin, 120–126. Boston: McGraw-Hill.

Children's Defense Fund. 1992. *The State of America's Children, 1992*. Washington, D.C.: Children's Defense Fund.

Clark, R. 1983. *Family Life and School Achievement: Why Poor Black Children Succeed or Fail*. Chicago: University of Chicago Press.

Collins, P. H. 1991a. "The Meaning of Motherhood in Black Culture and Black Mother-

Daughter Relationships." In *Double Stitch: Black Women Write About Mothers and Daughters*, ed. P. Bell-Scott et al., 42–60. Boston: Beacon Press.

———. 1991b. *Black Feminist Thought: Knowledge, Consciousness, and the Politics of Empowerment*. New York: Routledge.

Cook, D. A., and M. Fine. 1995. " 'Motherwit': Childrearing Lessons from African-American Mothers of Low Income." In *Children and Families "At Promise": Deconstructing the Discourse of Risk*, ed. B. B. Swadener and S. Lubeck, 118–142. Albany, N.Y.: SUNY Press.

Comer, J. P., and N. M. Haynes. 1991. "Parent Involvement in Schools: An Ecological Approach." *The Elementary School Journal* 91 (3): 271–277.

Corsaro, W. A. 1985. *Friendship and Peer Culture in the Early Years*. Norwood, N.J.: Ablex.

———. 1988. "Routines in the Peer Culture of American and Italian Nursery School Children." *Sociology of Education* 61: 1–14.

———. 1993. "Interpretive Reproduction in the 'Scuola Materna.' " *European Journal of Psychology of Education* 8 (4): 357–374.

——— 1994. "Discussion, Debate, and Friendship Processes: Peer Discourse in U.S. and Italian Nursery Schools." *Sociology of Education* 67: 1–25.

———. 1995. "Transitions in Early Childhood: The Promise of Comparative, Longitudinal Ethnography." In *Essays on Ethnography and Human Development*, ed. A. Colby, R. Jessor, and R. Shweder, 419–457. Chicago: University of Chicago Press.

———. 1997. *The Sociology of Childhood*. Thousand Oaks, Calif.: Pine Forge Press.

Corsaro, W. A., and K. B. Rosier. 1992. "Documenting Productive-Reproductive Processes in Children's Lives: Transition Narratives of a Black Family Living in Poverty." In *Interpretive Approaches to Children's Socialization*, ed. W. A. Corsaro and P. J. Miller, 67–91. New Directions for Child Development 58. San Francisco: Jossey-Bass.

———. 1994. "Transition Narratives and Reproductive Processes in the Lives of Black Families Living in Poverty." Paper presented at the XIII World Congress of Sociology, July 1994, Bielefeld, Germany.

Dodson, J. 1988. "Conceptualizations of Black Families." In *Black Families*. 2d ed., ed. H. P. McAdoo, 77–90. Newbury Park, Calif.: Sage.

Duneier, M. 1992. *Slim's Table: Race, Respectability, and Masculinity*. Chicago: University of Chicago Press.

Edin, K., and L. Lein. 1997. *Making Ends Meet: How Single Mothers Survive Welfare and Low-Wage Work*. New York: Russell Sage.

Ellison, C. 1990. "Family Ties, Friendships, and Subjective Well-Being among Black Americans." *Journal of Marriage and the Family* 52: 298–310.

Entwisle, D., and L. A. Hayduk. 1984. *Early Schooling: Cognitive and Affective Outcomes*. Baltimore: Johns Hopkins University Press.

Epstein, J., and H. Becker. 1982. "Teachers' Reported Practices of Parent Involvement: Problems and Possibilities." *Elementary School Journal* 83: 103–113.

Franklin, A. J., and N. Boyd-Franklin. 1985. "A Psychoeducational Perspective on Black Parenting." In *Black Children: Social, Educational, and Parental Environments*, ed. H. P. McAdoo and J. L. McAdoo, 194–210. Newbury Park, Calif.: Sage.

Furstenburg, F., Jr. 1993. "How Families Manage Risk and Opportunity in Dangerous Neighborhoods." In *Sociology and the Public Agenda*, ed. W. J. Wilson, 231–258. Newbury Park, Calif.: Sage.

Garbarino, J., K. Kostelny, and N. Dubrow. 1991. "What Children Can Tell Us About Living in Danger." *American Psychologist* 46 (4): 376–383.

Gecas, V. 1979. "The Influence of Social Class on Socialization". In *Contemporary Theories About the Family*, vol. 1, ed. W. R. Burr et al., 365–404. New York: Free Press.

Gibbs, J. 1990. "Developing Intervention Models for Black Families: Linking Theory and Research." In *Black Families: Interdisciplinary Perspectives*, ed. H. E. Cheatham and J. B. Stewart, 325–351. New Brunswick, N.J.: Transaction.

Goodwin, M. H. 1990. *He-Said-She-Said: Talk as Social Organization among Black Children*. Bloomington: Indiana University Press.

Grant, L. 1984. "Black Females' 'Place' in Desegregated Classrooms." *Sociology of Education* 57: 98–111.

Gresham, J. H. 1989. "The Politics of Family in America." *The Nation* 249 (4): 116–122.

Gurin, P., G. Gurin, and B. M. Morrison. 1978. "Personal and Ideological Aspects of Internal and External Control." *Social Psychology Quarterly*, 41 (4): 275–296.

Harkness, S., C. Super, and C. Keefer. 1992. "Learning to Be an American Parent: How Cultural Models Gain Directive Force." In *Human Motives and Cultural Models*, ed. R. G. D'Andrade and C. Strauss, 163–178. Cambridge, U.K.: Cambridge University Press.

Harris, K. M. 1996. "Life After Welfare: Women, Work, and Repeat Dependency." *American Sociological Review* 61: 407–426.

Harrison, A. O., M. N. Wilson, C. J. Pine, S. Q. Chan, and R. Buriel. 1990. "Family Ecologies of Ethnic Minority Children." *Child Development* 61: 347–362.

Heath, S. B. 1982. "Ethnography in Education: Defining the Essentials." In *Children In and Out of School: Ethnography and Education*, ed. P. Gilmore and A. A. Glatthorn, 33–55. New York: Harcourt Brace Jovanovich.

———. 1983. *Ways with Words: Language, Life, and Work in Communities and Classrooms.* Cambridge, U.K.: Cambridge University Press.

———. 1989. "Oral and Literate Traditions among Black Americans Living in Poverty." *American Psychologist* 44: 367–373.

———. 1990. "The Children of Trackton's Children: Spoken and Written Language in Social Change." In *Cultural Psychology: Essays on Comparative Human Development*, ed. J. Stigler, R. Shweder, and G. Herdt, 496–519. New York: Cambridge University Press.

Hendrix, B. 1980. "The Effects of Locus of Control on the Self-Esteem of Black and White Youth." *Journal of Social Psychology* 112: 301–302.

Hill, R. B., A. Billingsley, E. Ingram, M. R. Malson, R. H. Rubin, C. B. Stack, J. B. Stewart, J. E. Teele. 1989. *Research on African-American Families: A Holistic Perspective.* Boston: University of Massachusetts at Boston, William Monroe Trotter Institute.

Holliday, B. G. 1985. "Developmental Imperatives of Social Ecologies: Lessons Learned from Black Children." In *Black Children: Social, Educational, and Parental Environments*, ed. H. P. McAdoo and J. L. McAdoo, 53–69. Newbury Park, Calif.: Sage.

Hooper, K. L., and A. Neal. "City's Racial Trouble Is Unfinished History." *Indianapolis Star*, 21 February 1993.

Indianapolis Public Schools Planning Department. 1 March 1981 (unpublished). "Chronological Summary: Court-Related Actions and Events, I.P.S. Desegregation Case."

Indianapolis Public Schools, various unpublished documents. IPS Administration Building, Public Relations Office, 120 E. Walnut St., Indianapolis, IN 46204-1312.

Indianapolis Star:
15 February 1973. "Board Offers 3-Way Plan to Desegregate 14 Schools."
17 May 1989. "IPS Wants $67 Millon for Desegregation."
5 August 1989. "State Dodging Desegregation Costs, IPS says."

Jarrett, R. L. 1997. "African American Family and Parenting Strategies in Impoverished Neighborhoods." *Qualitative Sociology* 20 (2): 275–288.

———. Unpublished paper. "Community Context, Intrafamilial Processes, and Social Mobility Outcomes: Ethnographic Contributions to the Study of African-American Families and Children in Poverty."

Kohn, M. L. 1969. *Class and Conformity: A Study in Values.* Homewood, Ill.: Dorsey Press.

Ladner, J. 1978. "Growing Up Black." In *Psychology of Women: Selected Readings*, ed. J. Williams, 212–224. New York: W. W. Norton.

Lareau, A. 1989. *Home Advantage: Social Class and Parental Intervention in Elementary Education.* London: Falmer Press.

———. 1987. "Social Class Differences in Family-School Relationships: The Importance of Cultural Capital." *Sociology of Education* 60: 73–85.

Lefcourt, H. M. 1972. "Recent Developments in the Study of Locus of Control." In *Progress in Experimental Personality Research*, vol. 6, ed. B. A. Haher, 1–39. New York: Academic Press.

Lefcourt, H. M., and G. W. Ladwig. 1965. "The American Negro: A Problem in Expectancies." *Journal of Personality and Social Psychology* 1: 377–380.

Lerner, M. J. 1980. *The Belief in a Just World: A Fundamental Delusion.* New York: Plenum.

Lewis, D. 1975. "The Black Family: Socialization and Sex Roles." *Phylon* 36: 221–237.

Lipset, S. M., and R. Bendix. 1962 (1987). "Psychological Factors in Social Mobility: Intelligence and Motivation." In *Structured Social Inequality*, ed. C. S. Heller, 282–292. New York: Macmillan.

MacLeod, J. 1987. *Ain't No Makin' It: Leveled Aspirations in a Low-Income Neighborhood*. Boulder, Colo.: Westview Press.

Martin, E., and J. Martin. 1978. *The Black Extended Family*. Chicago: University of Chicago Press.

————. 1986. "The Black Woman: Perspectives on Her Role in the Family." In *Ethnicity and Women*, ed. W. A. Van Horne, 184–205. Milwaukee: University of Wisconsin Press.

McAdoo, H. P. 1978. "Factors Related to Stability in Upwardly Mobile Black Families." *Journal of Marriage and the Family* 40: 761–776.

————. 1986. "Strategies Used by Black Single Mothers against Stress." In *Slipping Through the Cracks: The Status of Black Women*, ed. M. C. Simms and J. M. Malveaux, 153–166. New Brunswick, N.J.: Transaction.

Metcalf, G. R. 1983. *From Little Rock to Boston: The History of School Desegregation*. Westport, Conn: Greenwood Press.

Mills, C. W. 1959. *The Sociological Imagination*. New York: Oxford University Press.

Minkler, M., and K. M. Roe. 1993. *Grandmothers as Caregivers: Raising Children of the Crack Cocaine Epidemic*. Newbury Park, Calif.: Sage.

Nobles, W. W. 1988 (1976). "African-American Family Life: An Instrument of Culture." In *Black Families*. 2d ed., ed. H. P. McAdoo, 44–53. Newbury Park, Calif.: Sage.

Oakley, A. 1981. "Interviewing Women: A Contradiction in Terms." In *Doing Feminist Research*, ed. H. Roberts, 30–61. London: Routledge & Kegan Paul.

Ogbu, J. U. 1980. "Origins of Human Competence: A Cultural-Ecological Perspective." *Child Development* 52: 413–429.

————. 1988. "Black Education: A Cultural-Ecological Perspective." In *Black Families*. 2d ed., ed. H. P. McAdoo, 169–183. Newbury Park Calif.: Sage.

Poole, T. G. 1990. "Black Families and the Black Church: A Sociohistorical Perspective."In *Black Families: Interdisciplinary Perspectives*, ed. H. E. Cheatham and J. B. Stewart, 33–48. New Brunswick, N.J.: Transaction.

Rist, R. C. 1970. "Student Social Class and Teacher Expectations: The Self-Fulfilling Prophecy in Ghetto Education." *Harvard Educational Review* 40: 411–451.

————. 1973. *The Urban School: A Factory for Failure*. Cambridge, Mass.: M.I.T. Press.

Robinson, J. L., and W. B. Choper. 1979. "Another Perspective on Program Evaluation: The Parents Speak." In *Project Head Start: A Legacy of the War on Poverty*, ed. E. Zigler and J. Valentine, 467–476. New York: Free Press.

Roof, J., and R. Wiegman. 1995. *Who Can Speak? Authority and Critical Identity*. Urbana: University of Illinois Press.

Rosenthal, R., and L. Jacobson. 1968. "Pygmalion in the Classroom." New York: Holt, Rinehart & Winston.

Rosier, K. B., and W. A. Corsaro. 1993. "Competent Parents, Complex Lives: Managing Parenthood in Poverty." *Journal of Contemporary Ethnography* 22 (2): 171–204.

Seeley, D. 1984. "Educational Partnership and the Dilemmas of School Reform." *Phi Delta Kappan* 65: 383–393.

Sidel, R. 1992. *Women and Children Last: The Plight of Poor Women in Affluent America*. New York: Penguin Books.

————. 1996. *Keeping Women and Children Last: America's War on the Poor*. New York: Penguin Books.

Silverstein, B., and R. Krate. 1975. *Children of the Dark Ghetto*. New York: Praeger.

Slaughter, D. T., and E. G. Epps. 1987. "The Home Environment and Academic Achievement of Black American Children and Youth: An Overview." *Journal of Negro Education* 56 (1): 3–20.

Spencer, M. B. 1990. "Parental Values Transmission: Implications for the Development of African-American Children." In *Black Families: Interdisciplinary Perspectives*, ed. H. E. Cheatham and J. B. Stewart, 111–130. New Brunswick, N.J.: Transaction.

Stacey, J. 1990. *Brave New Families: Stories of Domestic Upheaval in Late Twentieth Century America*. New York: Basic Books.

Stack, C. 1974. *All Our Kin: Strategies for Survival in a Black Community*. New York: Harper & Row.

Stephan, W. G. 1991. "School Desgregation: Short-Term and Long-Term Effects." In *Opening Doors: Perspectives on Race Relations in Contemporary America* , ed. H. J.

Knopke, R. J. Norrell, and R. W. Rogers, 100–118. Tuscaloosa: University of Alabama Press.

Stevenson, H., C. Chen, and D. Uttal. 1990. "Beliefs and Achievement: A Study of Black, White, and Hispanic Children." *Child Development* 61: 508–523.

Sudarkasa, N. 1988. "Interpreting the African Heritage in Afro-American Family Organization." In *Black Families*. 2d ed., ed. H. P. McAdoo, 27–43. Newbury Park Calif.: Sage.

Swadener, B. B., and S. Lubeck. 1995. *Children and Families "At Promise": Deconstructing the Discourse of Risk*. Albany N.Y.: SUNY Press.

Tabachnick, B. R., and M. N. Bloch. 1995. "Learning In and Out of School: Critical Perspectives on the Theory of Cultural Compatibility." In *Children and Families "At Promise": Deconstructing the Discourse of Risk*, ed. B. B. Swadener and S. Lubeck, 187–209. Albany, N.Y.: SUNY Press.

Taylor, R. J., L. M. Chatters, M. B. Tucker, and E. Lewis. 1992. "Developments in Research on Black Families: A Decade Review." In *Cultural Diversity and Families*, ed. K. G. Arms, J. K. Davidson, and N. B. Moore, 11–32. Dubuque, Iowa: WCB Brown and Benchmark.

Toomey, D. 1989. "How Home-School Relations Policies Can Increase Educational Inequality: A Three-Year Follow-up." *Australian Journal of Education* 33 (3): 284–298.

U.S. Department of Commerce, Economics and Statistics Administration, Bureau of the Census. 1990 CPH-3-179. 1990 Census of Population and Housing. *Population and Housing Characteristics for Census Tracts and Block Numbering Areas. Indianapolis IN MSA.*

Valentine, J., and E. Stark. 1979. "The Social Context of Parent Involvement in Head Start." In *Project Head Start: A Legacy of the War on Poverty*, ed. E. Zigler and J. Valentine, 291–313. New York: Free Press.

Van Galen, J. 1987. "Maintaining Control: The Structuring of Parent Involvement." In *Schooling in Social Context: Qualitative Studies*, ed. G. W. Noblit and W. T. Pink, 78–92. Norwood, N.J.: Ablex.

Wahlberg, H. J. 1984. "Families as Partners in Educational Productivity." *Phi Delta Kappan* 65: 397–400.

Ward, W. E. 1986. "Comment on Brown et al.'s "Locus of Control, Sex Role Orientation, and Self-Concept in Black and White Third- and Sixth-Grade Male and Female Leaders in a Rural Community." *Developmental Psychology*, 22 (1): 95–96.

Warren, S. 1994. "Crispus Attucks High School" In *Encyclopedia of Indianapolis,* ed. D. J. Bodenhamer and R. G. Barrows, 481–483. Bloomington: Indiana University Press.

Warren, S., and D. G. Vanderstel. 1994. "School Desegregation" In *Encyclopedia of Indianapolis*, ed. D. J. Bodenhamer and R. G. Barrows, 1220–1222. Bloomington: Indiana University Press.

Young, V. 1970. "Family and Childhood in a Southern Negro Community." *American Anthropologist* 72: 269–288.

———. 1974. "A Black American Socialization Pattern." *American Ethologist* 1: 405–413.

Zigler, E., and S. Muenchow. 1992. *Head Start: The Inside Story of America's Most Successful Educational Experiment*. New York: Basic Books.

Index

abuse, 217, 219; *see also* violence, domestic; discipline, physical

activities: alternatives to neighborhood, 36, 194, 242, 245; *see also* extra-curricular activities; church, children's activities in

adaptability, mothers' valuation of, 83, 174–175

adolescence, anticipated loss of control during, 80, 101, 190, 244

adoption: effective, by extended family members, 124, 168; informal 127, 240, 281n. 5, 281n. 6

AFDC, *see* Aid to Families with Dependent Children

affection, between teachers and children, 60, 110

Aid to Families with Dependent Children (AFDC): benefit levels, 3, 265, 275n. 2, 276n. 5, 281n. 1; "cheating," 4, 265, 282n. 1; child support payments, and 281n. 2; explanation of program, 275n. 2; education and training requirement, 275n. 2; receipt of, mothers', 1, 7–8; resistance to receipt of, 119, 124, 219–220; work, combined with, 264–265; *see also* employment, choice of, over AFDC

alternative schools and programs, 270, 273–274 table 2; *see also* parent involvement/ participation in schooling, alternatives to traditional classrooms

Anderson, E., 83, 200, 241, 248, 249, 261

Anyon, J., 287n. 9

Aquila, F. D., 278n. 17

"at-risk" label, 68, 104, 259

attendance zones, 277n. 16

attitudes: translation of, into practice, 244; *see also* fatalistic attitudes

authority, of author, 2–5

autonomy: children's bids for, 36, 243; children's display of, 35, 53–54, 103, 104, 175–176, 181, 255; contradictory goals of, and protection, 245–246; daughters vs sons, for, 286n. 4; empty talk about, 21, 35; encouragement of, blacks', 246–247; encouragement of, mothers', 51–54, 66, 81–83, 148–150, 151–152, 155–156, 165, 167, 245–247, 286n. 4; encouragement of, teachers', 35, 59, 86, 287n. 9; misbehavior, as, 35, 255

awards, received by children, 88, 285–286n. 6

and combating, 197; socialization strategies, on, 13, 74, 212; strategies to combat, 200, 222, 241–242
neglect, *see* child neglect
networks, *see* support networks
Nobles, W. W., 249

Oakley, A., 276–277 n. 8
Ogbu, J. U., 246, 247, 248, 255
one-upmanship, 183
outcomes, of other children, 196, 249

parent expectations: behavior, for, 35; blacks compared to whites, 239; decline of, 117, 180, 243; high, for children's achievement, 28, 50–51, 99, 156, 234; post-secondary education, for, 177, 280n. 8; self, for, 28, 119; unintended effects of, 253
parent involvement/participation in schooling, 20; alternatives to traditional classrooms, and, 13, 54–56, 142, 158, 164, 224, 231–232, 239; bused students' parents, of, 31–32, 38, 41–42, 112–113, 115, 278n. 17; children's resistence to, 37, 39, 100, 282n. 12; communication of values through, 41, 115, 258; customizing children's schooling, and, 38–39, 279n. 4; emphasis on, 207, 208, 257–258; excessive, 37–38, 42, 230; Follow Through component, as, 85; Head Start program component, as, 276n. 7; in-home routines, 26–27, 117–118, 139, 223, 239; mothers' academic abilities, and, 100, 224; parent-teacher partnerships, and, 100; preschool preparation, 133–134, 224, 239; teachers' descriptions of, generally, 108, 109, 134–135; teachers' descriptions of, specific parents, 37, 65–66, 92, 112, 140–141, 205; teachers' unawareness of, 13, 115; visiting classrooms, 32, 38, 54, 100, 135, 161, 223; withdrawal from, with negative reports, 114–115; *see also* extracurricular activities; teacher expectations; racial bias of teachers, mothers' withdrawal response to
parent-teacher conferences: significance of, for teachers, 13, 112, 115, 135–136, 282n. 13, 287n. 12

participation in study, rationales for, 173, 283nn. 2, 3
peer interaction: importance of, for children, 196, 242, 245; *see also* Head Start center, interaction style in; relationships, children with peers
peer pressure, to downplay education, 79–80, 90
perfectionism, children's, 230, 234, 253, 254, 287n. 15
poverty level, 169; full-time work, and, 123–124; Head Start requirement for, 276n. 7; neighborhood rates of, 269, 271–272 table 1; of Head Start center families, 277n. 11
pregnancy, of mothers' teenaged daughters, 144, 148, 178–180
private transportation: access to, 105, 126, 281n. 7; neighborhood access rates, 270, 271–272 table 1, 282n. 13

race, of teachers, 270, 273–274 table 2
race relations, in Indianapolis, 285n. 3
racial bias of teachers, 256, 257, 259; mothers' perceptions of, 138–139, 145, 163–164, 207–209, 243; mothers' withdrawal response to, 164, 208; reluctance to mention, 208
racial composition, of IPS system, 278n. 17
racial difference, *see* cultural/racial difference
Reagan era, program cuts, 276n. 7, 281n. 3
recreational activities, *see* extracurricular activities
relationships: children, with fathers, 22, 97, 153–154, 161–162, 193, 220–222; children, with peers, 59, 84, 91, 104, 118, 161, 183–184, 186–187, 201, 226; children's parents, between, 98, 153–154, 220–222; mothers with own parents, 102, 170, 283n. 1, 286n. 1; researcher and research participants, 9, 276n. 8, 277nn.9, 12, 282n. 9, 285n. 1
religion, contradictory role of, 237, 280n. 5
religiosity, 13, 218

underclass, 11, 251; *see also* "street" culture
Uni-Gov Act, 1969, 278n. 17

Vanderstel, 278n. 17
violence: domestic, 105, 130, 149; personal encounters with, 73–74; *see also* neighborhood characteristics, drug, gang, and violence activity

War Over the Family, The: 275n. 3
Warren, S., 278n. 17

welfare: usage of term, 275n. 2; *see also* Aid to Families with Dependent Children (AFDC)
Welfare Reform Bill, 1996, 276n. 6
white flight, 278n. 17
whites, mothers' attitudes toward, 174, 285n. 3
Who Can Speak?, 275n. 4
Wiegman, R., 275n. 4

Young, V. 283–284n. 6

Katherine Brown Rosier is an award-winning teacher and assistant of sociology at Louisiana State University. Her primary research interests center on families, children, and social policy.